序　言

商業英文要求的重點在於——精、簡、明、確，因此寫作起來格外不易，也更須要技巧。例如承作契約時，決定用Shall或will，可能就是日後萬一發生索賠時，成功與否的重要關鍵，一點也馬虎不得。而整個貿易流程之繁雜，往往令不熟悉這個領域的工作者，感到暈頭轉向，稍一不慎就可能造成鉅額的損失，甚至破壞公司長期辛苦建立起來的聲譽。

我們針對這些困擾，編成「**商業英語實務**」一書，收錄國內外大貿易商精彩的來往信函，供讀者參考，以從中學習有效實用的商業英文。全書按照貿易流程的先後次序編排，共分為六大部分：一、商業英語必備知識；二、交易關係；三、買賣合同；四、買賣契約的履行；五、外貿附帶事項；六、電報與電傳。把繁雜吃力的實務系統化、簡單化，並對每個階段的注意事項、處理技巧、及信函寫作要領，均詳加解說，使您輕輕鬆鬆就能掌握貿易的訣竅，做起貿易來，格外得心應手。

本書經過多次審慎校訂，如有疏漏，望各界不吝批評指正。

編者　謹識

Editorial Staff

● 編著 / 卓美玲

● 修編 / 林順隆

● 校訂

劉　毅・陳怡平・陳瑠琍・王慶銘
林佩汀・劉瑞芬・鄭明俊

● 校閱

Edward C. Yulo・Nick Veitch
Thomas Deneau・Francesca A. Evans
Joanne Beckett・Stacy Schultz

● 封面設計 / 張鳳儀

● 版面設計 / 曹馨元・許靜雯・張俊齡

● 打字

黃淑貞・倪秀梅・蘇淑玲・吳秋香

目 錄

本書另附有高品質錄音帶四捲500元，由美籍電台播音員錄音，配合學習，效果更佳。

PART Ⅰ

Preliminaries

商業英語必備知識

第1章

書信的初步籌備工作

Preliminary Arrangement

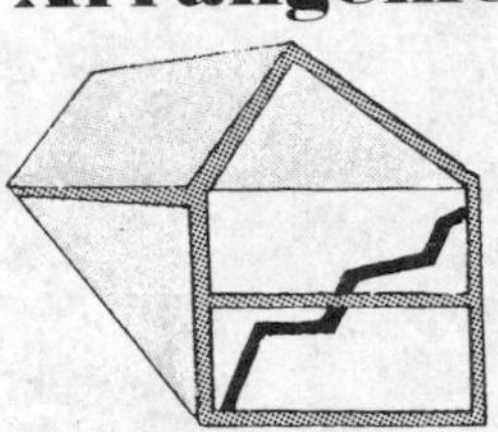

門面給人第一印象，極具說服力。適當的信紙、正確精美的打字印刷，常能發揮意想不到的效果。本著這個基本概念，先來談談信的格式及體裁。

A 信　紙 Paper

商業信紙一般都採用美國規格（American Size）的打字用紙 8½″× 11″（約長 21.6*cm*，寬 27.9*cm*），白色或淺色強韌的良質紙。打字用紙以上述正規打字紙為佳，印刷用紙則分為A版與B版兩種，各有 0～6 號的規格。0號為最大（A版為 841×1189*mm*，B版為 1030×1456*mm*），號碼愈大，規格越小，按長：寬＝1：$\sqrt{2}$ 的比例切割。信紙只能用一面，切勿為了節約，兩面都用。較隨便的信件（如memo 等）只要用 half size 就可以了。

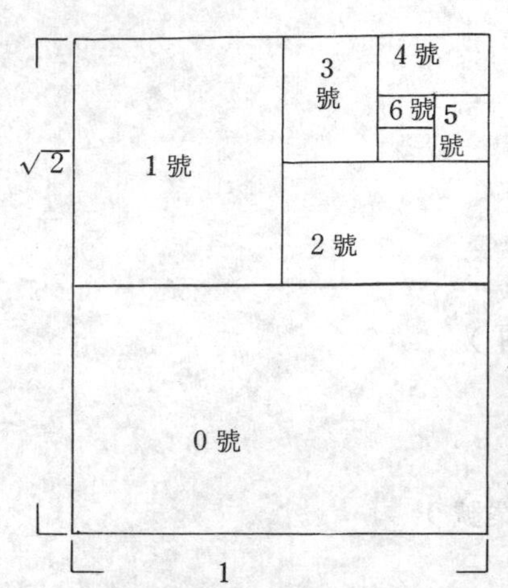

如左圖，

A1,B1 長：寬＝1：$\sqrt{2}$　A版面積 1m²

A2,B2 長：寬＝$\frac{\sqrt{2}}{2}$：1　B版 1.5m²，再按左圖切割

A3,B3 長：寬＝$\frac{1}{2}$：$\frac{\sqrt{2}}{2}$

A4,B4

A5,B5

A6,B6

商業信紙頂端（即Letterhead）必須印有下列各項，其印刷之整潔、簡明與美觀影響收信人的印象，不可不注意。

1. Firm Name　公司名號
2. Address　地址
3. Cable Address　電報簡號
4. Codes Used　密碼
5. Line of Business　營業項目
6. Bankers　交易銀行
7. Telephone　電話號碼
8. Telex　電傳號碼
9. P.O. Box　信箱號碼
10. Trade Mark　商標
11. Year of Establishment　創立年份

B Parts of the Letter

商用英文書信由必要構成部分，及特殊構成部分組合而成，特殊構成部分之使用與否，視情況而定。

必要構成部分有：

(1) Letterhead（信頭）
(2) Date（發信日期）
(3) Inside Address（收信人姓名）
(4) Salutation（開頭稱呼語）
(5) Body of the Letter（本文）
(6) Complimentary Close（結尾謙稱）
(7) Signature （簽名）

特殊構成部分有：

(8) Reference Number（參照號碼；案號）
(9) Particular Address（特定稱呼）
(10) Letter Subject（標題；主旨）
(11) Identification Marks（關係人姓名第一個字母，識別記號）
(12) Enclosure Directions（附帶文件說明）
(13) Postscript（P.S.）（補述；追記）

通常信紙上各項位置都按下列圖形排列：

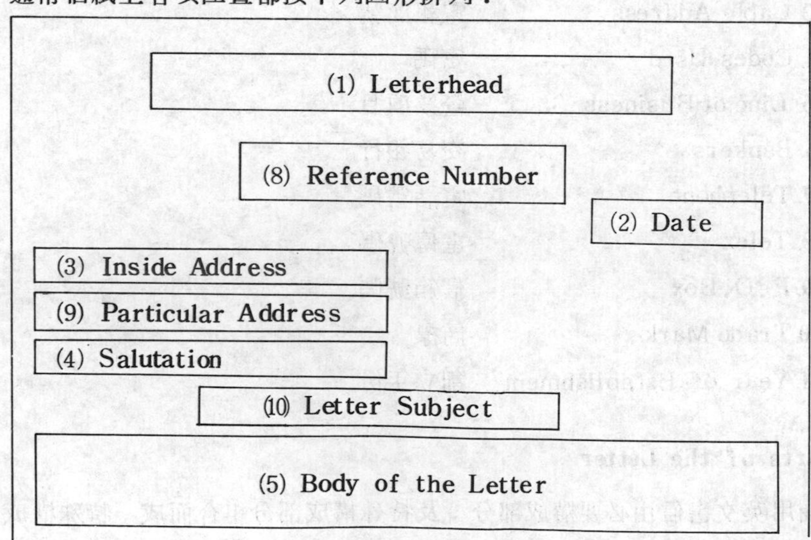

(6) Complimentary Close

(7) Signature

(11) Identification Marks

(12) Enclosure Directions

(13) Postscript

實際書信如下：

THE GENERAL TRADING CO., LTD

Cable Address:
GENERAL TAIPEI
Telex:
GENERAL TP 3628
Codes Used:
Acme ; Private

Importers & Exporters
36 Nanking East Road,
Taipei, Taiwan, R.O.C.

Branches:
Taipei
London
New York

April 1, 19—

Hong Kong Chamber of Commerce
International Trade Bldg.
38 Kowloon, Hong Kong

Dear Sirs,

Established in 1940, we have been expanding our business operations around the world as a leading general exporter and importer in Taiwan.

As we are now planning to incorporate our business activities in your market as general base in Asia, we will be much obliged for your introduction to a most reliable importer handling sundries and textile goods。

Concerning our financial status and reputation, please direct all enquiries to Bank of Taiwan, Taipei and The International Trading Co., Ltd. in Taipei.

Thank you very much for your co-operation. We hope to hear from you soon.

Yours faithfully,
THE GENERAL TRADING CO., LTD.
David Wang
David Wang
President

DW/ ht
Enc. Pamphlet 1

第2章

信函各部分的解說

Explanation of Each Part

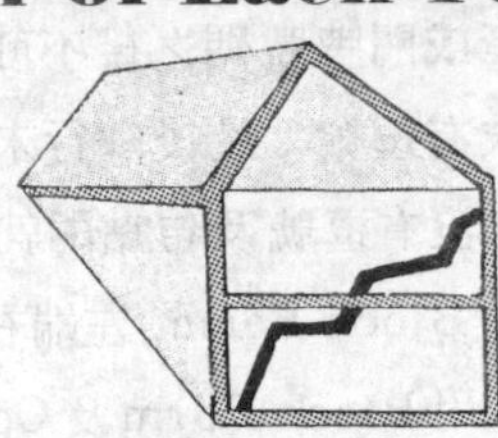

A.信頭 Letterhead

Letterhead印有公司的名號、地址、電報簡號、營業項目、密碼、電話及TELEX號碼、創立年份。如下所示：

THE MAO YUAN ELECTRIC CO.,LTD.

Code Used :	552 Tun Hwa North Road,	Cable Address:
Bentley's ;	Taipei, Taiwan	TAIWANTAIPEI
Private		Telex: TY3658
Business Line :	Established in 1940	Telephone:
Electric Appliances		TAIPEI941-2919

若無印刷之Letterhead時，要在打字紙右上方打上Sender's Address（發信人地址）。

1. 22-20 Tun Hwa North Road,
Taipei, Taiwan, R.O.C.（Indented Form, Close Punctuation）

2. 18 Railroad Ave.
Pearl River, New York, N.Y. 10016
U.S.A. （Block Form, Open Punctuation）

【說明】*1.* 第幾區或門牌號碼之後不可打逗點。

2. 各行末有逗號，最後一行末有句點稱爲Close Punctuation。各行末沒有逗號及句點的就稱爲Open Punctuation。左端垂直者稱爲Block Form，左端右凹則稱爲Indented Form。美國式主要採用Block Form及Open Punctuation，英國式多用Indented Form與Close Punctuation。（詳見第三章）

3. Ave. 是Avenue的縮寫，縮寫單字後需打句點。

4. N.Y.10016是美國的郵遞區號，英國倫敦是London E.C. 4之類的郵遞區號。

B.發信日期 Date

有Letterhead的信紙，日期寫在右上端，沒有Letterhead時就寫在Sender's Address的正下方，當然也有寫在Letterhead下方的，但以寫在右上方的格式較爲普遍。

美式	英式
June 3, 1986	3rd June, 1986

以Close Punctuation書寫時，於行末的年代之後需附上句點。注意英式採用1st，2nd，3rd，15th的寫法，不論英式或美式，年代前都必須加上逗號。本文中若省略月份只寫日期時，必須使用序數並加上冠詞，如the 15th。由於這種序數寫法不可以省略，故只寫1st. 2nd. 是不對的。

C.收信人姓名地址 Inside Address

Inside Address的第一行寫收信人姓名或公司名號，有時候包含收信人職稱，或只有職稱而無姓名，通常連地址只要三～四行即可，其主要目的爲便於檔案之處理，故可簡略。其書寫順序是由小單位到大單位，再到國名。請詳細區分以下二例：

1. Manchester Trading Co., Ltd.,
16-18 Worsley Road,
Swinton, Manchester,
England. (Indented Form, Close Punctuation)

2. Messrs, W. Schulhof & Co.
65 Rue Veydt
Brussels 5, Belgium (Block Form, Open Punctuation)

Ltd. 是Limited 的縮寫，意爲股份有限公司，在英國常用。美國主要用Inc. (Incorporated)。美國的ZIP code是Zone Improvement Plan Number之略，意爲地區改善計劃號碼，有五位數字，如New York, N. Y. 10016 。第一位數字分別代表九大區域，以下兩位數代表郵政地區，最後兩位是現今的Postal Zone Number。倫敦市則以字首字母如E.C.(Eastern Central)表示九大區域，以下的數字區分爲更小的30 個地區。州名一定要用簡字。

對個人的尊稱用Mr. Mrs. Miss 等，如果在公司名號之後再接上人名時用Messrs., 沒有人名時就什麼都不必加。由公司名號決定用不用 the，要給公司內某人時，在公司名號上頭加上個人姓名，職務名稱則接於人名之後。

同時寫出收件人的姓名及職稱時，職稱放在姓名之後。若職稱太長則寫於下一行。若只寫職位而無姓名，就先寫職位名稱，之後再寫公司名號。

3. *Mr. F. Lawrence, President*
Wholesale Supplies Co., Ltd.

481 University Ave.

Toronto 2, Canada

4. *Mr. F. Lawrence*

Vice President and Manager

Wholesale Supplies Co., Ltd.

481 University Ave.

Toronto 2, Canada

寫給銀行時，收件人一定要寫The Manager。若寄給個人則依尊稱、性別及收件人數而有不同。

5. The Manager,

The Bank of Bombay, Ltd.,

Kandivli, Bombay,

India.

D.開頭稱呼語 Salutation

Salutation是信的起頭招呼語，相當於中文的敬啓者。美國式寫給個人時用Dear Sir, Dear Mr. —，寫給公司則用Gentlemen：英國式寫給個人時用法與美國式相同，給公司時就用Dear Sirs。詳細情形如下表所示：

收信人		尊稱	實例	Salutation
男性	單數	Mr.(Mister) Esq.(Esquire) Dr.(Doctor)	Mr. E. Hemingway Howard Underson, Esq. Dr. R.P. Watson	Dear Sir Dear Mr.—
男性	複數	Messrs. (Messieurs)	Messrs. Wilson & Co.	Dear Sirs Gentlemen
女性	未婚單數	Miss	Miss Janet Parker	Dear Madam
女性	未婚複數	Misses	Misses Lucy and Bessy Smith	Dear Ladies Dear Mesdames
女性	已婚單數	Mrs. (Mistress)	Mrs. Lucy Wood	Dear Madam
女性	已婚複數	Mmes. (Mesdames)	Mmes. Lucy Cole and Jane Bennett	Dear Ladies Dear Mesdames

E.本文 Body of the Letter

Body of the Letter 是書信的本文，用 Indented Form 時，各個段落起頭須與右端間隔五～十個字母開打。Block Form 則採左端對齊的形式，不必間隔，各段落間，相隔 double spacing 以上，各行間隔single spacing, 但若信件過短時，可另外安排適當的間隔。通常可能的話，最好一張信紙寫完，若超過一張，從第二張起用和第一張相同而沒有 Letterhead 的信紙，在信紙上端記下收信人姓名、頁數及日期，如下：

Messrs. R.P. Blackmur & Co. —2— May 5, 19—

最後一頁最少要寫二～三行，不能只有 Complimentary Close 和 Signature。

F.結尾謙稱 Complimentary Close

Complimentary 是最後的祝詞，相當於中文的「敬上」。最後需加逗號。

美式	英式
Yours very truly,	Yours faithfully,
Very truly yours,	Faithfully yours,
Yours truly,	
Truly yours,	

特別表示敬意時（英美用法相同）：

Yours respectfully, Respectfully yours,

表示親密時（英美用法相同）：

Cordially yours, Sincerely yours, 或 Yours sincerely,

G.簽名 Signature

簽名乃表示信文執筆者負責之意，爲防止假冒，務要親自簽上不易模仿的字跡。如果是以公司名義簽署，則應打上大寫的公司名號，再由公司授權簽署的人簽名，然後打上簽署者姓名，其下再打上職務名稱，例如：

General Trading Co., Ltd.

A.A. Weaver

A.A. Weaver

Sales Manager

若公司並未授權此事，則簽名時須在姓名前面加上By或Per ，或是在公司名稱前加上For或P.P.（Per Procuration）。

例如：

1. General Trading Co., Ltd.

By *David Wang*

David Wang

2. **For** General Trading Co., Ltd.

David Wang

David Wang

商業英文中，通常使用的職務名稱如下：

President 董事長

Vice-President 副董事長

Managing Director 常務董事

Executive Director 執行董事

Chief Manager, General Manager 總經理

Manager 經理

Sales Manager 銷售部經理

Export Manager 出口部經理

Business Manager 業務部經理

Assistant Manager, Sub-Manager 襄理；副理

Chief of Section 科、課長

Clerk 職員；辦事員

營業部門名稱如下：

Head Office 總公司

Division 部門

Departement 部門

Bureau 局、部

Section 科、課

Branch 分公司

Office 辦公室、辦事處

Laboratory 實驗室

H.識別記號 Identification Marks

於信末附上執筆人及打字員姓名的第一個字母，以示負責或便於必要時查考。通常寫在左下方。執筆人寫左側，打字員寫右側，這時雖寫名字的簡寫，但不必加縮寫符號（句點）。

如：EK/SM　　EK:SM　　EK–SM

ek/sm　　EK/sm

I.附帶文件說明Enclosure Directions

寄送附帶文件時，要在 Identification Marks（識別記號）下方加以標明，以提醒發信部門，避免遺漏，又可引起收信人的注意。當附件只有一樣時，標註Enc.即可，一件以上時，則要標註 Enclos.，右側接打附件的名稱及數量。例如：

1. Enc. Catalog 1

2. Enclos. Catalog 3

Price List 2

J.補述 Postscript（P.S.）

若寫完信之後還須再附加任何項目時，就得寫上補述，類似中文信的附筆。有時這並非把忘了寫的事情補上，而是故意特別引起對方的注意。P.S.的位置在Enclosure Directions下方，寫完P.S.之後，再把簽署人姓名的第一個字母加在最後。

例如：**NT**/SM

P.S. We have just received a telegram from our buyer stating "QUOTE 500 1-BAND TRANSISTOR SHIPMENT JULY". Please send us your quotation urgently. **NT**.

K.特定稱呼 Particular Address

想讓公司某部門全體職員看這封信，或希望某人注意收看此信時，應使用特定稱呼。有時也叫Attention Line或Attention Notation。通常寫在Inside Address下方，方法如下：

Messrs. Wilson & Co.
Bracken House, Cannon Street
Australia

Attention: Mr. H. Lees

Dear Sirs,

Wholesale Supplies Co., Ltd.
481 University Ave.
Torando 2, Canada

Attention: Sales Department

Dear Sirs,

此時，即使Attention是單數，開頭稱呼語，仍然用複數，例如Dear Sirs，或Gentlemen。Attention也可以寫成att.或attn.

L.標題 Letter Subject

在本文中央的上方簡單地寫出提要，並在提要下畫線，以引起對方注意，使收信人一眼便看出來信的主旨，以利業務處理。老式的寫法於Letter Subject前加上Re：或Subject：，現多已揚棄不用。(re是拉丁文的in the matter = in re 之略)。此外應注意，標題不必是完整的句子，只要簡單扼要地寫出主旨即可。

例如：

<u>Your Order 3045 ：Portable TV</u>

M.參照號碼 Reference Number

貿易往來函件繁多，為了便於參照處理或歸檔保管，必須標明參照號碼。一般都寫在 Inside Address 上方，Letterhead 下方，可以按部門、產品、地區或客戶加以分類，例如：

Your Ref. MA — 108

Our Ref. RS — 285

第3章

書信的格式

Styles of the Letter

信件各部分的安排，就整體形式而言，可分爲三類，即 Indented Form（鋸齒式），Block Form（齊頭式）及Modified Block Form（折衷式）。用 Indented Form時，Inside Address 各行往右斜下，本文各段落起首要向右退五～十個字母開打，簽名部分也需順次右斜。Block Form的各部分都齊頭打，左端是垂直的，如下圖所示：

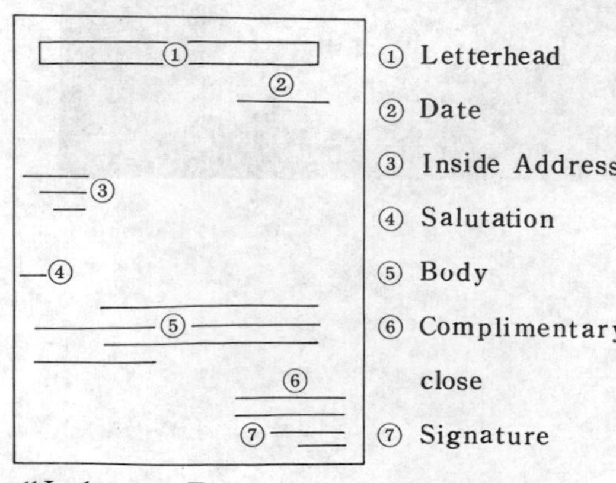

≪Indented Form≫

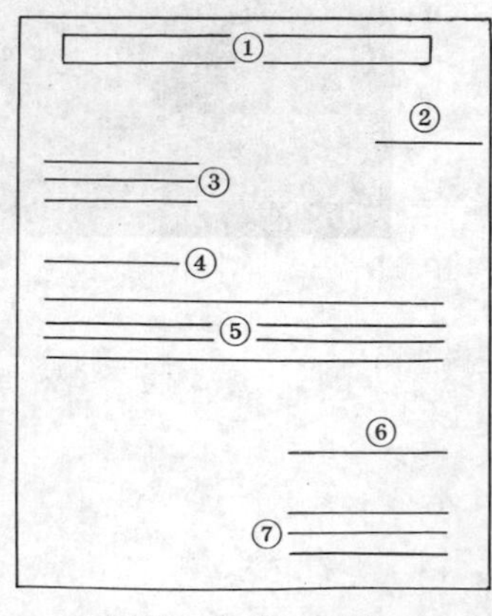

≪Block Form≫

英國式多採用 Indented Form，其優點是各部分清晰明瞭，但打字時較費事。美國式多採用Block Form，它的優點是便於打字，不易出錯，但較不易閱讀。折衷兩者優點的Modified Block Form（又稱Mixed Form或Semi-block Form）除了本文呈鋸齒式之外，其餘各部分齊頭打，是較為理想的格式。

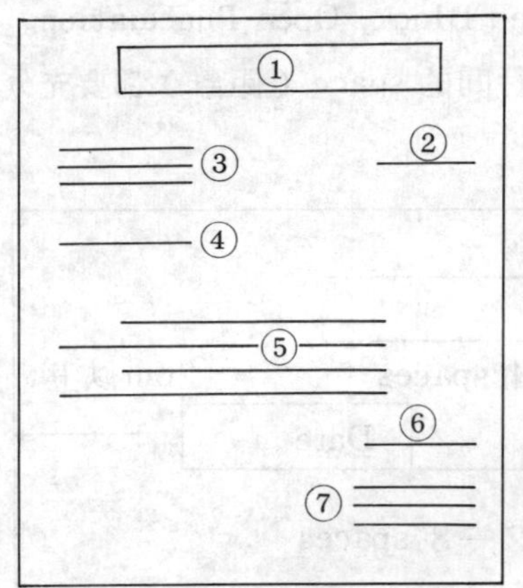

《Modified Block Form》

此外，若就 Punctuation（標點）而言，英文書信可以分為Open Punctuation 及Close Punctuation兩類。Close Punctuation就是發信日期、收信人姓名地址、及結尾謙稱部分的段末加逗點。而句尾加句點之謂。Open Punctuation 是以上三部分的段末或句尾都不加標點符號者。近來使用Open Punctuation 較Close Punctuation 更為頻繁。

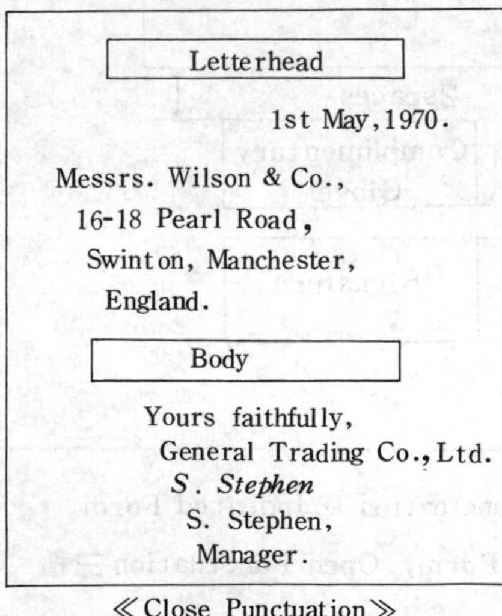
Letterhead

1st May, 1970.

Messrs. Wilson & Co.,
16-18 Pearl Road,
Swinton, Manchester,
England.

Body

Yours faithfully,
General Trading Co., Ltd.
S. Stephen
S. Stephen,
Manager.

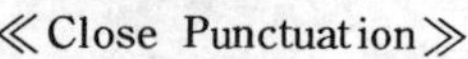
《Close Punctuation》

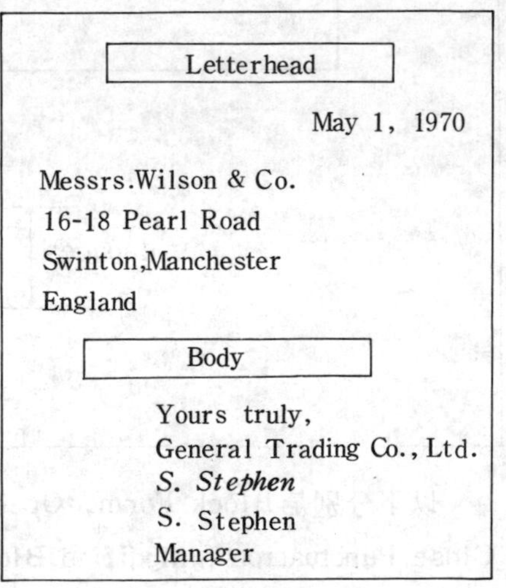
Letterhead

May 1, 1970

Messrs.Wilson & Co.
16-18 Pearl Road
Swinton,Manchester
England

Body

Yours truly,
General Trading Co., Ltd.
S. Stephen
S. Stephen
Manager

《Open Punctuation》

整體而論，最理想的形式應該是Modified Block，Open Punctuation。其他如信件左右的空白margin(邊緣)及各行間的space（距離）都要充分注意。各部分的間隔如下：

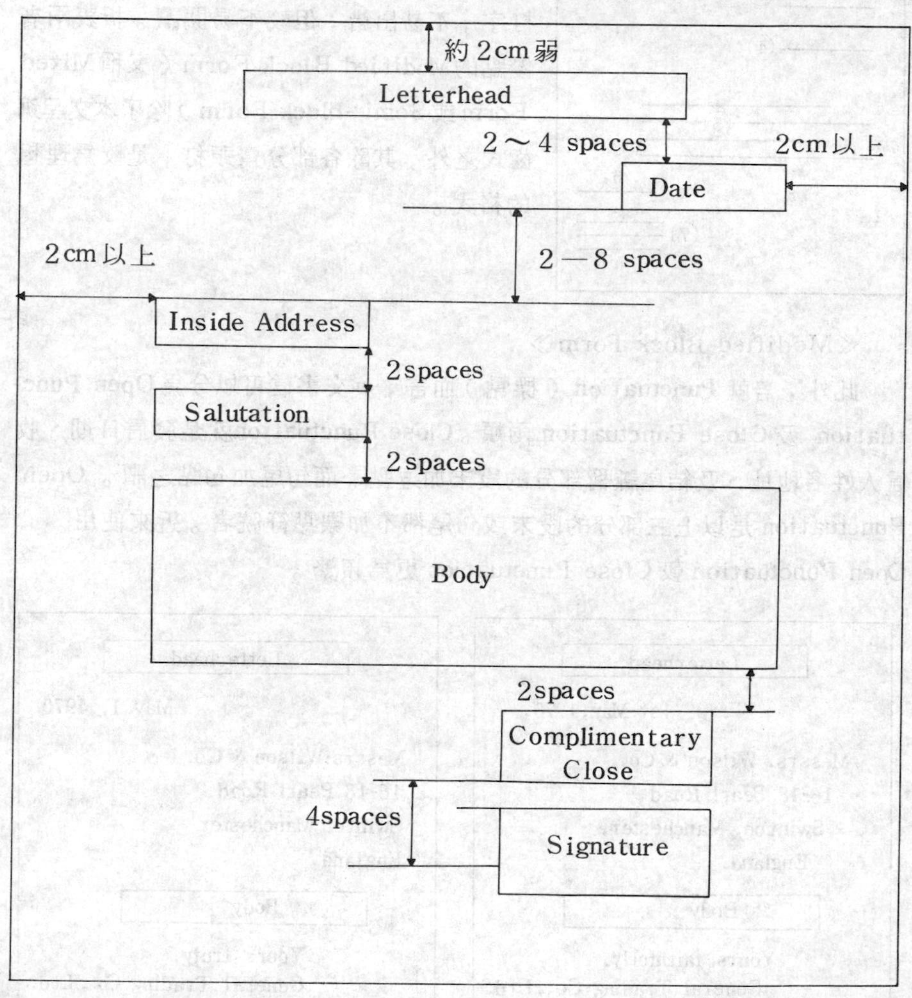

以下分別是Block Form，Open Punctuation 及 Indented Form，Close Punctuation 和Modified Block Form，Open Punctuation 三種形式的書信實例。

Business Machine Co., Ltd.

Cable Address:
BUSINESS TAIPEI
Telex: TK4328
Codes Used:
Acme; Private

Importers & Exporters of
Business Machine
22 Nanking West Road,
Taipei,
Taiwan, R.O.C.

Branches:
Hong Kong
London
New York

13th May, 19—

Wholesaler Business Machine Co., Ltd.,
5 Winsley Street, London W1,
England.

Dear Sirs,

Printing Machine

Thank you very much for your letter of April 1 offering a proposal to commence negotiation in the sale of your business machines.

We are now in demand for your machine, rotary offset with high efficiency, Model ROH-650. We would like to have a fully detailed pamphlet concerning the above machine. Also, please send us your latest catalog and technical information for the above with price list and possible delivery date as soon as possible.

If your price is reasonable and delivery is superior to other suppliers, we will be pleased to place an order with you.

Yours faithfully,
Business Machine Co., Ltd.,
Ted Wang
Ted Wang
Import Manager.

TW/RI

(Indented Form; Close Punctuation)

Business Machine Co., Ltd.

Cable Address:	Importers & Exporters of	Branches:
BUSINESS TAIPEI	Business Machine	Hong Kong
Telex: TK4328	22 Nanking West Road	London
Codes Used:	Taipei	New York
Acme; Private	Taiwan, R.O.C.	

May 13, 19—

Wholesaler Business Machine Co., Inc.
63 Fourth Avenue, New York, N.Y.10003

Gentlemen:

Printing Machine

Thank you very much for your letter of April 1 offering a proposal to commence negotiation in the sale of your business machines.

We are now in demand for your machine, rotary offset with high efficiency, Model ROH-650. We would like to have a fully detailed pamphlet concerning the above machine. Also, please send us your latest catalog and technical information for the above with price list and possible delivery date as soon as possible.

If your price is reasonable and delivery is superior to other suppliers, we will be pleased to place an order with you.

Very truly yours,
Business Machine Co., Ltd.
Ted Wang
Ted Wang
Import Manager

tw/ht

(Block Form; Open Punctuation)

Business Machine Co., Ltd.

Cable Address:	Importers & Exporters of	Branches:
BUSINESS TAIPEI	Business Machine	Hong Kong
Telex: TK4328	22 Nanking West Road	London
Codes Used:	Taipei	New York
Acme; Private	Taiwan, R.O.C.	

May 13, 19—

Wholesaler Business Machine Co., Inc.
63 Fourth Avenue, New York, N.Y. 10003

Gentlemen:

Printing Machine

Thank you very much for your letter of April 1 offering a proposal to commence negotiation in the sale of your business machines.

We are now in demand for your machine, rotary offset with high efficiency, Model ROH-650. We would like to have a fully detailed pamphlet concerning the above machine. Also, please send us your latest catalog and technical information for the above with price list and possible delivery date as soon as possible.

If your price is reasonable and delivery is superior to other suppliers, we will be pleased to place an order with you.

Very truly yours,
Business Machine Co., Ltd.
Ted Wang
Ted Wang
Import Manager

TW-HT

(Modified Block Form; Open Punctuation)

A.信封 Envelope

信封通常用白色的，大小規格主要分兩類。

a. Business Size　西式七號（16.5 cm × 9.2 cm）
主要作爲商用。

b. Official Size　西式四號（24 cm × 10.5 cm）
主要用於公文及契約。

除此之外，也可以用白色鑲藍邊的航空專用信封，務求質輕堅韌。

B.發信人名稱地址 Sender's Address

發信人的名稱、地址應該打字或印在信封左上角或封蓋上。間隔視信封大小空 Single, Double, Triple Spaces，務必與 Inside Address 的 Form（形式）和 Punctuation（標點）一致。

C.收信人名稱地址 Addressing

收信人名稱地址和 Inside Address 寫法不同，不可省略。寫在信封中下偏右，收信人姓名和國名一定要分行書寫。

D.郵寄指示 Mail Direction

郵寄方式可寫在信封的左、右下角上。

航空信： By Air Mail, AIR MAIL, PAR AVION

掛號信： Registered

限時信： Special Delivery，英國用 Express Delivery

小　包： Parcel Post

General Trading Co., Ltd.
552 Tun Hwa North Road
Taipei, Taiwan
R.O.C.

Stamp

Messrs. R.P. Blackmur & Co.
316 North Flower Street
San Francisco, California
U.S.A.

PAR AVION

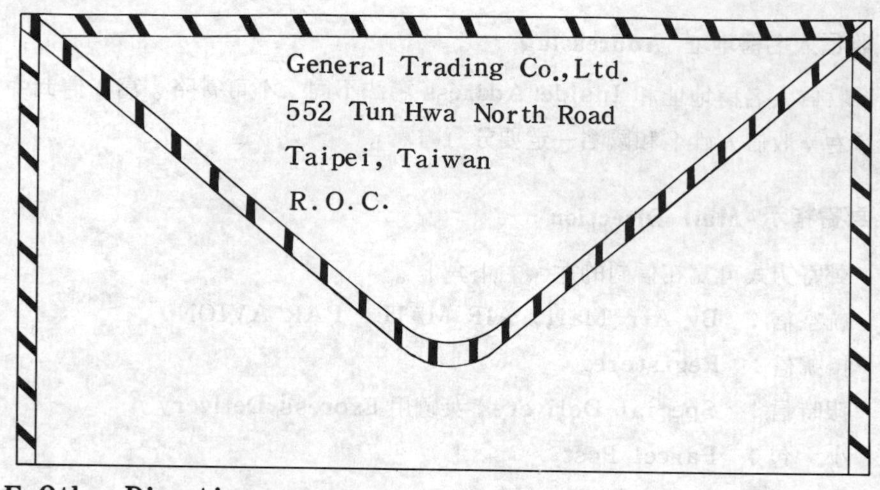

E. Other Directions

其他，若要特別提醒對方注意時，可將以下用語寫於左下角。

Printed Matter （印刷品）
Sample Matter（樣品）
Sample of No Value （免費樣品）
Strictly Confidential（密件）
Please forward to ～（請轉交給～）
Poste restante（留局待領，〔英〕）
c/o Postmaster （煩郵政局長轉交）
With Compliments（致候）
Photo（照片）
Private & Confidential（親展）
Personal（親啓）
Urgent（急件）
Immediate（急件）
General Delivery（留局待領，〔美〕）
Introducing Mr. ～ （介紹～先生）

Kindness of Mr. ～ （託～先生）

F.信件折疊與插入 Folding and Inserting

一封商務（business）用的 half-size 信紙折疊時，要先上下對摺，上部留1.5 cm ，然後由右側摺到⅓處，左側再摺疊過去，但要留下一點空間，不要摺滿，將信紙正面朝向信封背面放入，如圖所示：

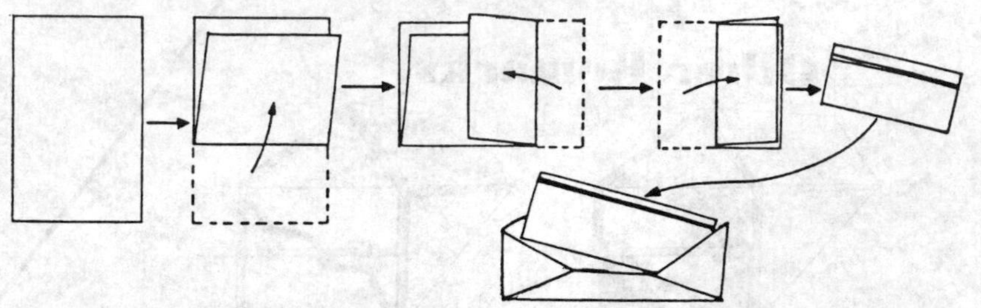

若是官方（Official）用的 Standard Size 信紙時，要由下往上折，上部留下 1.5 cm，裝入信封，如圖：

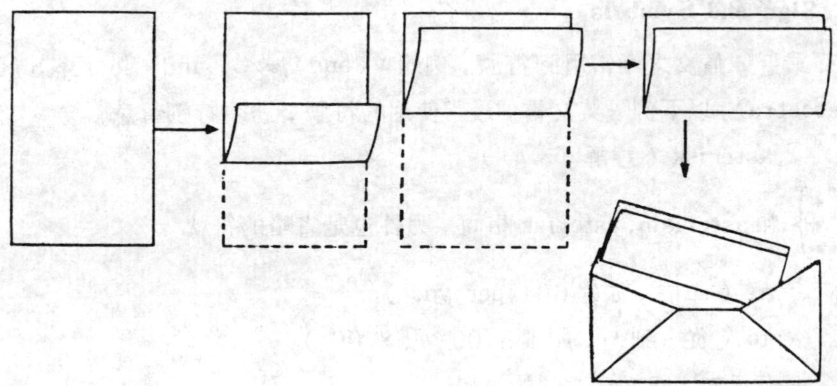

第5章 其他要點

Other Remarks

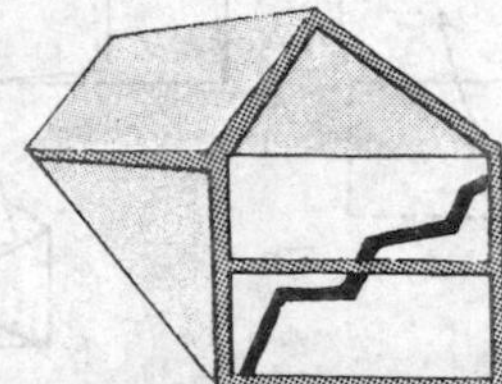

A. Sign and Symbols

最近，信文之中常用到符號，例如&(and)，&C. and (so forth) (etcetra)，以下例舉英文書信最常使用的符號，務須特別留意。

*　asterisk（註解，參照）

⁂ / *** 　和 asterism，asterisk 相同，另外也是省略的符號

@　at（單價，如@ 604 per yd.）
　to（從～到…，如$ 5.00 @ $8.00 ）

∧　表示文字與文字之間的遺漏

¢　cent

†　dagger 加在單字之後，表古字，或廢棄不用的字

> / < 　表示字源，衍生字

$ / $ 　dollar

… 省略（例如文章中途的省略）

number

¶ Paragraph

d. pence（辨士，英貨幣名稱）

£ pound（英鎊）

lb. pound（磅，重量單位）

§ section

pp. 從幾頁到幾頁

Nos.8,9 8號和9號

oz. ounce（盎司）

cu. in. cubic inch（立方英吋）

sq. in. square inch（平方英吋）

e.g. for example

ibid. ibidem在同處，在同書〔頁、句、章等〕

i.e. 也就是；換言之

op.cit. opere citato（拉丁語＝in the work cited）在已引用的書中

v. / vs. } vide supra（拉丁語＝see above）參照上面，參照上述

B. Punctuation

以下列舉標點符號，在商用場合時的代表性用法。

省略號 Apostrophe ’ 表所有或省略（如The girl’s here.）

冒 號 Colon ： 說明內容等。

逗 號 Comma ， 還未說完的話中間的停頓。

破折號 Dash — 強調。

連字號 Hyphen - 語氣轉折。

括號 Parentheses ( ) and Brackets〔 〕 內容之說明，補充。

句號 Period . 表示結束。

引號 Quotation Mark “ ” ‘ ’ 用於會話或引用句子時。

分號 Semi-colon ; 並列相同的內容。

C. Other Remarks

當單字打到行末而未能打完時，應該按音節（syllable）斷開，後面加上連字號，再接打於下一行。引用書名、報紙、雜誌名稱時，要用斜體字（Italic），或在字下劃橫線（underline）以表示斜體。縮寫時，要打上句號（period）。

PART Ⅱ

Business Relations

交易關係

第1章

建立商務關係

Establishment of Business Relations

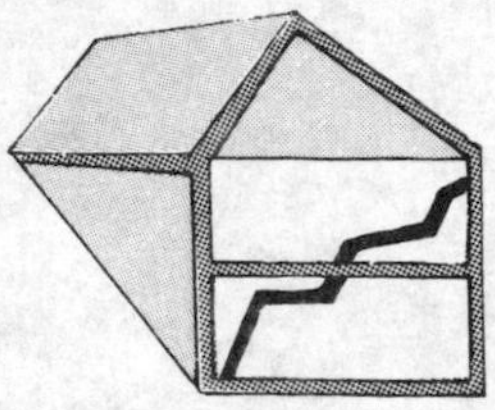

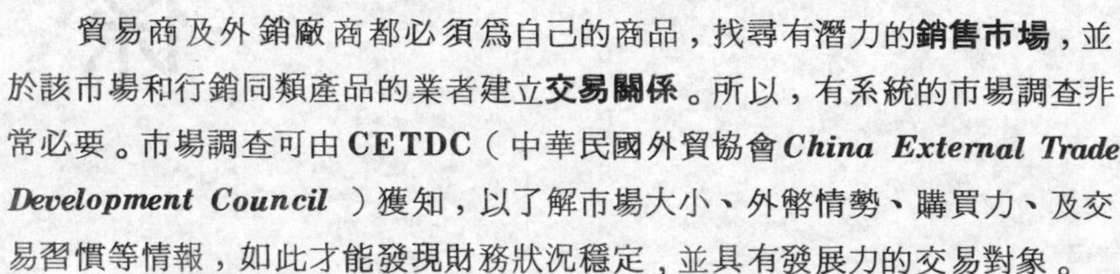

貿易商及外銷廠商都必須爲自己的商品，找尋有潛力的**銷售市場**，並於該市場和行銷同類產品的業者建立**交易關係**。所以，有系統的市場調查非常必要。市場調查可由**CETDC**（中華民國外貿協會***China External Trade Development Council***）獲知，以了解市場大小、外幣情勢、購買力、及交易習慣等情報，如此才能發現財務狀況穩定，並具有發展力的交易對象。

然後，可以利用商業報章雜誌刋登的廣告，直接請求交易，此時信文要求的重點如下：

1. 本公司產品優良，且潛力十足，如與我方交易必可獲利。

2. 公司營業之具體內容、及商品的優秀特徵。

3. 明示交易內容、交易條件、信用保證者，並希望對方也告知這些條件。

4. 附寄公司簡介、價目表及目錄。

5. 表示强烈的交易意願。

*　　　*　　　*

✤ 市場調查的線索來源：

經由經濟部、外交部、領事館、工商會館、貿易團體、外滙銀行、民間調查機構、及公司派遣的調查組織等。

✤ 發現交易對象的方法：

1. 借助工商名册（Kelly's Directory之類）。
2. 商業報章專業雜誌內的廣告。
3. 委任本公司駐國外職員。
4. 委託當地工商會館。
5. 派遣主管或職員赴國外考察。
6. 透過客戶、熟人、朋友之介紹。
7. 透過外滙銀行介紹。
8. 借助貿易市場之展售。
9. 透過總公司、同行之介紹。
10. 利用公司之代理商。

1 報紙廣告 Newspaper Advertisement

【實務須知】

- ***years of research and technological development*** ⇨長年的研究和技術發展
- earn〔ɜn〕*v.* 博得；帶來
- ***applicable patents*** ⇨可以應用的專利
- ***development program*** ⇨發展計畫
- ***for information concerning～*** ⇨關於～的資料
- ***refer to*** ⇨查詢
- affiliations〔ə,fɪlɪ'eʃən〕*n.* 聯盟；關係
- ***a fort of our future*** ⇨本公司未來的交易據點

<實 例>

The Bangkok Trade Times, March 18

Seek Agent for Electric Home Appliances

Taiwan's most rapidly developing manufacturer of Electric Home Products, "Prospect" (Mao Yuan Electric) offers you an ideal business opportunity.

Years of research and technological development have earned our company a foremost position in electrical engineering in Taiwan. A vast number of applicable patents have helped stimulate our development program over the past ten years.

Our main lines of products include:

TV, Portable Radio, Tape Recorder, Radio-phonograph, Car Radio, Car Stereo, Video Tape Recorder, Medical Instruments, Electronic Industrial Instruments, Electronic Desk Calculators, etc.

For information concerning our business outline, please refer to Bank of Taiwan and International Commercial Bank of China. Our affiliations also include RCA in New York City, U.S.A., with which we have engaged a business relationship for several years. We are a medium sized company but we are growing fast and we would like you to be a fort of our future!

The Mao Yuan Electric Co., Ltd.
552 Tun Hwa North Road, Taipei
Taiwan, R.O.C.

曼谷貿易時報，3月18日

尋求家電製品代理商

在台灣，發展最迅速的家電產品製造商──「遠景」(懋源電氣)提供您理想的生意機會。

長年的研究和技術發展，已使本公司在台灣的電氣工程界，獲得領先的地位。過去十年來，大量可以應用的專利，有助於使我們的發展計畫得到鼓勵。

本公司主要的產品包括：

電視機、手提收音機、錄音機、收音電唱機、汽車收音機、汽車音響設備、錄影機、醫療儀器、工業用電子儀器、桌上型電子計算機等等。

有關本公司業務概況的資料，請向台灣銀行及中國國際商業銀行查詢。我們的聯盟尚包括美國紐約市的RCA公司，幾年來本公司一直和其維繫交易關係。我們是一家中型公司，但是成長迅速，希望您成爲本公司的交易據點！

懋源電氣有限公司
中華民國台灣台北市敦化北路552號

**

appliance〔ə'plaɪəns〕*n.* (*pl.*) 用具；裝備　*electric appliances* 電化製品
stimulate〔'stɪmjə,let〕*v.* 鼓舞；激勵
portable〔'portəbḷ〕*adj.* 可攜帶的；可移動的
RCA爲Radio Corporation of America（美國無線電公司）的縮寫。

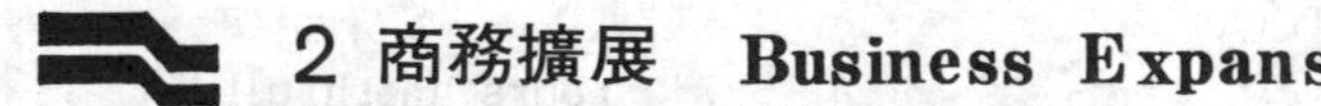

2 商務擴展　Business Expansion

【實務須知】

· ***incorporate our business activities*** = *extend our activity*
⇨擴展我們的交易活動

- ***financial status and reputation*** ⇨財務狀況和聲譽
- ***be much obliged for your introduction*** = *shall be obliged if you will introduce* ⇨感激您的介紹
- ***most reliable importer*** ⇨很值得信賴的進口商

<實例>

Dear Sirs,

Established in 1950, we have been expanding our business operations around the world as a leading exporter and importer of business machines.

Now we are planning to incorporate our business activities in your market as general base in Asia. We will be much obliged for your introduction to a most reliable importer handling business machines.

Our line of business includes :

Typewriter, Copying Machines, Calculators, Printing Machines, Cash Register, Addressing Machines, etc.

Concerning our financial status and reputation, please direct all enquiries to Bank of Taiwan, The First Commercial Bank, Taipei or The National Cash Register Co., Ltd. in Taipei.

Thank you very much for your co-operation. We hope to hear from you soon.

Yours faithfully,

敬啓者：

本公司成立於1950年，商務經營已經擴展至全世界，成爲首要的商業機器進出口商。

現在本公司正計畫在貴市場中，擴展我們的交易活動，做爲亞洲的總基地。若蒙介紹一家經銷商業機器最可靠的進口商，則不勝感激。

本公司的商品包括：

打字機、影印機、計算機、印刷機、收銀機、姓名住址印刷機等等。

關於本公司的財務狀況和聲譽，請寫信查詢台灣銀行、第一商業銀行台北分行、或是在台北的國民收銀機有限公司。

非常感謝您的合作。希望很快得到回信。

**

cash register 收銀機

addressing machine 姓名住址印刷機

enquiry〔ɪn'kwaɪrɪ〕*n.* 調查；詢問（= *inquiry*）

3 美國出口商的提案 American Exporter's Proposal

【實務須知】

- ***in the hope of opening an account with you*** = *with a desire to enter into business relation with you* ⇨希望能和貴方開啓交易關係
- ***leading exporters*** ⇨首要的出口商
- ***enjoying an excellent reputation*** ⇨享有極佳的聲譽
- ***be satisfied with our services*** ⇨對本公司的服務感到滿意
- ***the extent of our reliabilities*** ⇨我們值得信賴的程度
- ***objective information*** ⇨客觀的資料

<實例>

Gentlemen :

As your name and address were listed in The Textile Magazine, we are writing in the hope of opening an account with your company.

We are one of the leading exporters of first class cotton and rayon goods and are enjoying an excellent reputation through fifty years' business experience. We are sure that you will be quite satisfied with our services and the excellent quality of our goods.

We enclose herewith a pamphlet introducing our business standing and outline, the complete catalog of our goods, and some samples, from which you will readily observe the extent of our reliabilities.

If you need more objective information concerning our credit, please refer to The Bank of America, New York and Kahn Co., Ltd., Chicago.

We are looking forward to your early and favorable reply.

Very truly yours ,

Encls. Pamphlet 1
Catalog 1
Sample 3

敬啓者：

因爲紡織品雜誌列有貴公司的大名及地址，故寫信希望能和貴公司開啓交易關係。

本公司是高級的棉花、人造絲製品首要的出口商之一，歷經五十年的商務經驗，一直享有極佳的聲譽。我們確信貴公司必定會對本公司的服務、及產品優良的品質甚感滿意。

茲隨函附寄一本介紹本公司業務聲望及概況的小册子、完整的產品目錄、及一些樣品。從中您將很快發現，本公司值得信賴的程度。

如果貴公司需要關於本公司信用方面更客觀的資料，請向紐約的美國銀行、和芝加哥卡恩有限公司查詢。

期待貴公司儘快回覆好消息。

附寄 手册 1
目錄 1
樣品 3

**

rayon〔ˈreɑn〕*n.* 人造絲 herewith〔hɪrˈwɪθ〕*adv.* 同此；附此
pamphlet〔ˈpæmflɪt〕*n.* 小册子 catalog〔ˈkætl̩,ɔg〕*n.* 目錄
reliability〔rɪ,laɪəˈbɪlətɪ〕*n.* 可信賴性；可靠性 credit〔ˈkrɛdɪt〕*n.* 信用

實用 例句

【必備詞彙】

- publication〔,pʌblɪˈkeʃən〕*n.* 刊物
- ***open market*** ⇨打開市場
- ***your approaching them directly*** ⇨您直接和他們接洽
- ***in compliance with your request*** ⇨依從您的要求
- ***upon publication*** = ***upon hearing from you*** ⇨一刊登出來

⁂ ⁂ ⁂

1. We are seeking ***new business connections*** in your city and would appreciate your ***inserting*** the following information in your publication.

   本公司正在貴城找尋新的交易關係，若蒙將下列資料登載於貴刊上，則不勝感激。

   * insert〔ɪn'sɝt〕*v.* 刊載

2. Our firm was ***established*** in 1940 and has enjoyed an excellent ***reputation*** for these items.

   本公司成立於1940年，已經因為這些品目，而享有極佳的聲譽。

3. We wish to ***open a market*** in your district. Please introduce us to a reputable firm ***interested in*** porcelain goods.

   本公司想打開貴地區的市場。請將我們介紹給對瓷器有興趣、且聲譽良好的公司。

   * porcelain〔'porslɪn〕*n.* 瓷器

4. Messrs. Chang & Co. is one of our most trustworthy ***concerns***. As they are now making a proposal to ***act as*** an agent for Taiwan Silk Goods, we advise your approaching them directly.

   張氏公司是最值得我方信賴的公司之一。既然他們現在提議做台灣絲織品公司的代理商，我建議您直接和他們洽商。

   * Messrs. 用於商號名稱之前；用於姓名之前，為Mr.之複數
   trustworthy〔'trʌst,wɝðɪ〕*adj.* 值得信賴的
   concern〔kən'sɝn〕*n.* 公司；商店

5. ***In compliance with*** your request, we are sending herewith the names and addresses of the most reputed companies in this city.

   依從您的要求，我們隨信附寄本城最受好評的公司之名稱及地址。

6. ***As requested***, we have arranged to insert your advertisement in the next ***issue*** of our magazine. Upon publication we will send a copy directly ***to your attention***.

應您的要求，我們已安排在下一期雜誌上，刊載貴公司的廣告。一刊登出來便會即刻寄一分影本以供查照。

⁂ ⁂ ⁂

第2章 信用查詢

Credit Inquiry

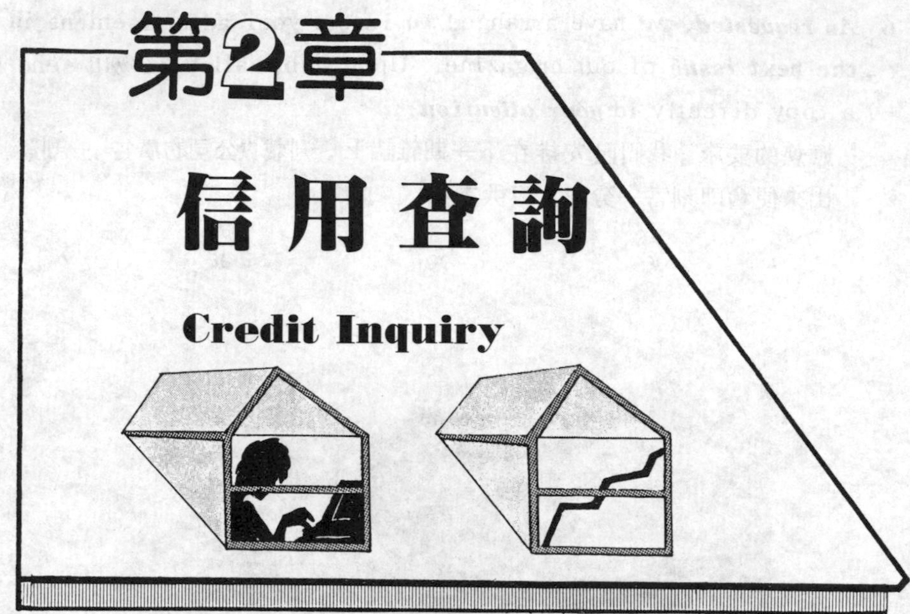

信用查詢的主要目的，是預防貿易上的糾紛。國際貿易的交易對象，大多是透過工、商會團體或老客戶的介紹，以及在報章雜誌上登廣告而獲得的。然而，在與他們從事正式交易前，必須先對其信用狀況做一番徹底的調查。

與外國公司做生意，危險性要比與國內公司做生意來得高，稍有不愼可能就會損失巨額資金，遭受嚴重的打擊，有的甚至不得不宣告倒閉。所以，一定要弄清楚對方的信用狀況才行！有人說信用調查即是針對**3C's of Credit**做調查。所謂的**3C's**指的是**Character**, **Capital**和**Capacity**。**Character**是表示對方的誠信、營業方針與公司性質；**Capital**是表示資產、財力、資金等。**Capacity**則表示營業能力、利潤和發展性。信用查詢可分爲向銀行查詢的Bank Reference（備詢銀行）和向客戶查詢的Trade Reference（備詢商號）兩種。Bank Reference固然正確又具信用，但是以數字表示的資料，不易對對方的實際狀況有所了解。

詢函的時候，切記包含以下項目：

1· 對方的名稱、地址。

2· 對方與我方的關係、調查的原因。

3· 絕對保密，不傷及對方信譽。

4· 謝辭，感謝其付出的心力，並說明願適時予以回報。

5· 爲使其便於回覆，應寄上利於回答的格式信紙及回郵信封。

信用查詢關係對方的信譽，應該認清自己的責任範圍排除主觀意識，客觀而公正地執行。特別是有不利被查詢者的回答時，不可明示其姓名，譬如寫成Mr.M～，或是 the firm you asked in your letter of May 10～等，以防秘密外洩。

*　　　　*　　　　*

✦ 以下是信用查詢的方法：

1· 委託本國駐外經濟參事機構調查。

2· 委託貿易徵信所調查（inquiry agency）。

3· 自行派調查團調查。

4· 委任本公司駐外人員調查。

5· 委託國內商會或進出口公會調查。

6· 委託當地熟悉的商號代爲調查。

7· 函請對方提供的商號備詢人（House Reference）告明。

1 備詢銀行 Bank Reference

【實務須知】

· ***would appreciate your providing us with*** ～ = *appreciate if you will furnish us with* ～ ⇨ 若蒙提供～則不勝感激

- ***any pertinent information*** ⇨任何相關資料
- a proper evaluation ⇨適切的評價
- ***strictly confidential*** ⇨絕對保守秘密
- ***upon receipt of your report*** ⇨在接到您的報告時
- look forward to = *expect* ⇨期待

＜實 例＞

Dear Sir,

The Mao Yuan Electric Co., Ltd

At the request of our client we would appreciate your providing us with any information you might have concerning the above-mentioned company.

Our client, The Bangkok Trading Co., Ltd., Bangkok Custom Bldg., has a desire to enter into business relations with the above firm. We should be much obliged, therefore, if you could supply us with any pertinent information which would help make a proper evaluation for our client.

Any information, of course, is strictly confidential and expenses will be gladly paid by us upon receipt of your report.

We look forward to your early reply.

Yours faithfully,

敬啓者：

燃源電器有限公司

應客戶的要求，若蒙提供您所擁有關於上述公司的任何資料，則不勝感激。

我們的客戶──位於曼谷惠顧大廈的曼谷貿易有限公司，想和上述公司締結交易關係。因此，若蒙提供任何相關資料，有助於替我們的客戶做適切的評價，則不勝感激。

當然，任何資料絕對保守秘密，收到您的報告後，我們樂意付出費用。

期待您早日回信。

**

request〔rɪˈkwɛst〕*n.* 要求；請求
client〔ˈklaɪənt〕*n.* 客戶；顧客

2 備詢商號 Trade Reference

【實務須知】

- ***listed in the April 1 issue*** ⇨登載於4月1日發行的刋物
- ***trade reference*** ⇨交易客戶的信用備詢處
- ***close engineering agreement*** ⇨密切的工程合約
- actual relations ⇨實際關係
- business prospect ⇨業務展望
- ***similar opportunity arises*** ⇨類似的機會發生

<實 例>

Gentlemen :

The Mao Yuan Electric Co., Ltd., Taipei , Taiwan

Your name was listed in the April 1 issue of The Bangkok Trade Times as an important trade reference by the above company which is seeking capable dealers in our area.

They are reputed to be one of the most reliable electronics product manufacturers working under a close engineering agreement with your company.

We shall appreciate it if you will kindly inform us of your actual relations with them, and your opinion on their business prospects in the future by answering the questions in the attached papers.

We assure you that all information will be kept in strict confidence. We will be very glad to reciprocate your assistance when a similar opportunity arises.

Thank you very much for your continued assistance and cooperation.

Yours very truly,

敬啓者：

台灣台北市懋源電氣有限公司

貴公司名號登載於４月１日發行的曼谷貿易時報上，爲上述公司重要的信用備詢處，該公司正在本地尋找有能力的貿易商。

他們被譽爲最可靠的電子產品製造商之一，在和貴公司訂立密切的工程合約下生產。

若蒙好意回答所附文件上的問題，以告知本公司您和他們的實際關係、以及對他們未來業務展望的意見，則不勝感激。

我方確保所有資料將嚴守秘密。當有類似的機會時，我方將很樂意回報貴公司的協助。

非常感謝貴公司持續的協助和合作。

**

dealer〔'dilɚ〕*n*. 貿易商；商人

manufacturer〔,mænjə'fæktʃərɚ〕*n*. 製造商

attached〔ə'tætʃt〕*adj*. 附上的　confidence〔'kɑnfədəns〕*n*. 秘密

reciprocate〔rɪ'sɪprə,ket〕*v*. 回報

3 答覆查詢 Reference Reply

【實務須知】

- ***most responsible dealers*** ⇨ 最負責的貿易商
- ***textile goods*** ⇨ 紡織品
- quality goods ⇨ 品質優良的貨物
- ***their financial status is stable*** ⇨ 他們的財務狀況穩定
- ***rated as A1 company*** ⇨ 被評定爲第一等的公司
- ***can deal freely without risk*** ⇨ 可放心交易而安全無虞
- ***your proposed business negotiations*** ⇨ 你們提出的商務交涉
- ***in making a decision*** ⇨ 在做決定上

<實 例>

Gentlemen :

The Wolesale Textile Supplies Co., Ltd.

The firm mentioned in your letter of August 19 is one of the most responsible dealers of textile goods.

The company was established in 1920, and has supplied our firm with quality goods for over fifty years.

They have always provided complete satisfaction with delivery, moderate prices and superior quality. Moreover, their financial status is quite stable.

We believe that they may be rated as an A1 company with which you can deal freely without risk. Of course, this is our personal opinion and we assume no responsibility in your proposed business negotiations.

We hope the above is satisfactory and will help you in making a decision.

Very truly yours,

敬啓者：

Wolesale 紡織有限公司

貴公司8月19日來信所提到的公司，是最負責的紡織品貿易商之一。

該公司成立於 1920 年，供應我方品質優良的貨物已經逾五十年之久。

他們提供的交貨、適中的價格、和優良的品質，始終令人完全滿意。

而且，他們的財務狀況相當穩定。

相信他們可以被評定爲第一等的公司，可放心與之交易而安全無虞。當然，這是我方私人的意見，對你們所提出的商務交涉，本公司不負任何責任。

希望以上所述能令貴公司滿意,並有助於您做決定。

** ―――――――――――――

moderate〔ˈmɑdərɪt〕*adj*. 適中的　assume〔əˈsjum〕*v*. 負責；承擔

superior〔səˈpɪrɪɚ〕*adj*. 優良的

【必備詞彙】

- ***you inquired about*** ⇨貴公司查詢～
- ***a delay in payment*** ⇨付款的延誤
- ***in response to your inquiry*** ⇨答覆貴公司的查詢
- ***bankruptcy of his company is very likely*** ⇨他的公司非常有可能會破產
- ***our inability to let you know*** ⇨本公司無法讓貴公司知道
- ***a credit agency*** ⇨徵信所

⁂　⁂　⁂

1. The company ***you inquired about*** in your letter of April 1 is considered to have an excellent business reputation. Several times we have sold goods amounting to eight million dollars, but have never experienced ***a delay in payment***.

貴公司4月1日來信查詢的公司，被認爲擁有優良的商業聲譽。本公司曾經賣過好幾次高達八百萬元的貨物，但是從未碰過付款的延誤。

* ***amount to*** 共達；總計

2. Please furnish us with your frank opinion on their financial status, way of doing business and reputation in your city.

   請坦白提供本公司，有關他們的財務狀況、交易方式、及在貴城的聲譽。

3. ***In response to your inquiry*** about Mr. T, we are very sorry to say that we had to press him for payment many times, and were finally obliged to take legal steps to recover the balance of our account.

   答覆貴公司查詢有關T先生的事,很抱歉,我方必須說，有好幾次本公司必須催促他付款，而最後不得不採取法律途徑，以取得帳款的差額。

   * recover〔rɪˈkʌvɚ〕*v*. 取得

   * balance〔ˈbæləns〕*n*. 差額

4. The person in question is reported to be in a difficult financial condition and unable to meet the obligation. Under the circumstances ***bankruptcy of his company is very likely***. Therefore we advise you not to enter into any business relation with him.

   據說您所詢問的人財務狀況很困難，無法償還債務。有鑑於此，他的公司很可能會破產。因此勸告貴公司不要和他締結任何交易關係。

   * ***meet the obligation*** 償還債務

5. We regret ***our inability to let you know*** anything positive concerning the above firm. It would be advisable for you to instruct ***a credit agency*** to investigate the matter.

   很抱歉，本公司無法讓貴公司知道關於上述公司任何肯定的資料。貴公司指示徵信所調查這件事將是明智的。

* advisable〔 əd'vaɪzəbḷ 〕*adj*. 可行的；明智的

6. We will keep any information you give us in strict confidence and gladly reciprocate your assistance when a similar occasion arises.

貴公司提供的任何資料，本公司將嚴守秘密，當有類似的機會發生時，我方將樂意回報貴公司的協助。

* reciprocate〔 rɪ'sɪprə,ket 〕*v*. 回報

※ ※ ※

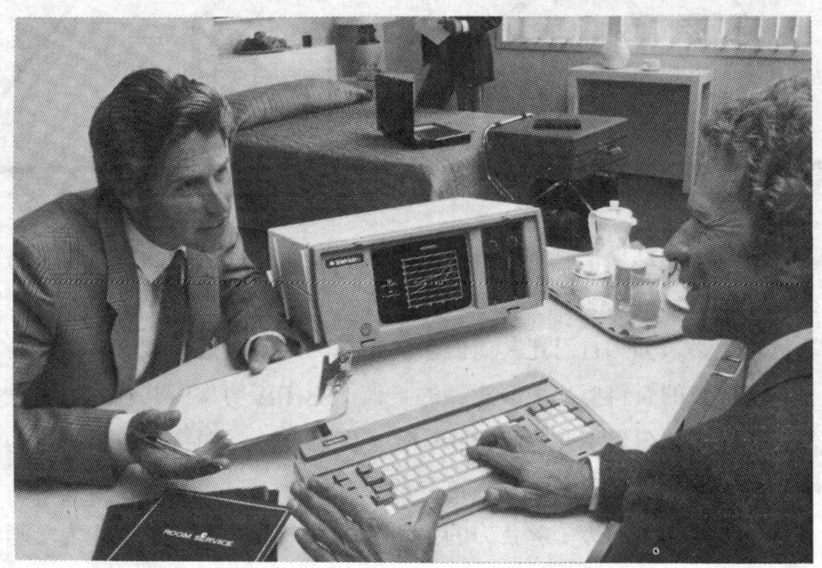

信用調查的結果，確定對方有令人滿意且穩固的**信用狀態**時，就可開始進行實際的**交易提案**。

這時，必須強調自己比其他競爭者優秀的地方，以爭取有利的機會。爲此，提出客觀的資料要比主觀意識的東西，更能證明您所具備的有利條件。此外，從衆多競爭對手將自己***identify***（**突出化**），明確地打出自己的特色，給予深刻強烈的印象，是非常重要的。

另外，爲了讓對方了解我方的信用狀況、公司狀態、營業能力，應該備妥公司簡介、目錄、樣品册、報表、主要往來商號一覽表，不只希望贏得交易機會，也要將自己的PR（*public relations*）打通。信文內容應注意下列要點：

1. 陳述向對方申請交易的過程。這時，若能舉出較具權威的介紹者就更好了。

2. 希望交易的商品、營業內容——即交易型態，說明是本人或代理人

託售或直接交易。

3. 說明公司的交易資歷、營業能力、資金、發展潛力。

4. 說明交易條件、交易內容、付款條件。

5. 必要時提供備詢商號(Trade Reference)。

6. 進口時說明本公司的推銷能力,出口時強調本公司產品之優點。

7. 以吸引對方採取行動的言辭,做強而有力的結尾。

付款條件中,特別需要明確提出的問題,包括有否信用狀及其種類,滙票期限、裝運文件的交割條件等,所以要使用到這類特別用法及字彙。

* * *

1 交易提案 Trade Proposal

【實務須知】

- ***a negotiating firm for establishing a base sales point*** ⇨建立銷售據點的交涉公司
- ***specializing in your commodities*** ⇨專營您這方面的商品
- ***in these lines*** ⇨在這些貨品方面
- ***add to your line of business*** ⇨增加您營業的種類
- ***a superior competitive position*** ⇨優越的競爭地位
- ***letter of credit*** ⇨信用狀
- ***a draft may be drawn at sight*** ⇨可見票付款的滙票;可開立即期滙票
- ***standing***〔'stændɪŋ〕*n.* 信用狀況

<實 例>

Dear Sirs,

Your name has been listed by the Hong Kong Chamber of Commerce as one of the leading dealers of business machines in your city and a negotiating firm for establishing a base sales point with reliable dealers.

As the enclosed pamphlet shows, we have been specializing in your commodities for over twenty years. Our wide experience in these lines will surely add to your line of business. Moreover, our broad range of business affiliations with many companies in surrounding cities places us in a superior competitive position.

We would like very much to open an account with you, and hope that a mutually agreeable consideration of interests can be arranged.

Enclosed is a sample letter of credit under which a draft may be drawn at sight.

For further information as to our standing, please refer to The Shanghai Commercial & Savings Bank, Hong Kong.

Looking forward to your prompt reply, we remain,

Yours faithfully,

敬啓者：

貴公司的大名已經被香港商會列爲貴城首要的商業機器貿易商之一，也是與可靠的貿易商建立銷售據點的交涉公司。

如附寄的小册子所示，本公司專營您這方面的商品已經達二十年以上。以本公司在這些貨品方面廣博的經驗，必然能增加貴公司營業的種類。再加上和附近城市許多公司間廣濶的商業聯盟，使本公司處於優良的競爭地位。

非常渴望和貴公司開啓交易關係，也希望在利益方面能協商相互合意的報酬。

隨函奉寄一張可以開立即期滙票的信用狀樣本。

有關我方信用狀況更進一步資料，請查詢上海商業儲蓄銀行香港分行。

期待貴公司儘快回信。

** ______

range〔 rendʒ 〕*n*. 範圍　affiliation〔 ə,fılı'eʃən 〕*n*. 聯盟；關係

agreeable〔 ə'griəbḷ 〕*adj*. 愉快的；合意的

2 應徵代理店 Agency Application

【實務須知】

- market〔 'mɑrkıt 〕*v*. 出售；交易
- ***customer market here*** ⇨本地的顧客市場
- ***moderate price*** = *inexpensive*, *reasonable*, *competitive*, *low price*, *etc*. ⇨適中的價格
- ***make～thorough success*** ⇨使～全然成功
- ***terms and conditions of your business*** ⇨貴公司的交易條件及狀況
- brochure〔 bro'ʃʊr 〕*n*. 手册（= *pamphlet*, *booklet*, *tract*）

• ***further information*** ⇨進一步的資料

<實 例>

Dear Sirs,

Application for Agency

We are very interested in your advertisement of March 18 seeking an agent here.

Since our establishment in 1940, we have been marketing various German and British electric & electronic products. Recently, however, they have opened a direct sales office here and no longer need our specialized services.

The general customer market here is quite interested in Taiwanese products of moderate prices but fine quality like yours. With our long experience in marketing, we would like to offer our services as your agent for Bangkok.

As the top wholesaler here we are confident of making your business operation in this area a thorough success. If you are interested in our proposal, please let us know the terms and conditions of your business. Details of our business and references are stated in the attached brochure.

If any further information is required, please let us know. As your agent in Bangkok we believe we can assure your operations here will be met with complete satisfaction.

Faithfully yours,

Enc. Pamphlet 1

敬啓者：

應徵代理商

本公司對貴公司3月18日在本地尋求代理商的廣告，甚感興趣。

本公司成立於1940年，銷售德國、英國各種電氣和電子產品。然而他們最近已經在這兒開設直接銷售處，不再需要本公司專門的服務。

本地一般的顧客市場，對像貴公司這樣的台灣產品，價錢適中，但品質優良，甚感興趣。本公司願以長久的銷售經驗，提供服務，做您曼谷的代理商。

身爲此地首要的批發商，我方有信心促使您在本區的商務經營，獲得全然成功。如果貴公司對本公司的提議感興趣,請告知貴公司的交易條件及狀況。有關本公司商務及備詢的詳細資料，均載於附寄的手册上。

如果需要任何進一步的資料，敬請告知。若有幸爲貴公司的曼谷代理商，本公司相信可以確保，貴公司對此地的業務必定完全滿意。

附寄　手册 1

** ———————————

specialize〔ˈspɛʃəl,aɪz〕*v.* 特殊化；專攻

wholesaler〔ˈhol,selɚ〕*n.* 批發商　operation〔,ɑpəˈreʃən〕*n.* 業務經營

【必備詞彙】

- ***be not represented*** ⇨ 尚無代理店
- ***with our sufficient capital and intimate knowledge of business***
  ⇨ 以本公司充足的資金和深入的商務知識
- ***a draft at*** 90 ***d/s on D/A*** ⇨ 承兌後交單據，見票九十天後付款滙票

- ***liberal term*** ⇨ 寬大的條件
- ***best interests are considered*** ⇨ 最大利益已考慮進去
- ***in this offering*** ⇨ 這個提議
- ***the Taiwanese electrical products purchase*** ⇨ 台灣電器產品的購買
- ***buying agent*** ⇨ 採購代理商 ＜比較＞ ***selling agent*** ⇨ 銷售代理商

⁂ ⁂ ⁂

1. As we have learned from our customer Mr. Chin that you are anxious to extend your activity in our market and ***are not represented*** at present, we would like to recommend our company as a most suitable agent for your products. ***With our sufficient capital and intimate knowledge of business***, we are sure that we can help you establish a ***successful business corporation*** in our area.

   從客戶金先生那兒得知,貴公司渴望在本地市場擴展業務活動,而目前尚無代理店，因此想毛遂自薦，作貴產品最適宜的代理商。以本公司充足的資金和深入的商務知識,我方確信,可以幫助貴公司在本區設立成功的商務公司。

   * recommend〔ˌrɛkəˈmɛnd〕*v*. 推薦

2. As we have marketed your line of products in large quantities, we are confident you will be quite satisfied with our services.

   由於一直大量銷售貴公司這一類的產品,本公司有自信,您必定會對我方的服務相當滿意。

3. As to payment, we will draw you ***a draft at*** 90 ***d/s on D/A***. These are very ***liberal terms*** and we feel your ***best interests are considered in this offering.***

至於付款方面，本公司將以承兌交單的條件，開立見票九十天後付款的滙票。這些條件非常寬大，我方認爲此提議已考慮到貴公司最大的益。

* ***d/s = days after sight*** 見票後……天付款

D/A = documents against acceptance 承兌交單；承兌後交單據

4. Having heard your name from First National City Bank, New York, we are approaching you ***with a keen desire*** to enter into a successful business relationship.

本公司從紐約國家市立第一銀行得知貴公司大名,此刻和您接洽,渴望締結成功的交易關係。

5. We assure you of the utmost cooperation and expect to establish a mutually profitable business relationship in the near future.

本公司向貴公司確保,必定全力合作,並期望未來不久即能建立相互有利的交易關係。

* profitable〔ˈprɑfɪtəbl̩〕*adj.* 有利的

6. We believe this is an excellent opportunity for you to strengthen your situation in regard to the ***Taiwanese electrical products purchase,*** and we are quite willing to offer our services as your ***buying agents*** in this area.

相信這是極佳的機會，來加強貴公司對台灣電氣產品的購買情勢，本公司極樂意提供服務，以爲貴公司在此地的採購代理商。

* ***in regard to*** 關於

⁂ ⁂ ⁂

第4章

介紹公司的印刷品

Printed Materials introducing the company

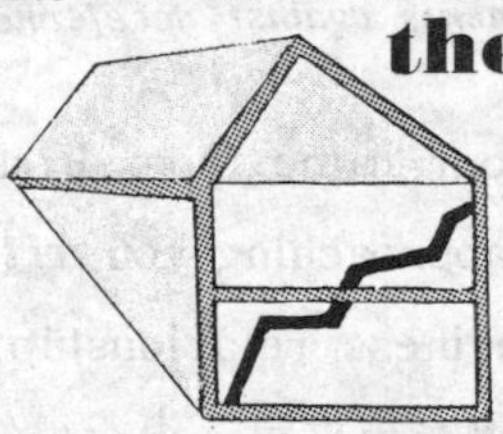

在申請交易之際，若只憑信件敍述，無法使對方充分了解我方狀況。公司中應經常備有**Pamphlet**（手册）、**Catalog**（目錄）、**Statements**（財務報表）等，做爲公司簡介資料，隨時可以寄給對方。這不僅可以說明本身的業務內容，並有藉著了解與好感達成交易的積極效果，千萬馬虎不得。這類資料就某種意義而言，是信件所無可比擬的客觀資料，可資對方嚴密研討，所以，千萬不要吝惜金錢，必以能充分引起對方興趣的高尚品味爲重。它們可算是無聲的說服利器，效果非同小可。

1 商務概況 Business Outline

【實務須知】

- *make great strides* ⇨ 有長足的進步
- *electronic industrial & medical instrument* ⇨ 工業及醫療用電子儀器

• ***authorized capital*** ⇨ 額定資金
• ***incorporate*** 〔ɪn'kɔrpə,ret〕 *v*. 合併；組成

<實 例>

Guide To Prospect

Ever since its inception more than half a century ago, The Mao Yuan Electric Company has been making great strides under the motto "Create And Apply New Ideas." The staff members of our company have been endeavoring for a higher living standard, and are dedicated to the improvement of society through the manufacture of unique products, electronic home devices and industrial equipment.

Chronological History (1930 — 1985)

1930 Mr. Jen-chieh Wu, president, establishes The Mao Yuan Company.

1940 Production of AC tube radio begins.

1946 Assembly conveyor system adopted.

1950 Hsinchu plant established.

1959 Company renamed The Mao Yuan Electric Co., Ltd.

1966 TV production started.

1970 Engineering agreement concluded with RCA.

1973 Production-Tape Recorder, Radio-phonograph, Electronic Industrial & Medical Instruments begins.

1977 World-wide sales network incorporated.

Business Outline

Authorized Capital	US$14,200,000.00
Issued Capital	US$ 4,141,400.00

Established	April, 1930
Incorporated	May, 1959
Head Office & Main Plant & Central Research Laboratory	552 Tun Hwa North Rd., Taipei
Hsinchu Plant	31 Chung Cheng Rd., Hsinchu
Branches	Tachih, Peitou, Sanchung, Yungho, Chungho, Chingmei, Mucha

遠景指南

懋源電氣公司自從五十多年前創立以來，一直本著「創造並應用新構想」的座右銘，而獲得長足的進步。本公司全體員工爲更高的生活水準而努力，經由製造卓越的產品、家庭電子裝置、及工業設備，致力改善社會。

年代紀事（1930～1985）

1930　董事長吳仁傑先生創立懋源公司。

1940　開始生產交流電收音機。

1946　採用整體自動輸送裝配作業系統。

1950　設立新竹廠。

1959　公司更名爲懋源電氣有限公司。

1966　開始生產電視機。

1970　和美國無線電公司締結工程合約。

1973　開始生產錄音機、無線電唱機、工業及醫療用電子儀器。

1977　合併遍及全世界的銷售網。

業務概況

額定資金　　美金一千四百二十萬元正

發行資金	美金四百一十四萬一千四百元正
創立	1930年4月
組成有限公司	1959年5月
總公司、主廠、研究實驗中心	台北市敦化北路552號
新竹廠	新竹市中正路31號
分廠	大直、北投、三重、永和、中和、景美、木柵。

**

inception〔ɪnˈsɛpʃən〕*n.* 開始；開端

make great strides 突飛猛進；大有進步

dedicate〔ˈdɛdəˌket〕*v.* 獻身；致力

chronological〔ˌkrɑnəˈlɑdʒɪkl̩〕*adj.* 按年代的

conveyor〔kənˈveɚ〕*n.* 自動輸送裝置

conclude〔kənˈklud〕*v.* 締結；訂立

2 商務介紹 Business Introduction

【實務須知】

- ***the central research laboratory*** ⇨研究實驗中心
- ***push forward research*** ⇨全力研究
- ***rigidity yielding "Trust"*** ⇨嚴格產生「信用」
- ***precision gauges and meters*** ⇨精密的計量器
- ***labyrinthine circuit*** ⇨錯綜複雜的電路

<實 例>

Activity for Electric Living in the Future

The central research laboratory is engaged in analyzing the wonders of the "world of electronics", with its limitless potentiality for the future. The carefully selected technical staff, with superb research facilities and the traditional frontier spirit, have a variety of achievements behind them, and are now pushing forward research on all kinds of electronic instruments.

Rigidity Yielding "Trust"

Check after check —— this is the field which is placed under the severest control of Prospect technical superiority. No product is sent out to the market unless our veteran inspectors give it an approval, after rigid checkups with precision gauges and meters. Prospect products which enjoy a high reputation come through control that some may consider too rigid.

Traditional Techniques Tackling Electronics

Electronic equipment requiring top-level technical skill …… a table calculator with 600 transistors and 1,900 diodes, and other electronic equipment with labyrinthine circuit are manufactured through the full use of our technical skill and contemporary electronic knowledge and experience.

未來電氣化生活的活動

研究實驗中心致力分析「電子世界」的奧妙，具有未來無限的潛力。經過細心挑選的技術人員，以優越的研究設備、和傳統的拓荒精神，已經獲得各種不同的成就，而目前正全力研究各類電子儀器。

嚴格產生「信用」

檢查再檢查——是遠景優越技術最嚴格管制下的領域。除非經過本公司熟練的品管人員，以精密的計量器嚴格檢驗後，予以批准，否則產品不會發送到市場上。享有高度聲譽的遠景產品，是歷經有些人可能認爲太嚴格的管制而產生的。

傳統處理電子學的技術

電子設備需要尖端的科技……一個桌上型計算機有六百個電晶體，以及一千九百個兩極眞空管，而其它電子設備有錯綜複雜的電路，這些都是經由本公司充分運用科技，和現代的電子知識及經驗製造出來的。

** ——————

potentiality〔pə,tɛnʃɪ'ælətɪ〕*n.* 潛力

superb〔sʊ'pɝb〕*adj.* 極好的；上等的

frontier spirit　拓荒精神　veteran〔'vɛtərən〕*adj.* 老練的

inspector〔ɪn'spɛktɚ〕*n.* 品管人員；檢查員

checkup〔'tʃɛk,ʌp〕*n.* 檢查；審核

transistor〔træn'zɪstɚ〕*n.* 電晶體

diode〔'daɪod〕*n.* 兩極眞空管

3 財務報表
Statements of Accounts (1)

【實務須知】

- statements of accounts ⇨財務報表；對帳單
- Balance Sheet ⇨資產負債表
- ***current asset*** ⇨流動資產 <比較> current liability ⇨流動負債
- ***accounts receivable*** ⇨應收帳款
- ***less allowance for doubtful accounts*** ⇨減備抵壞帳
- ***inventory***〔'ɪnvən,torɪ〕***n.*** 存貨
- ***work in process*** ⇨在製品
- ***finished goods*** ⇨製成品
- ***government contract inventory*** ⇨政府訂購貨品存貨
- ***less accumulated depreciation & amortization*** ⇨減累積折舊與攤銷
- ***investment & advances*** ⇨投資及預付款
- ***current maturities of long term debt*** ⇨長期負債到期債款
- ***note payable*** ⇨應付票據
- ***account payable*** ⇨應付帳款
- ***accrued liability*** ⇨應計負債
- 6% note, payable in annual principal installment of $200,000 ⇨年繳二十萬元，年息百分之六的應付債券
- ***less current maturity*** ⇨減到期債款
- ***authorized*** 2,000,000 ***shares of*** $.50 ***par value*** ⇨面值五十分額定的二百萬股份
- ***capital in excess of par value of common stock*** ⇨普通股面值的過剩資金

<＜實 例＞

Balance Sheets

December 31, 19—

Assets		**Liabilities**	
Current assets		***Current Liabilities***	
Cash	$478,422	Current Maturities of	
Accounts receivable		long term debt	$475,000
less allowance for		Notes payable to	
doubtful accounts	$22,800	bank	$2,500,000
Inventories		Accounts payable	$1,475,697
Raw materials, parts		Accrued liability	$986,789
and supplies	$390,579	Total current liability	
Work in process	$564,396		$5,437,486
Finished goods	$468,016	***Long-term Debt***	
Government contract		6% note, payable in annual	
inventories	$5,004,004	principal installments of	
Prepaid expenses	$286,799	$200,000, less current	
Total current		maturity	$300,000
assets	$1,105,917	7% note, payable in annual	
Property, Plant and Equipment		principal installments of	
Land	$1,128,870	$275,000, less current	
Buildings, Machinery		maturity	$2,675,000
& Other equipment		Total Long-term debt	
	$12,387,202		$2,975,000
Less accumulated depreciation		***Stockholders' Equity***	
& amortization		Common stock — authorized,	
	(−) $5,682,929	2,000,000 shares of $.50 par	

Total property $7,833,143

Investments & Other Assets

Investments in & advances to Subsidiary Company $1,020,000

Other $497,264

Total Investments $1,517,264

Total $20,409,577

value $769,444

Capital in excess of par value of common stock $3,416,079

Retained earnings $7,811,568

Total Stockholders' Equity $11,997,091

Total $20,409,577

資產負債表

19—年 12 月 31 日

資產

流動資產

現金	$478,422
應收帳款減備抵壞帳	$22,800

存貨

原料、零件、和庫存貨	$390,579
在製品	$564,396
製成品	$648,016
政府訂購貨品存貨	$5,004,004
預付費用	$286,799
流動資產總計	$1,105,917

負債

流動負債

長期負債到期債款	$475,000
應付銀行票據	$2,500,000
應付帳款	$1,475,697
應計負債	$986,789
流動負債總計	$5,437,486

長期負債

年繳二十萬元，年息百分之六應付債券，減到期債款	$300,000
年繳二十七萬五千元，年息百分之七應付債券，減到期債款	$2,675,000

廠房設備	
土地	$1,128,870
建築物、機器及其它設備	$12,387,202
減累積折舊與攤銷	(−) $5,682,929
財產總計	$7,833,143
投資及其它資產	
對附屬公司的投資和預付款	$1,020,000
其它	$497,264
投資總計	$1,517,264
總計	$20,409,577

長期負債總計	$2,975,000
股東權益	
普通股一面值五十分，額定的二百萬股份	$769,444
普通股票面價值的過剩資金	$3,416,079
保留盈餘	$7,811,568
股東權益總計	$11,997,091
總計	$20,409,577

**

raw material 原料　part〔pɑrt〕*n.* 零件

supply〔səˈplaɪ〕*n.* 庫存品　property〔ˈprɑpətɪ〕*n.* 財產；所有權

common stock 普通股　subsidiary〔səbˈsɪdɪ,ɛrɪ〕*adj.* 附屬的；補助的

Stockholders' Equity 股東權益　***retained earnings*** 保留盈餘

4 財務報表

Statements of Accounts (2)

【實務須知】

- statements of operations and retained earnings ⇨ 營業活動和保留盈餘表
- net sales ⇨ 銷貨淨額
- ***cost of goods sold*** ⇨ 銷貨成本
- gross profit ⇨ 毛利
- ***earnings before income tax*** ⇨ 稅前收益

- ***income tax refund*** ⇨所得稅退款
- statement of source and application of funds ⇨資金來源及應用表（即財務狀況變動表）
- ***net profit for year*** ⇨年淨利
- depreciation and amortization ⇨折舊與攤銷
- net change in property, plant and equipment ⇨廠房和設備的淨變更
- ***reduction of long-term debt*** ⇨長期負債的減少
- ***increase in working capital*** ⇨營運資金的增加
- net earnings ⇨營業淨收益
- expenditure for property ⇨地產的支出
- ***company funded research*** ⇨公司研究基金

＜實 例＞

Statement of Operations and Retained Earnings

(Year ended December 31)

Net Sales	$26,314,403	
Cost of Goods Sold	$20,237,586	
Gross Profit	$5,666,817	
Other Expenses	$5,237,146	
Earnings before income tax	$429,671	
Income Tax Refund		
Net Earnings	$429,671	
Retained earnings(beginning of year)		$7,811,568
Retained earnings(end of year)		$8,241,239

Statement of Source and Application of Funds

(Year ended December 31)

Source of Funds

Operations

Net profit for year	$429,671
Depreciation and amortization	$820,978
Other expenses which required no fund	$30,014
Total	$1,280,663
Net change in property, plant and equipment	(−$38,391)
Proceeds from sale of stock	$1,305
Total	−$37,356
Total	$1,243,307

Application of Funds

Reduction of long-term debt	$475,000
Increase in investments and other assets	$75,000
Increase in working capital	$693,307
Total	$1,243,307

Financial Highlights

Net Sales $26,314,403

Earnings before income tax refund $429,671

Net earnings $429,671

Working Capital $6,314,991

Expenditure for property $225,786

Depreciation $820,978

Equity of shareholders $12,427,797

Company funded research $1,397,000

營業活動和保留收益報表

（至年底12月31日）

銷貨淨額	$26,314,403
銷貨成本	$20,647,586
毛利	$5,666,817
其它費用	$5,237,146
稅前收益	$429,671
所得稅退款	
營業淨收益	$429,671
保留盈餘（年初）	$7,811,568
保留盈餘（年尾）	$8,241,239

資金來源及應用表（財務狀況變動表）

（至年底12月31日）

資金的來源		
營業活動		
年淨利		$429,671
折舊與攤銷		$820,978
不須資金的其他費用		$30,014
總計		$1,280,663
廠房和設備的淨變更		(−$38,391)
銷售股票的收入		$1,035
	總計	−$37,356
	總計	$1,243,307
資金的應用		
長期負債的減少		$475,000
投資及其它資產的增加		$75,000
營運資金的增加		$693,307

總計　　　$1,243,307

財務重點

銷貨淨額　$26,314,403

所得稅退款前的收益　$429,671

營業淨收益　$429,671

營運資金　$6,314,991

地產費用　$225,786

折舊　$820,978

股東權益　$12,427,797

公司研究基金　$1,397,000

** ―――――――――――――

retained〔rɪ'tend〕*adj.* 保留的　expense〔ɪk'spɛns〕*adj.* 費用；支出

investment〔ɪn'vɛstmənt〕*n.* 投資　assets〔'æsɛts〕*n.* (*pl.*) 資產

depreciation〔dɪ,priʃɪ'eʃən〕*n.* 折舊

proceeds〔'prosidz〕*n.* (*pl.*) 所得

highlight〔'haɪ,laɪt〕*n.* 重點；最精采之部分

5 電視目錄　TV Catalog 

【實務須知】

- ***outstanding reception*** ⇨ 博得壓倒性的好評
- AC radio ⇨ 交流電收音機
- has characterized ⇨ 具……特色
- really portable color portable ⇨ 眞正手提的手提彩色電視
- ***true-to-life*** ⇨ 逼眞
- ***walnut grain finish*** ⇨ 最後再塗上一層優美的胡桃色紋理

- ***recessed carrying handle*** ⇨鉗進式手提把手
- 12″ viewable ⇨十二吋畫面
- ***automatic degaussing and noise canceller*** ⇨自動中和四週之磁場以防禦磁雷及噪音消除器
- slide-rule dial ⇨滑動顯示之計量盤

<實 例>

Prospect ……Outstanding Reception the World Over

Long before the AC radio——the first primitive radio—was perfected the name Prospect was born. And with it came the Prospect reputation for reliability.

Reliability —— dependable performance —— has characterized Prospect from the early days of experimental broadcasting to the "Golden Days of radio."

Then, when Prospect pioneered in TV, the same standards were applied. Today Prospect TV, Radios, and Tape Recorders are famed for dependability the world over.

And that is what you can expect when you select Prospect — the finest engineering and styling, the ultimate in brilliant, dependable performance.

We are your constant assurance of maximum enjoyment.

Model CL-40 Color TV

At last — a really portable color portable!

The ultimate result of Prospect's electronic research and pioneering. Great color performance that will stay great for years to come—rich, bright, true-to-life. And a cabinet to match the performance — compact—slimlined —

handsome walnut grain finish— deluxe, recessed carrying handle. 12″ viewable. Preset tuning. AGC.AFC. Automatic degaussing and noise cancellers. Front mounted speaker and controls plus easy-to-read UHF slide-rule dial.

遠景……**博得全世界壓倒性的好評**

早在交流電收音機 —— 第一架原始收音機 —— 改良前，遠景的名字就已經誕生了。隨之而來的是遠景可靠的聲譽。

可靠性 —— 可靠的性能 —— 從早期的實驗廣播，到「收音機的黃金時代」，一直都是遠景的特色。

當遠景開拓電視機時，也採用了同一標準。今天遠景的電視機、收音機和錄音機，無不以可靠聞名全球。

您在選擇遠景時，可以期待 —— 最精良的設計與樣式、極爲出色、可靠的性能。

本公司是您最高享受的永久保證。

CL-40型　彩色電視機

終於 —— 一架眞正手提的手提彩色電視機！

遠景電子研究和開拓的最終成果。絕佳的彩色性能，將來還是一樣棒——豐富、鮮麗、逼眞。與性能相稱的外殼 —— 細緻 —— 細條紋型 —— 最後再塗上一層優美的胡桃色紋理 —— 豪華型、鉗進式手提把手。十二吋畫面。可預先調整的頻道。自動調音控制、自動頻率控制。自動中和四週磁場以防禦磁雷、及自動噪音消除器。前端開口的喇叭和操縱裝置，再加上易讀的 UHF 滑動顯示之計量盤。

** ______________________________

AC = alternating current 交流電 broadcast〔ˈbrɔd,kæst〕*v.* 廣播

cabinet〔ˈkæbənɪt〕*n.* 電唱機或電視機之外殼

deluxe〔dɪˈlʊks〕*adj.* 豪華的

6 收音機目錄 Radio Catalog

【實務須知】

- ***pocket-size power*** ⇨ 袖珍型的動力
- *AFC = Automatic Frequency Control* ⇨ 自動頻率控制
- *AGC = Automatic Gain Control* ⇨ 自動調音控制
- ***distortion-free RF circuit*** ⇨ 永不失眞的收音機頻率電路
- ***impact-proof case*** ⇨ 耐碰撞的外殼
- ***penlite batteries*** ⇨ 小型電筒的電池

＜實 例＞

Portable Radio Model FR-158

Pocket-size Power! Music — sports — news — wherever you go — with this highly sensitive, compact AM/FM portable. Exactly engineered for brilliant reception. 9-transistor, 3-diode, super-heterodyne circuit. Dynamic speaker. AFC, AGC and distortion-free RF amplifier. Impact-proof case, telescopic antenna. Earphone, smart carrying case and penlite batteries included.

Enter the world of Prospect — the world where design and dependability are combined. In glowing color television. In crystal-clear black-and-white television. In full-fidelity

radio.
From tiny transistors to studio-styled tape recorders, and everything in between, Prospect quality is uncomparable quality.
That is why we invite you to compare!

FR-158型手提收音機

袖珍型的動力！音樂——運動——新聞——無論您到那裡——攜帶這架高敏感度、細緻的AM/FM手提收音機。
精確設計以達到出色的收聽效果。九個電晶體、三個兩極眞空管、超級外差式電路。動力喇叭。自動頻率控制、自動調音控制、和永不失眞的收音機頻率擴音器。耐碰撞的外殼、伸縮自如的天線。包括耳機、別緻的手提盒、和小型電筒的電池。
請跨進遠景的世界——綜合了設計和可靠性的世界。在鮮明的彩色電視裡。在透明清晰的黑白電視裡。在完全傳眞的收音機裡。
從微小的電晶體到廣播室型態的錄音機，及介於兩者間的每一件產品，遠景的品質是無可比較的。
那就是我們邀請您來比較的原因！

**———————

portable〔ˈportəbḷ〕*adj.* 手提的
compact〔kəmˈpækt〕*adj.* 細密的；細緻的
telescopic〔ˌtɛləˈskɑpɪk〕*adj.* 能自由伸縮的
antenna〔ænˈtɛnə〕*n.* 天線　fidelity〔faɪˈdɛlətɪ〕*n.* 傳眞性

第5章

答覆提案

Response to Proposal

在允諾交易提案之前，一定要充分考慮其可行性，以冷靜、科學的態度檢討現狀與發展潛能，以免將來枝節橫生。特別是面臨締結代理商契約時，必定要就商域問題，一地區一代理商的原則着手，進行充分的**市場調查**，以便完全**了解申請對象的信用狀態**。此外，在締結基本交易條約之初，不要忘了彼此交換目錄、樣品册、價目表、說明書、技術資料等，仔細研討。由於面對的是商業習慣、法律、民族性迥異的對象，如果用尋常的知識來應對，恐怕極易產生誤解，招致事後的紛爭。爲避免無謂的摩擦，必須彼此將**交易條件**一併寫明於契約中。如此充分的事前協調，會使紛爭減低至最小限度，倘若發生紛爭，也比較容易解決，可謂對內、對外交易的鐵則。

若沒有往來交易的意願，可陳述理由，委婉拒絕。只要明確申訴無法達成交易的理由，必然可以獲得對方的諒解，所謂「買賣不成仁義在」，大可不必以強硬姿態拒絕交易。況且，即使現在無法進行交易，保存在自已的 file（檔案）中，可望贏得將來的交易機會。

 1 接受提案 Proposal Accepted 

【實務須知】

- *credit inquiry* ⇨信用調查
- *the favorable result* ⇨有利的結果
- *justified our decision* ⇨證明我方的決定是正確的
- *general terms and conditions of business* ⇨商務的一般條件及狀況
- memorandum〔 ˌmɛməˈrændəm 〕*n.* 約定書；買賣契約書
- documents in duplicate ⇨一式二份的文件
- documents in triplicate ⇨一式三份的文件
- *with your signature and seal* ⇨加上貴方的簽名封印
- *for your file* ⇨以供查照
- *formal business relations* ⇨正式的交易關係

〈實 例〉

Dear Sir,

Your Agency Application

Thank you very much for your proposal of May 2. We are pleased to inform you that we have completed the required credit inquiries, and the favorable results have justified our decision to enter into a business agreement with you.

Before entering into a final agreement, however, we would like to affirm the general terms and conditions of business.

The attached memorandum is prepared for your approval and alteration as required. If you have no objection to any of its articles, please send the duplicate with your signature and seal, and retain the original for your file.

We are quite anxious to start formal business relations and assure you we will provide the lowest possible prices for an initial order.

Looking forward to a mutually prosperous business relationship, we remain,

Yours faithfully,

Enc. Memorandum

敬啓者：

貴方代理店的申請

非常謝謝貴公司5月2日的提議。很高興通知貴公司，本公司已經完成必要的信用查詢，有利的結果證明，決定和貴公司締結交易契約是正確的。

然而，在締結最後的契約前，本公司想確定商務的一般條件及狀況。

附寄的約定書是依據要求，爲貴公司的贊成和變更而準備的。如果貴公方對任何條款都不反對，請將副本簽名封印寄回，原件保留以供查照。

本公司很渴望開始正式的交易關係，並向您確保，首次訂單一定提供可能的最低價格。

期待一次互相都很順利的交易關係。

附寄　約定書

**

enter into 締結　　alteration〔ˌɔltəˈreʃən〕*n.* 變更

original〔əˈrɪdʒənl̩〕*n.* 原件；原文

2 拒絕提案 Proposal Rejected

【實務須知】

- ***in response to*** ⇨答覆
- ***in compliance with our policy*** ⇨依從本公司的策略
- ***a sole agent for one country*** ⇨一個國家一間獨家代理店
- ***prior to receiving your proposal*** ⇨接到貴公司的提案前
- ***decline from*** ⇨拒絕
- ***extending our activity more extensively*** ⇨更廣泛地擴展交易活動

〈實　例〉

Dear Sirs,

Thank you very much for your proposal of May 15 offering us your services as Bangkok Agents for our products.

In response to our advertisement seeking a selling agent, we have received and considered a great number of proposals. However, in compliance with our policy of a sole agent for one country, which avoids unnecessary competition and trouble among dealers, we are obliged to select only one firm.

We regret to inform you that we made our decision prior to receiving your proposal. Therefore, we will have to decline from entering into a business relationship with your company.

We shall keep your name and address, however, in our file so that we may call upon you when extending our activity more extensively in that area.

Thank you for your kind proposal. We hope a friendly business relationship will be possible in the future.

Yours faithfully,

敬啓者：

非常謝謝貴公司5月15日的提案，提供您的服務，做爲本公司產品的曼谷代理商。

玆接到也考慮了許多響應本公司尋找銷售代理商之廣告的提案。。然而依從本公司一個國家一間獨家代理店的策略，以避免銷售公司間無謂的競爭和麻煩，却不得已只選擇一家公司。

很抱歉通知貴公司，本公司在接到您的提議前，就下了決定。因此，勢必得拒絕和貴公司締結交易關係。

然而，本公司會將貴公司的名字及地址存檔，以便當我方在該地區更廣泛地擴展交易活動時，可以請貴公司協助。

謝謝貴公司好意的提議。希望未來可能締結友善的交易關係。

** ———

competition 〔ˌkɑmpəˈtɪʃən〕 *n.* 競爭

dealer 〔ˈdilɚ〕 *n.* 銷售公司；商人

實用例句

【必備詞彙】

- ***upon careful investigation*** ⇨經過仔細調查
- ***get a complete line of merchandise*** ⇨得到全部商品
- D/A ***without*** L/C ⇨不用信用狀的承兌交單
- draft〔dræft〕*v.* 草擬
- ***our margin is almost negligible*** ⇨我方幾乎無利可圖
- term〔tɜm〕*n.*(*pl.*)〔商〕(付款、價格等的)條件
- ***our line of merchandise*** ⇨本公司的商品
- competitive〔kəm'pɛtətɪv〕*adj.* 經得起競爭的

⁂　⁂　⁂

1. ***Upon careful investigation*** of your market, we have come to the conclusion that we had better postpone extending our activity until we ***get a complete line of merchandise*** suitable for your market in price and design.

   經過仔細調查貴市場,本公司的結論是,最好將擴展活動延緩,直到我方得到適合貴市場的價格和設計的全部商品。

   * postpone〔post'pone〕*v.* 延緩

2. Because of our agent agreement with The Philip Trading Co., Ltd., we are not allowed to contact you directly. Therefore, please approach the following agents in your city.

   因爲本公司和菲力普貿易有限公司有代理契約,故不能直接和貴公司聯繫。因此,請與下列的貴城代理商接洽。

3. We usually adopt an L/C base, while you require ***D/A without L/C***. On this point we hesitate entering into a business relationship with your company.

本公司通常採用信用狀爲基本的條件，而貴公司却要求不用信用狀的承兌交單。對這點我方猶豫是否和貴公司締結交易關係。

* L/C = *letter of credit* 信用狀
* D/A = *documents against acceptance* 承兌交單

4. The agreement you ***drafted*** is sufficient for us concerning payment. As to the sales amount, however, we suggest a sum of $10,000,000 a year.

貴公司草擬的契約在付款方面，符合我方條件。然而，關於銷售額，我方建議一年總額一千萬元。

* sufficient 〔səˈfɪʃənt〕 *adj*. 足夠的；充分的

5. Upon examination of the draft, we request that you delete article 8 and insert the following clause.

檢查草約後，本公司要求貴公司刪除第八條，並插入下列條款。

* delete 〔dɪˈlit〕 *v*. 刪去
* insert 〔ɪnˈsɝt〕 *v*. 挿入

6. Our catalog will indicate the fine quality of our products in detail. Our prices have been reduced to a point where ***our margin is almost negligible***. Therefore, we are sure the ***terms*** will be agreeable and beneficial to your company. Moreover, we are sure ***our line of merchandise*** is quite competitive.

本公司的目錄會詳細指出產品精良的品質。而價格已經降到我方幾乎無利可圖的地步。因此，我方確信這些條款對貴公司來說，是可以同意而且有利的。何況，可以確信本公司的商品相當具有競爭力。

第6章 契約

Agreement

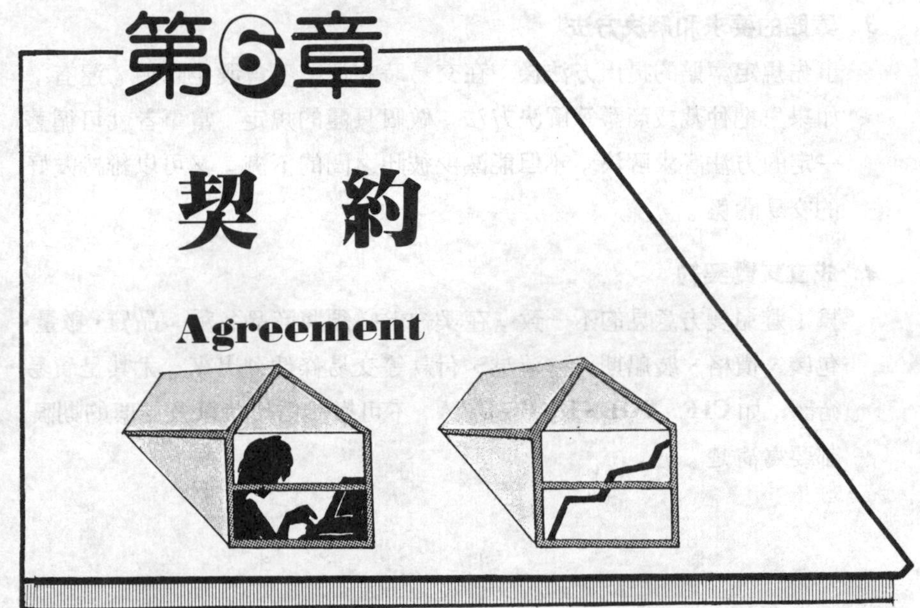

買賣當事人在建立交易關係，進行個個商品的買賣之前，基於雙方的同意，可針對交易的一般條件締結**基本交易條件協定書**（***Memorandum of the Agreement on General Terms and Conditions of Business***），事先將全部的交易條件訂定下來，在每次交易時可以省下往返討論各交易條件的手續，使每次的交易能夠迅速、順利地進行。協定書中的基本交易條款，具體而言有：

1. 買賣當事人的資格

買賣當事人可分爲**本人對本人**（***Principal to Principal***）和**本人對代理人**（***Principal to Agent***）二種，在協定書上必須規定清楚，以免日後發生紛爭。本人是指自己參與交易，風險由自己承擔。而代理人是「本人」的代表，達成交易後向「本人」收取手續費。

2. 基本的交易條件

基本的交易條件包括價格形態、報價、定貨、信用狀、付款條件、保險、裝運、不可抗力、品質等。應該採用什麼樣的條件，必須明確地記載在協定書上。

3. 索賠的要求和解決方法

事先規定索賠的提出方法後，在交易時才比較不會發生麻煩。還有，如果先把仲裁或商議等解決方法，做個具體的規定，當事者就可循著一定的方法謀求解決，不但能減少彼此之間的不滿，又可以維持友好的交易關係。

4. 成立買賣契約

爲了避免雙方意見的不一致，在契約上必須將商品名稱、品質、數量、包裝、價格、裝船期、啓運港、付款等交易條件列出來。尤其是貿易術語，如**CIF**、**FOB**、**D/P**、**D/A**，不可撤銷信用狀以及支票的期限都要寫淸楚。

* * *

✦ 承作契約書應留意要點

契約書是爲了防範交易過程中發生的抱怨、紛爭於未然而承作，必須將當事人的意圖充分反映在契約上。當然其內容必須是合法而有效的。在承作契約書的時候，應該注意下列各點：

1. 辭句要簡潔、易於了解。
2. 條文不可矛盾，務須前後一致。
3. 相關條文不能矛盾，須確實地表現事實。
4. 妥當安置法律行爲的證據。
5. 句子需簡短而直接，較長的句子要細分。儘量不用被動句型。時式原則上以現在式爲主。

此外必須特別注意，絕對要避免英文上意義內涵不明確的用法，而以簡單明瞭爲尙。

* * *

✦ 契約用字須知

契約中 **shall** 表示未履行契約的債務時，就構成違約行爲；**will** 較 shall 不具強制力，多用於無需法律強制時；**may** 則用於顯示契約的權利、權限、特權時。所以，用 The term "F.A.Q." shall mean 才對，而不可以用 The term "F.A.Q." means。確切的日期用 **on**，「到某月某日之前」用 **by** 或 **before**。**on** 代表當天，**by** 則不包括當天，例如，by May 1 時，指到 April 30 爲止。**from** May 31, 亦不包括當天，意指從 June 1 開始。**commencing** 包括當天。這類用字需嚴加小心，不可大意視之。應該滙集有關人員，確實研討，並且在遣詞用字上，要和對方徹底地溝通。這種嚴密的工作步驟，可以避免日後產生解釋上的問題。確實達到預防的效果。

1 買賣契約 Sales Agreement 

【實務須知】

- witnesseth〔'wɪtnɪsɪθ〕*v.*〔古〕於(文書)上簽名作證
- business〔'bɪznɪs〕*n.* 業務性質，說明雙方的地位
- ***their unit to be quoted*** ⇨ 所報的單價
- ***unless otherwise specified*** ⇨ 除非另行規定；除非另有聲明
- ***considered "firm"*** ⇨ 被視爲「確定的」
- ***date of dispatch*** ⇨ 遞出的日期
- ***orders are binding*** ⇨ 訂單具約束力
- ***banker's irrevocable letter of credit*** ⇨ 銀行的不可撤銷信用狀
- confirmation of sale ⇨ 買賣的確認書
- ***full invoice amount*** ⇨ 發票全額
- conclusive proof ⇨ 決定性證據

- seller's option ⇨賣方的選擇
- ***W. A. = With Average*** ⇨單獨海損賠償
- ***by the duly authorized presentation*** ⇨以正當授權提出
- ***Force Majeure*** ⇨不可抗力，一般包括：

war：戰爭	blockade：封鎖
revolution：革命	insurrection：暴動；叛亂
mobilization：動員	strike：罷工
lockout：停工	civil commotion：內亂
riot：騷動；暴動	act of God：天災
plague：疫病	epidemic：傳染病
fire：火災	flood：洪水

<實 例>

Sales Agreement

This agreement made on the 1st day of 19 — by A & B Company, Ltd. (in this agreement called Seller), 552 Tun Hwa North Road, Taipei, Taiwan, R.O.C. and C & D Company, Inc. (in this agreement called Buyer), 458 Manhattan, New York, U.S.A.

witnesseth that：

whereas, Seller is engaged in the manufacture of electric & electronic goods and desires to sell them to Buyer, and whereas, Buyer desires to purchase electric & electronic goods from Seller subject to terms and conditions stated in this agreement. Now, therefore, it is agreed as follows:

1. ***Business***： Both parties shall act as Principals, each

paying expenses for business, sales and purchases.

2. ***Goods*** : Goods in business, their unit to be quoted, and their modes of packing goods shall be as stated in the attached list.

3. ***Prices*** : Unless otherwise specified in telegram or letters, all prices submitted by Seller or Buyer Shall be understood C.I.F. New York in U.S. Dollars.

4. ***Offers*** : Unless otherwise stated in each telegram, all cable offers are to be considered "firm" subject to reply being received within ten (10) days from and including the date of dispatch.

5. ***Orders*** : Except in cases where firm offers are accepted by Buyer, no orders are binding until acknowledged in letters by Seller.

6. ***Letter of Credit*** :

Buyer shall open banker's Irrevocable Letter of Credit in favor of Seller by telegram or mail immediately upon confirmation of sale. Unless otherwise specified in each order, Buyer shall open L/C so that Seller may receive it within fifteen (15) days after order at latest. The credit shall be made effective fifteen (15) days beyond the contracted time of shipment.

7. ***Payment*** : Seller shall draw drafts under credits at 30 days after sight, documents attached, for

the full invoice amount.

8. ***Shipment*** : Seller shall ship all goods sold to Buyer within the period stipulated. The date of Bill of Lading shall be taken as the conclusive proof of the day of shipment. Unless clearly stated in the Order Sheet, the port of shipment shall be at the Seller's option.

9. ***Force Majeure*** :

Seller is not responsible for the non-delivery or the delay in shipment caused by prohibition of export, refusal to issue export license or permit, arrests and restraint of rulers, government and people, war or warlike operations, blockade, revolution, insurrection, mobilization, strikes, lockouts, civil commotions, riots, act of God, plague or other epidemics, destruction of goods by fire or flood, or any other causes beyond Seller's control. In the event of the afore-mentioned causes arising, documents proving its occurrence or existence shall be submitted by Seller to Buyer without delay. The order will be considered cancelled as far as the causes continue to exist.

10. ***Delayed Shipment*** :

If Seller fails to ship the goods within the period stipulated, Buyer shall have a right to cancel the order thus unshipped and Seller shall bear the loss incurred in consequence.

11. ***Marine Insurance*** :

Seller shall effect marine insurance on all shipments on W.A. for an amount of the invoice plus ten (10) percent. Special insurance, if required additionally by Buyer, shall be covered for account of Buyer.

12. ***Inspection***: Unless otherwise stated, Seller shall undergo the export inspection by Taiwan STS authorized by Chinese Govenment and take the certificates issued by the above.

13. ***Claims*** : Claims, if any, shall be made by cable within fifteen(15) days from the date of the final landing of the goods at destination.

14. ***Arbitration*** :

Any claim or dispute which cannot be disposed of by mutual agreement, shall be settled in Taiwan by Taiwan International Commercial Arbitration Association according to the rule of the association above. Arbitration may be initiated by Buyer or Seller giving thirty (30) days' notice in writing to the other party.

15. ***Period of Agreement*** :

This agreement will be effective for a period of three (3) years from the 1st day of July, 19— to the thirtieth day of June, 19— and will be automatically extended for a period of one year unless either party gives the notice of termination at thirty (30) days prior to the termination date.

16. ***Proper Law*** :

This agreement shall be governed by the Laws of Taiwan.

In witness whereof, the parties have executed this agreement in duplicate by the duly authorized presentation.

Seller A & B Co., Ltd. President

....

Buyer C & D Co., Inc. President

....

買賣契約

本契約訂立於 19 一年元旦，由中華民國台灣台北市敦化北路 552 號的A & B有限公司（本契約中稱爲賣方），與美國紐約曼哈坦 458 號的C & D股份公司（本契約中稱爲買方）共同訂立。

以資證明：

鑑於賣方從事電氣和電子產品的製造，欲將貨品賣給買方，且鑑於買方在本契約所列的條款和情況爲條件下，欲向賣方購買電氣及電子產品。因此，現在經協議如下：

1. **業務性質**：雙方應充當本人，各付商務、銷售和採購費用。
2. **貨　　品**：商務上的貨品所報的單價，和貨物包裝款式，應如附列的明細表所記載。
3. **價　　格**：除非於電報或信裡另行規定，否則所有由賣方或買方提出的價格，應以美元、到紐約的運費、保險費在內價說明。

4. 報　　價： 除非每封電報另行聲明，否則在從遞出日期（當天包括在內）算起十天內接到回覆的條件下，所有電報報價均視同「確定報價」。

5. 訂　　貨： 除了確定報價已為買方接受的情況外，在賣方以信件認可前，訂單皆不具約束力。

6. 信 用 狀： 買方在買賣確定時，應立刻以電報或郵件，開立以賣方為受款人的銀行不可撤銷信用狀，除非於每份訂單另行規定，買方應開立信用狀，以便賣方至遲在訂貨十五天內收到。應使信用狀於約訂的裝船日期十五天後生效。

7. 付款條件： 賣方應憑信用狀，以發票全額開立見票三十天後付款滙票，附寄文件。

8. 貨物裝運： 賣方應於規定期限內，裝運賣給買方的所有貨物。提單日期將視為裝船日期的決定性證據。除非於訂單另行聲明清楚，裝運港口應由賣方選擇。

9. 不可抗力： 賣方不須負責因禁止出口、拒絕簽發出口許可證或准許證、統治者、政府或人民的拘捕和禁止出港、戰爭或軍事行動、封鎖、革命、叛亂、動員、罷工、停工、內亂、暴動、天災、疫病或其它傳染病、火災或洪水損毀貨物、或其它任何超出賣方所能控制的原因，而引起的未交貨或延遲裝運。萬一發生前述原因，賣方必須立刻向買方提出證明原因發生或存在的文件。只要原因繼續存在，訂單將視同取消。

10. 延遲裝運： 若賣方不能於規定期限內裝運貨物，買方有權取消未裝運貨物的訂單，賣方應負擔因此所招致的損失。

11. 海上保險： 賣方所有的船貨，須按發票總額加百分之十，投保單獨海損賠償的海上保險。若買方額外要求，特別的保險費應由買方負擔。

12. 檢　　驗： 除非另行聲明，賣方應接受中華民國政府授權的台灣遠東公證行的出口檢驗，並得到上述公司簽發的合格證書。

13. 索　　賠：如果有任何索賠，應從貨物登陸目的地的最後一天算起，十五天內以電報索賠。

14. 仲　　裁：任何不能相互協調處理的索賠或爭論，應由台灣國際商業仲裁協會，依據上述協會的規則在台灣解決。仲裁可由買方或賣方發起，寫信給對方給予三十天的通告。

15. 契約期限：本契約有效期限三年，從19—年7月的第一天起，至19—年6月的第三十天止，且會自動延長一年，除非任何一方在終止日期前三十天，發出終止通告。

16. 適用法規：本契約適用台灣的法律。

爲證明此事，雙方簽章使這份正當授權所提出的一式兩份契約生效。

賣方　A&B股份有限公司　董事長

………

買方　C&D股份有限公司　董事長

………

** ______

whereas〔hwɛr'æz〕*conj.* 鑑於　*n.* 正式文件之開場白

subject〔'sʌbdʒɪkt〕*adv.* 以～爲條件；遵照～

principal〔'prɪnsəpḷ〕*n.* 本人

in favor of 付給

CIF = ***cost, insurance & freight*** 運費保費在內價；起岸價格

stipulate〔'stɪpjə,let〕*v.* 規定

Bill of Lading 大提單

International Commercial Arbitration Association　國際商業仲裁協會

 2 代理契約 Agency Agreement 

【實務須知】

- represent 〔 ˌrɛprɪˈzɛnt 〕 *v.* 代表
- 50,000 pounds monthly and yearly 500,000 ⇨每月五萬英鎊，每年五十萬英鎊
- ***under condition of warranty*** ⇨在擔保的情況下
- ***draft by A being dishonored*** ⇨ *A*開的滙票遭退票
- Conciliation and Arbitration of the International Chamber of Commerce in Taiwan ⇨台灣國際商會的調解及仲裁
- ***final and binding*** ⇨視爲準則並具有約束力
- ***remain in force*** ⇨持續有效
- subsequent yearly ⇨下一年的
- ***bankruptcy or insolvency or breach*** ⇨破產或是無力清償債務或是違約
- in witness whereof ⇨以資證明～

<實 例>

Agency Agreement

This agreement, made in duplicate, between The A Co., Ltd., Taipei, Taiwan (hereafter called A) and The B Co., Ltd., Bangkok, Thailand (hereafter called B) stipulates the Agency Agreement under the terms and conditions stated and mutually agreed upon as follows:

1. A shall be represented by B as the Sole Agent for Bangkok for the sale of the electric & electronic goods manufactured by A as described in Article 4 .

2. A shall not establish any other Agents in Bangkok for the goods in Article 4 and B shall not represent any other person and sell any other goods similar to those of A.
3. Both A and B are quite free to sell or represent any other goods or person outside Bangkok.
4. The goods comprising this agreement are :
   1. Various TV's
   2. Various Radios
   3. Various Tape Recorders
   4. Various Radio-phonographs & Stereos
   5. Various Car Radios
5. A agrees to pay the commission for all orders at 5% to the total amount unless otherwise specified at the time of placing the order with A.
6. B agrees to sell A's products more than 50,000 in Pound Sterling monthly and yearly more than Stg. 500,000 in total.
7. A warrants to B that the products shall be free from defects in materials and workmanship under normal use and service, and to replace any defective parts under the condition of the warranty.
8. A shall quote prices in Pound Sterling on CIF Bangkok, unless otherwise stated, including the commission.
9. A shall draw a draft on indentors at 30 d/s, with all shipping documents attached, and send the copies of all documents to B.
10. In any event of the draft by A being dishonored, B shall

pay such draft and dispose of the shipped goods on B's own responsibility.

11. All orders shall be subject to confirmation of A, that is, they are not regarded as contract until A approves by cable.

12. Each party shall pay their own cabling and other expenses.

13. In the event of any dispute between the parties hereto owing to the claims which cannot amicably be settled between the parties it shall be settled under the Rules of Conciliation and Arbitration of the International Chamber of Commerce in Taiwan. The Award by such arbitration shall be final and binding upon the parties hereto.

14. Unless cancellation shall be effected by mutual consent, this agreement shall bc and remain in force from and after the 1st day of April, 19— until the 31st day of March, 19—. Thereafter this agreement shall be automatically extended for subsequent yearly periods commencing on the 1st day of April unless 90 days written notice of termination is given to the other party.

15. Regardless of the stipulation of Article 14, any party shall have the right to cancel this agreement immediately upon written notice in the event of the bankruptcy or insolvency and in the event of the breach within 30 days after written notice is given to the committing party.

16. In witness whereof the parties hereto have caused this agreement to be duly executed as of the day and year above written.

Attest Principals A Co., Ltd.
Signed

Attest Agents B Co., Ltd.
Signed

代理契約

本契約爲一式二份，是台灣台北的A有限公司（以下簡稱爲A）和泰國曼谷的B有限公司（以下簡稱爲B），在載明的條件和情況下，所規定的代理契約，雙方協議如下：

1. B擬代表A，作爲曼谷的獨家代理商，銷售A製造的電氣和電子產品，如第四條所描述之物品。
2. A不應在曼谷成立任何其他銷售第四條描述之物品的代理商，B不應再代表任何其他人銷售任何其它和A類似的貨品。
3. A和B兩者都可自由銷售或代表，任何曼谷以外的其他物品或人。
4. 本契約的貨品包括：
   1. 各類電視機
   2. 各類收音機
   3. 各類錄音機
   4. 各類收音電唱機和立體音響設備
   5. 各類汽車收音機
5. 除非在下訂單給A時另行規定，A同意支付所有訂單總額的百分之五做爲傭金。
6. B同意每月銷售超過五萬英鎊的A產品，每年總額超過五十萬英鎊。

7. A向B擔保，產品的原料和作工，在正常使用和保養下，不應有瑕疵，而且在此擔保的情況下，任何有瑕疵的零件可以更換。
8. 除非另行聲明，A應以到曼谷的運費、保險費在內價，包括傭金在內，用英鎊報價。
9. A應開立給委託訂購者見票三十天後付款的滙票，附上所有裝運文件，並把所有文件的副本寄給B。
10. 萬一任何A開的滙票遭退票，B應支付該滙票，並可以自做主張處理船貨。
11. 所有訂單皆以A的確認爲條件，亦即直到A以電報贊同，訂單才能視爲合約。
12. 每一方將自付電報和其它費用。
13. 至此爲止，萬一雙方間因索賠無法友好解決，而有任何爭論時，應依照台灣的國際商會的調解及仲裁規則來解決。至此爲止，以這種仲裁的判決爲準，雙方必須共同遵守。
14. 除非彼此同意取消，本契約將自19 —年4月的第一天起，持續有效至19 —年3月的第三十一天。其後本契約將自4月的第一天開始，自動延長至下一年期間，除非一方於九十天前將書面的終止通告送達對方。
15. 不受第十四條的規定限制，萬一破產或無力清償債務，或者萬一違約時，任何一方有權經由書面通知，於書面通知送達違犯的一方後三十天內，立刻取消本契約。
16. 至此爲止，以資證明雙方照以上載明的日期及年度，如期履行本契約。

立證據本人　　A有限公司

簽　章

立證據代理商　B有限公司

簽　章

** ______________________

duplicate〔'djupləkɪt〕*n.* 相同的東西；副本

stipulate〔'stɪpjə,let〕*v.*（條約或契約上）規定；記明

comprise〔kəm'praɪz〕*v.* 包括；構成

stereo〔'stɪrɪo〕*n.* 立體音響設備

sterling〔'stɝlɪŋ〕*n.* 英國貨幣（通常寫於金額之後，略作 *stg.*）

commence〔kə'mɛns〕*v.* 開始；著手

termination〔,tɝmə'neʃən〕*n.* 終止；結束

PART Ⅲ

Sales Contract

買賣契約

第1章 貿易詢價

Trade Inquiry

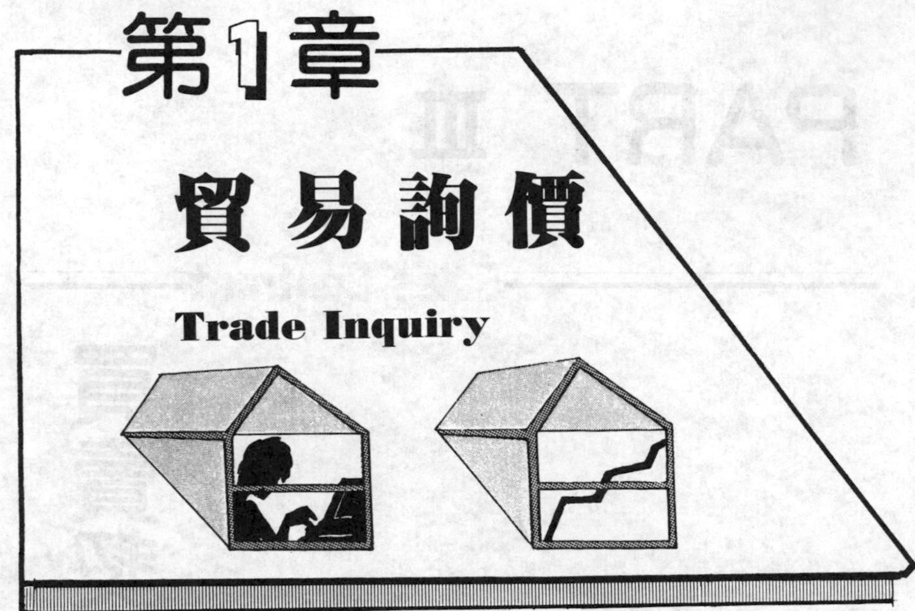

一旦訂立交易基本條約，就算進入實際的交易關係。首先，除了該公司的公司簡介、財務報表之外，還需索取樣品、目錄等，做爲了解信用狀態的資料。甚至要索取個別商品的詳細樣本、目錄、價目表，進行買賣的實際檢討。買方應該就欲採購的商品，要求賣方提供品質、價格、船期等相關資料，並表示有購買的希望，這就稱爲 ***inquiry***（詢價）。賣方接到詢價，應迅速確實地回覆，以免坐失商機。交易基本約定中，有關買賣條件應注意的事項爲：

1. 商品名稱
2. 交貨日期
3. 數量
4. 價格
5. 包裝
6. 保險
7. 付款條件

其中，比較固定的條件，如包裝、保險、付款條件，可依情況酌情省略，至於經常有變動的項目，不可省略。貿易並不是要賣方坐待詢價，由賣方積極地選擇合乎對方口味的產品，加以推銷尤為重要。為此，必須不斷獲取有關的新產品、商品行情、發展的最新資料，加以探討研究。

*　　　　*　　　　*

✦買賣條件中，應特別注意的術語及其有關事項：

A. 貨幣

交易貨幣於出口時，限定為U.S Dollar, Canadian Dollar, Swiss Franc, Sterling Pound, Deutsche Mark，日圓等十六國貨幣。C.I.F.、F.O.B. 等價格條件的寫法如下。

$10,000 ***CIF*** New York in U.S currency
U.S. $10,000 ***CIF*** Keelung
£100-65p ***FOB*** Calcutta in Pound Sterling
Stg. £100-65p ***FOB*** Keelung
Canada $10,000 ***CIF*** Montreal
Ex Ship New York U.S. $10,000
Ex Ship Customs New York U.S. $10,000

進口時無限定貨幣，由於外滙市場的變動危險，採本國貨幣較安全。

B. 價格條件

價格方面，可依交貨地點及價格構成要素分類。若以出口地及進口地來區分，可大致區分如下：

1. 出口地價格條件

出口地
- 現場交貨價 Loco（*Ex Works*，*Ex Godown*）
- *F.O.B.*
  - 車上交貨價 F.O.R, F.O.T.（*Free on Rail or Truck* 英）
  - F.O.B.（*Free on Board* 美＝內陸）
  - 船邊交貨價 F.A.S.（*Free Alongside Ship*）
  - 船上交貨價 F.O.B.（*Free on Board* 英）
  - F.O.B. vessel（美）
- *C.I.F.*
  - 運費、保險費在內價 C.I.F.（*Cost*，*Insurance & Freight*）
  - 成本、運費在內價 C & F
  - 成本、運費、保險費及傭金在內價 C.I.F. &C.（*Cost*，*Insurance*，*Freight & Commission*）

2. 進口地價格條件

進口地
- 目的港船上交貨價 Ex Ship
- 目的港駁船交貨價 Ex Lighter
- 目的港碼頭交貨價 Ex Quay（英），Ex Dock（美）
- 目的港海關倉庫交貨價 In Bond, Duty Unpaid
- 目的港海關倉庫完稅交貨價 Duty Paid, Ex Customs Compound
- （全部費用在內的）目的地交貨價 Franco（*Free Delivered*，*Free Domicile*）

前面所談，從 Loco 到 Franco 的各個階段，所有權乃是以交貨地點做界限的。所負擔的風險也一樣以此爲限，像 C.I.F，F.O.B. 都是在出口地船上轉移風險負擔的。在進口地價格條件的情況下，貨物到達交貨地之前發生的風險，由賣方負擔。爲了減少海上運輸的風險及海上運輸保險的範圍，大有從進口地價格條件轉移爲出口地價格條件的趨勢。此外，C.I.F.，F.O.B. 的條款下，所有權於支付貨款時轉移。

1 錄音機之詢價 Inquiry for Tape Recorder

【實務須知】

- ***your extensive consideration*** ⇨貴方廣泛的考慮
- ***with the prospects of great success*** ⇨因爲期望順利成功
- ***successful sale*** ⇨成功的銷售
- list〔 lɪst 〕*v.* 列於表上

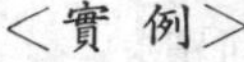

＜實　例＞

Dear Sirs,

Cassette Tape Recorder

Thank you very much for your extensive consideration in establishing business relations with our company. With the prospects of great success we wish to start off with an initial order for 500 sets of your most popular cassette tape recorder, Model CRC-137.

As the demand for inexpensive cassette tape recorders is high, we may expect a successful sale depending on the cost and quality of your machines.

Incidentally we shall be much obliged if you will send us your latest catalog listing your tape recorders and price list with samples.

Your prompt reply will be much appreciated.

Yours very truly,

敬啓者：

<u>卡式錄音機</u>

非常感謝貴公司廣泛的考慮，和本公司締結交易關係。因爲期望順利成功，我方希望以貴公司最受歡迎的CRC-137型，卡式錄音機五百台的首次訂單做爲開始。

因爲對價廉的卡式錄音機需求很高，以貴公司產品之價格與品質，我們可以期待一次成功的銷售。

附帶提起，若能寄來列有貴公司錄音機的最新目錄，和有樣品的價目表，則不勝感激。

我們將十分感謝您的早日回覆。

** ———————————

cassette〔kæ'sɛt〕*n*. 裝卡式錄音帶的扁盒

initial〔ɪ'nɪʃəl〕*adj*. 首次的；最初的

incidentally〔,ɪnsə'dɛntḷɪ〕*adv*. 附帶提起

2 紡織品之詢價
Request for Textile Goods

【實務須知】

- ***spot purchase*** ⇨ 現金購買
- measuring〔'mɛʒərɪŋ〕*n*. 測量
- ***an influx of orders*** ⇨ 訂單大量湧入；訂單紛至
- ***CIF Keelung*** ⇨ 到基隆港的運費、保險費在內價
- ***Irrevocable and Confirmed L/C*** ⇨ 不可撤銷確認信用狀
- repeat orders ⇨ 再次訂單

<實 例>

Dear Sirs,

Having heard from our chief supplier that your company is a leading firm specializing in cotton and rayon goods, we wish to make a spot purchase from you on the following fabrics, each measuring at least 50,000 yds.

1. First class tweed
2. First class black serges

Owing to an influx of orders after opening a new office in Hongkong, our stocks are nearly exhausted. This compels us to compile a large inventory immediately in order to meet the needs of our customers.

We shall appreciate your lowest possible prices CIF Keelung with immediate delivery.

We do business on an Irrevocable and Confirmed L/C by Bank of Taiwan, under which you may draw a draft at sight. For any information concerning our credit, please refer to the above bank.

If your goods are satisfactory in quality and delivery, we will place repeat orders with you in the near future.

Yours faithfully,

敬啓者：

從我方主要的供應商得知，貴公司是專門銷售棉花和縲縈貨品的首要公司，我方希望從您那兒現金購買下列的紡織品，每一種至少量五萬碼。

1. 最高級的斜紋軟呢
2. 最高級的黑色斜紋嗶嘰布料

由於在香港的新辦公處開幕之後，訂單紛至，本公司的存貨幾已用罄。故不得不立刻收集大批的庫存品，以迎合顧客的需求。

若蒙報知到基隆港的運費、保險費在內價之可能最低價，及保證立即交貨，則不勝感激。

本公司的交易方式是由台灣銀行開立不可撤銷確認信用狀,貴公司可憑此開立即期滙票。任何有關我方信用的資料，請向上述銀行查詢。

若貴公司貨品在品質及交貨上令人滿意，本公司在不久的將來，會再下訂單給您。

**

fabric〔ˈfæbrɪk〕*n.* 紡織品　compel〔kəmˈpɛl〕*v.* 迫使

compile〔kəmˈpaɪl〕*v.* 收集；編列

inventory〔ˈɪnvən,torɪ〕*n.* 庫存品；存貨

3 商業機器之詢價
Inquiry for Business Machine

【實務須知】

- ***commence negotiation in the sale of～*** ⇨開始商議～的買賣
- ***be in demand for*** ⇨需要
- rotary offset ⇨旋轉式迂迴管
- high efficiency ⇨高效率
- ***technical information*** ⇨技術資料

- ***delivery date*** ⇨交貨日期
- ***price is reasonable*** ⇨價格合理

＜實 例＞

Gentlemen :

Rossetti Printing Machine

Thank you very much for your letter of May 1 offering a proposal to commence negotiation in the sale of your business machines.

Upon reading the pamphlet introducing your company, we have learned that you are the Sole Agent of Rossetti Printing Machine. This interests us very much.

We are now in demand for your machine, rotary offset with high efficiency, Model ROH-650. We would like a fully detailed pamphlet concerning the above machine. Also, please send us your latest catalog and technical information for the above with price list and possible delivery date as soon as possible.

If your price is reasonable and delivery is superior to other suppliers, we will be pleased to place an order with you.

Yours very truly,

敬啓者：

羅塞帝印刷機

非常感謝貴公司5月1日來信，提出開始商議銷售商業機器的建議。

讀到介紹貴公司的手册時，我方知道您是羅塞帝印刷機的獨家代理商。這使本公司非常感興趣。

現在本公司需要高效率有旋轉式迂迴管的 ROH-650 型機器。希望有一份關於上述機器詳盡解說的手册，也請儘快寄來貴公司最新的目錄，和上述機器的技術資料、價格表和可能的交貨日期。

如果貴公司價格合理，交貨優於其它供應商，本公司將很樂意訂購。

**

sole agent 獨家代理商　pamphlet〔ˈpæmflɪt〕*n.* 手册

superior〔səˈpɪrɪɚ〕*adj.* 較優的

supplier〔səˈplaɪɚ〕*n.* 供應商

實用例句

【必備詞彙】

- ***quote your lowest prices*** ⇨ 報上貴公司最低的價格
- ***immediately ship*** ⇨ 即期裝運
- take pleasure in sending ⇨ 樂於寄上
- ***special discount*** ⇨ 特別的折扣
- ***if agreeable*** ⇨ 若蒙贊同

⁂ ⁂ ⁂

1. We are pleased to inform you that our government has cut the duty on rayon goods. Therefore please ***quote your lowest prices***

CIF Keelung only on those items which you can ***immediately ship.***

很樂意通知貴公司,我國政府已經降低縲縈貨物的關稅。因此僅就那些貴公司能立刻裝運的貨物請報到基隆運費、保險費在內價之最低價格。

* duty〔ˈdjutɪ〕*n.* 關稅

2. As requested in your letter of May 5, we ***take pleasure in sending*** a complete catalog which states our products in detail.

應貴公司5月5日來信要求，茲樂意奉寄一份詳細說明本公司產品的完整目錄。

3. If there is any further information, please contact us immediately.

如果有任何更進一步的消息，請立刻與本公司接洽。

* contact〔ˈkɑntækt〕*v.* 接洽；接觸

4. The enclosed catalog and price list will show our goods to be original in design and excellent in quality as well as competitive in price.

從附寄的目錄和價目表，可以看出本公司貨品設計新穎、品質優良、價格具有競爭力。

* original〔əˈrɪdʒənḷ〕*adj.* 新穎的；創新的

5. As this is a large order, we would like you to give us a ***special discount*** of 5% off the list price. ***If agreeable,*** we will be most anxious to place an order with you.

因為這是一筆大訂單，希望您照表列價格打百分之五的特別折扣。若蒙贊同，本公司極渴望訂購。

* ***place an order with*** ～下訂單給～；向～訂購

對於**詢價的回覆，不僅要求正確，更需具有把客戶胃口導向訂購的功能**。答覆當然是越快越好，因爲可能尙有衆多競爭者，如果第一步就遲了，那是最吃虧的。不過，首先還得做好**市場調查**，有自信且儘速正確地回信，告訴對方收到來信，同時向對方報價。回信時要點如下：

1. 對顧客洽詢事項，需經全力充分地搜集資料，務求詳盡正確地回覆，以免勞煩對方作第二次詢問。

2. 應隨函檢送買賣必備資料，諸如樣品、目錄、價目表等。若為另函投寄，需先加以說明。可視情況，向買方提供市場、資料的說明，以誘發其購買慾。

3. 向對方暗示，請他們下訂單。當然要避免使用強迫性字眼。

4. 若沒有對方所洽詢的物品時，可建議使用代替品。如果代替品也沒有，應該客氣地敍述理由。

*　　　　*　　　　*

✦ 數量品質重要術語

以下就數量、品質等條款及貿易術語加以說明，務必充分了解，因為有了這方面的正確知識，才能更順利地推展貿易。

A. 數量 Quantity

一、數量的種類：

1. 重量（*Weight*）

Ton：l / t　Long ton＝2,240 *lbs*.（英）　長噸

　　　s / t　Short ton＝2,000 *lbs*.（美）　短噸

　　　m / t　Metric ton＝2,204.6 *lbs*.　公噸

Ounce：oz＝28.35 *grams*（公克）（不用於貴重金屬或藥量）盎斯

Pound：lb.＝16 *ozs*＝454 *grams*　磅

Kilogram：kg.＝1000*g*.＝2.2045 *lbs*.　公斤

Hundred weight：cwt＝112 *lbs*.＝50.80 *kgs*.

（1 ton＝20 hundred weights）

2. 長度（*Length*）

1 ft.＝12 *inches* (in.)（英尺）

1 yard (yd.)＝3 *feet* (ft.)＝Approx. 91.4 *cm*（碼）

1 meter＝39.37 *in*＝3.28 *ft*.＝1.09 *yd*.（公尺）

3. 容積（*Capacity*）

1 dozen (doz.)＝12 *bottles*（打）

1 gallon (gal.)＝231 *cubic inches*＝4 *quarts*（加侖）

1 quart (gt.)＝2 *pints*（夸爾）

1 bushel＝Approx. 36 *kg*.（蒲式爾，英斗）

1 liter＝0.264 *gallon*（公升）

4. 包裝（*Packing*）・個數（*Number*）

10 barrels (*of*) butter（琵琶桶，36加侖）

5 quarters (*of*) barley（五夸特大麥＝8 *bushels*）

500 bales cotton（包；綑）

200 cases champagne（箱）

100 reams paper（令）

10 sets of instrument（套；件）

200 roles of matting（二百捲蓆子）

piece（件；個）

gross（籮 *great* $g. = 12^3 = 1778$

small $g. = 12 \times 10 = 120$）

5. **材積**（***Measurement***）

1 cubic foot（*cu. ft.* or *cut.* $= ft^3$）

1 cubic meter（*cu. m.* $= m^3$）

1 measurement ton = 40 cu. ft.

二、數量的決定：

貨物數量的檢定通常由衡量公證行（Sworn Measurer）辦理，以其所發出的證明為準，通稱為Certificate and List of Weight and/or Measurement 。

1. 數量因**決定地點**之不同區分為：

a. 裝船數量條款Shipped Weight Terms

b. 卸貨數量條款Landed Weight Terms

2. 數量因**包裝用具**是否合併計算區分為：

a. 毛重條款Gross Weight Terms

b. 淨重條款Net Weight Terms

3. 數量可以附加**容差條款**（***More or Less Terms***），而預測運送途中的減損，至多允許10％的容差。

a. Sellers have the option of shipping 5％ more or less on the contracted quantity.

b. One thousand metric tons 10% more or less at seller's option.

4. 訂單可因**可能認購數量**之上限、下限區分爲：

a. 最大可能認購數量 Maximum Quantity Acceptable

b. 最小可能認購數量 Minimum Quantity Acceptable

B. 品質 Quality

由於賣方和買方之間對品質要求不一致，往往產生誤解、抱怨，這是貿易理賠中占最重比例者。要避免這類不愉快事件發生，最確實的方法如下：

1. 以**樣品**（***Sample***）爲標準，稱爲***Sale by Sample***（按樣品買賣）。

Quality Sample	品質樣品
Seller's Sample	賣方提供的樣品
Buyer's Sample	買方提供的樣品
Counter Sample	與對方樣品類似的樣品；相對樣品
Original Sample	原始樣品；裝貨前所取出之樣品
Duplicate Sample	存驗樣品
Triplicate Sample	第三樣品
Advance Sample	先發樣品
Shipping Sample	裝船樣品；發貨樣品

2. 根據世界聞名的**商標或品牌**（***Brand or Trade Mark***），做爲品質的標準。

例如：Singer Sewing Machine　　Philips Radio

"Thermos" Flask　　Sony Radio

Kodak Film　　Scotch Whisky

Nikon Camera　　Ford car

3. 棉花、羊毛、小麥等農產品，自然材料都以**標準品**交易。稱爲***Sale by Standard***（按標準品買賣）。

具體來說有：

F. A. Q. (Fair Average Quality Term, 平均中等品質條件)

G.M.Q. (Good Merchantable Quality Term, 上好可銷品質條件)

4. 根據**最後決定品質的時間**，可區分為：

Shipped Quality Term 裝船品質條件

Landed Quality Term 卸貨品質條件

穀類則有

T. Q. (Tale Quale 裝船品質條件；現狀條件)

R. T. (Rye Terms 卸貨品質條件；裸麥條件)

S. D. (Sea Damaged 裝船品質條件；海損賣方擔保條件)

品質的決定需根據有權威的調查機構，如公證人 (Public Surveyor) 所簽發的：

Inspection Certificate (檢驗證明書)

Survey Report (公證報告)

來證明自己的品質，否則不予承認。

1 答覆詢價 Response to Inquiry 

【實務須知】

- ***inquiry of July 26 concerning*** ⇨ 7月26日有關～的詢價
- ***Chinese Government Good Design Award*** ⇨ 中華民國政府物品設計獎
- ***printed materials*** ⇨ 印刷品
- ***special delivery*** ⇨ 快遞

<實 例>

Dear Sirs,

Cassette Tape Recorder

Thank you very much for your inquiry of July 26 concerning your purchase of 500 sets of our popular cassette tape recorder, Model CRT-153.

In compliance with your request, we have enclosed herewith our latest tape recorder catalog with our price list No. 250. Among our best selling products, we recommend our Model CRT-508 because it has won the Chinese Government Good Design Award, and has been enjoying excellent sales ever since.

If satisfactory, we will send 400 sets from the production line. Owing to a rush of orders, this will be our maximum quantity for the present.

Together with the printed materials requested, we have sent samples, including several other models, by special delivery.

We are very pleased to have concluded business relations with you and hope that our appreciation will continue for a long time to come.

Yours very faithfully,

Encls. Pamphlet 1

Catalog 2

敬啓者：

<u>卡式錄音機</u>

非常感謝貴公司7月26日,有關購買本公司最流行的CRT-153 型卡式錄音機五百台的詢價。

按照貴公司要求,茲附寄最新的錄音機目錄，和第250號價目表 。在本公司銷售最佳的產品中，我們推薦 CRT-508型，因爲它曾經贏得中華民國政府物品設計獎，其後一直享有極佳的銷售量。

如獲滿意，我方會從生產線寄去四百台。由於訂單紛至，這是本公司目前可以提供的最大數量。

隨同您要求的印刷品，本公司以限時專送奉寄（包括數種其它款式的）樣品 。

非常高興和貴公司締結交易關係,也希望本公司的感激持續至未來很久之後。

附寄　手册 1

　　　目錄 2

** ———

in compliance with 依照；依從

maximum〔'mæksəməm〕*adj*. 最大的；最高的

2 價目表 Price List

Price List No. 250

August 25, 19−

Prices are subject to change without notice.
Please confirm when placing your order.
Please refer to catalog Model Number and specifications concerning design and capacity.

Model No.	Code word	Description	Price per unit	Shipment
CTR-505	TOP	Cassette, 3″ speaker Earphone, Battery Leather Case 2 7/16″ × 5 13/16″ × 8 ¾″	£6−38p	September
CRT-506	TOS	Cassette, 2 ½″ speaker Earphone, Battery Leather Case 2 ⅛″ × 5 ¼″ × 8 7/16″	£6−00	September
CRT-507	TOT	Cassette, 3 ½″ speaker AM radio, Earphone, Battery Leather case, AC & DC 3 ½″ × 6 ⅜″ × 8 ½″	£8−48p	September

CRT-508	TOX	Cassette, 3 ½″ Speaker Earphone, AC & DC, Battery Leather case 2 ¾″ × 5 ½″ × 8″	£6−58p	October (400 sets for May)
CRT-509	TOY	Cassette, 3 ½″ speaker Earphone, AM radio, Battery Leather case, AC & DC 2 ½″ × 6″ × 8 ½″	£8−59p	September
CRT-510	TOM	Cassette, 4 ¾″ speaker Earphone, Battery, AM/FM radio Leather case, AC & DC 3″ × 6 ½″ × 9″	£10−86p	August

Prices are C.I.F. & C. (5%) Calcutta in Pound Sterling.

Quantity available : More than 500 sets, 400 sets for CRT-508 before 30th May.

Packing : One in Cardboard case and ten dozens in wooden carton.

E. & O. E.

The Mao Yuan Electric Co., Ltd.

....

Sales Manager

第250號價目表

19－年8月25日

價格可能有變動不另通知。

下訂單時請先確認。

關於設計和性能請參照目錄的型號及明細表。

型號	密碼	品種、規格說明	單價	船期
CTR-505	TOP	卡式，3英吋喇叭 耳機，乾電池 皮套 2 7/16″×5 13/16″ ×8 ¾″	六英鎊三十八辨士	9月
CRT-506	TOS	卡式，2 ½英吋喇叭 耳機，乾電池 皮套 2 ⅛″×5 ¼″×8 7/16″	六英鎊正	9月
CRT-507	TOT	卡式，3 ½英吋喇叭 AM收音機，耳機， 乾電池 皮套，交直流兩用 3 ½″×6 ⅜″×8 ½″	八英鎊四十八辨士	9月
CRT-508	TOX	卡式，3 ½英吋喇叭 耳機，交直流兩用 乾電池 皮套		

		2 ¾″×5 ½″×8″	六英鎊五十八辨士	10月（5月四百台）
CRT-509	TOY	卡式，3 ½英吋喇叭 耳機，AM收音機， 乾電池 皮套，交直流兩用 2 ½″×6″×8 ½″	八英鎊五十九辨士	9 月
CRT-510	TOM	卡式，4 ¾英吋喇叭 耳機，乾電池， AM／FM收音機 皮套，交直流兩用 3″×6 ½″×9″	十英鎊八十六辨士	8 月

本價格是到加爾各答運費、保險費、傭金（百分之五）在內價，以英鎊計。

有效數量：超過五百台，在5月30日前CRT-508四百台。

包裝：每台用紙板盒包裝，每十打用大木箱包裝。

有 錯 當 查

懋源電氣有限公司

…………

銷售部經理

** ――――――――――――――

specification 〔,spɛsɪfɪˋkeʃən〕 ***n.*** (***pl.***) 明細表；詳細說明書

AC = ***alternating current*** 交流電

DC = ***direct current*** 直流電

C.I.F. & ***C.*** = ***cost, insurance, freight*** & ***commission***

運費保費傭金在內價

E. & ***O. E.*** = ***errors*** & ***omissions excepted*** 有錯當查

3 答覆詢價 Response to Inquiry

【實務須知】

- ***special air delivery*** ⇨航空快遞
- ***market is dull*** ⇨市場蕭條（不景氣）
- ***picking up in activity*** ⇨正活躍起來
- ***keep the prices effective*** ⇨價格保持有效

＜實　例＞

Dear Sirs,

Thank you for your letter of June 10 along with your excellent buying proposal.

We have already dispatched the samples and price list you requested by special air delivery.

As our market is now somewhat dull and prices generally low, you are very fortunate in making purchase at this time. European buyers, however, seem to be picking up in activity, so we advise you to buy the goods you requested before the recovery reaches a peak.

Accordingly, we cannot keep the prices effective more than three weeks from the date of this letter and we wish to receive your order by return mail.

We hope that this will meet with your immediate approval.

Yours very truly,

Encs. Price List 1
Sample book 3

敬啓者：

感謝貴公司6月10日來信，和極佳的購買提案。

本公司已經以航空快遞，寄去需索的樣品和價目表。

因爲本地市場目前有點蕭條，價格普遍低落，貴公司很幸運於此時機採購。然而，歐洲買主似乎逐漸活躍起來，所以勸您在景氣復甦到最高峰以前，購進需求的貨品。

按照情形，從這封信的日期算起，本公司不能保持此價格超過三星期仍然有效，希望接到信後，請即回示訂單。

希望這封信能獲得貴公司立刻贊同。

附寄 價目表1
樣品簿3

**
---

along with 隨同

dispatch〔dɪˈspætʃ〕*v.* 寄送；發送

reach a peak 達到頂點

accordingly〔əˈkɔrdɪŋlɪ〕*adv.* 按照情形；如前所說

by return mail 接到信後立刻；請即回示

實用例句

【必備詞彙】

- substitute sample ⇨替代的樣品
- ***assuring maximum quality*** ⇨確保最高的品質
- ***keep prices open*** ⇨價格保持有效
- ***subject to change without notice and without engagement*** ⇨可能有變動，不另通知也不保證
- ***we may draw on you at sight*** ⇨本公司可以開給貴公司即期滙票
- your specified documents ⇨您指定的文件
- market price ⇨市場價格
- ***execute your order*** ⇨履行貴公司的訂單

⁂ ⁂ ⁂

1. The commodity you required in your letter of June 25 is now out of stock. Therefore, we have sent ***substitute samples*** which we feel superior in price and quality and will meet your requirements.

   貴公司6月25日來信需索的商品現已無存貨。因此，茲寄送替代樣品，本公司認爲其價格低廉品質優良，必能迎合貴公司的需求。

   * ***out of stock*** 已無存貨；存貨告罄

2. A trial order will convince you this merchandise is superior to the product you requested since we have cut our prices nearly to production cost while ***assuring maximum quality.***

試訂一次,將使貴公司深信這種商品優於您需求的產品，因爲本公司在確保最高品質之餘，已把價格幾乎降到生產成本。

* convince〔kən′vɪns〕*v.* 使深信；說服

3. Owing to frequent fluctuations in the market price, it is impossible to ***keep the prices open*** for a week. Therefore, they are ***subject to change without notice and without engagement.***

由於市場價格經常變動，要保持價格一星期有效是不可能的。因此價格可能有變動，不另通知，也不保證。

* fluctuation〔ˌflʌktʃʊˋeʃən〕*n.* 不規則的變動

4. As this is our first business with you, we would like you to open an irrevocable L/C, against which ***we may draw on you at sight*** attaching your ***specified documents.***

因爲這是本公司和貴公司的第一筆交易,希望貴公司開立不可撤銷信用狀，憑此我方可以開給您即期滙票，並附上您指定的文件。

5. As present ***market prices*** are currently high, we are sorry that we are not in a position to ***execute your order*** at the price mentioned in your letter of April 25th.

因爲目前市場價格一般都很高，以貴公司4月25日信上提到的價格，我方無法履行訂單，至感抱歉。

* currently〔′kɝəntlɪ〕*adv.* 一般地；通行地

⁂ ⁂ ⁂

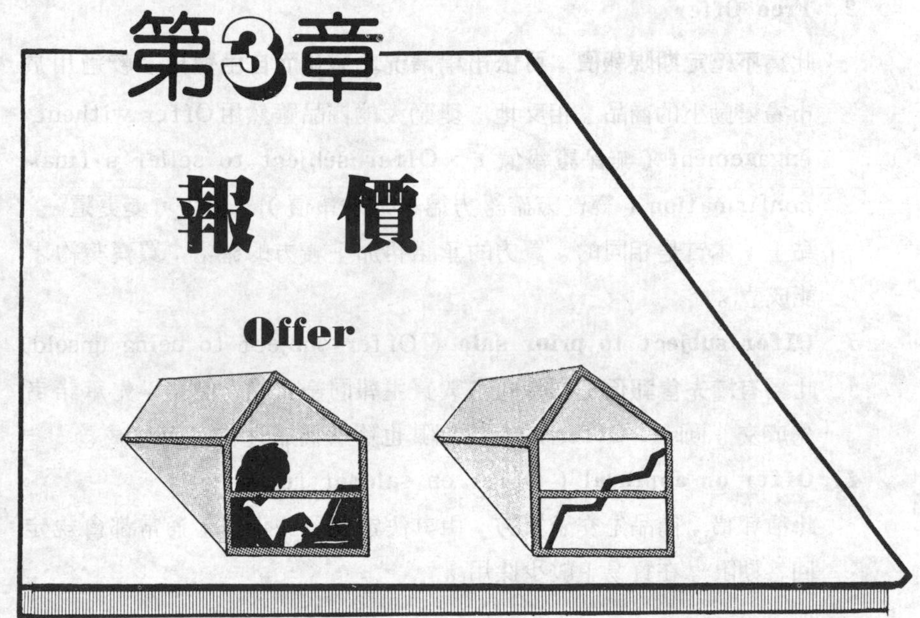

對於買方的詢價（ Inquiry ），具體的推銷方法就是**報價**（ ***Offer*** ），所謂報價，具體而言即賣方就希望出售的貨物之一定品質、數量、裝運日期、付款條件等，用電報或書信通知買方。對這份報價，買方若加以**承諾**（ ***Acceptance*** ），買賣契約即告成立。通常都是賣方向買方報價，但也有買方向賣方報價的情況，稱爲 **Buyer's Offer**（ *Buying Offer* ）和前者 **Seller's Offer**（ *Selling Offer* ）有別。報價共分四種：

1. Firm Offer

此爲**期限內有效報價**，由賣方規定一個期限讓買方答覆，在這期限內，即使市場價格發生變動，賣方也**不可取消報價或變更報價內容**。但期限一過，報價的效力自然消失。買方可用電報或電傳來答覆，不一定非用書信不可，在賣方收到買方對 Firm Offer 的回覆時即開始生效。不過，對雙方來講，用書信來答覆當然比較方便和可靠。

2. **Free Offer**

此爲**不確定期限報價，可依市場情況之變化而自由變更**，較適用於市場變動小的商品。相反地，變動大的商品雖然用Offer without engagement（無保證報價）、Offer subject to seller's final confirmation（經賣方確認方爲有效的報價）。但在可變更這一點上，本質是相同的。買方的承諾再加上賣方的確認，買賣契約才能成立。

3. **Offer subject to prior sale**（Offer subject to being unsold）

此爲**有權先售報價**，同時向多數買主報同一商品之價格，先承諾者先成交。同時，Offer 的有效期限也隨著商品之售完而消滅。

4. **Offer on approval**（Offer on sale or return）

此種報價，商品先交予買方，由其決定購買或退回，通常都會規定回答期限。在貿易上較少採用。

*

對賣方提出的Offer，買方請求變更交易條件（品質、數量、價格、裝船、付款日期）時，Firm Offer 就失去時效，產生新的Offer，是爲**Counter Offer**（還價），也就是說，**在對Offer完全無條件承諾（*absolute acceptance*）之前，不能成立契約**，在此之前常不斷討價還價，重新訂立Offer。貿易上的往來相當耗時，所以必須先考慮到市場情況的變更。爲了將風險減至最小，賣方往往在Firm Offer上規定回覆期限，根據「在某某日之前必須收到回音」的條件，以避免不必要的時間浪費。

*　　*　　*

✤ Payment

付款方式在貿易上極其重要，先付款時買方風險較大，後付款時賣方風險較大。在貿易上最常使用的是折衷的跟單滙票方式。

1. Cash in Advance（Cash with Order；C.W.O.）

訂貨時即須付款；就是在貨品送到前，先以Bank Bill（銀行滙票）或Bank Check（銀行支票）給付，在我國外滙市場上，屬於**預繳外滙**（***Surrender foreign exchange in advance***）。與此相對的是Deferred Payment（延期付款），及Progressive Payment（累進付款）。

2. Documentary Bill of Exchange with L/C

信用狀跟單滙票，就是貿易上的買賣雙方，用現金交換商品，將以現金交換爲原則的跟單滙票方式運用於貿易上。爲了使付款更爲確實起見，由銀行將買方（進口商）之信用明文記載於信用狀上，保證買方付款事宜。在此將跟單制度的流程以圖表示之：

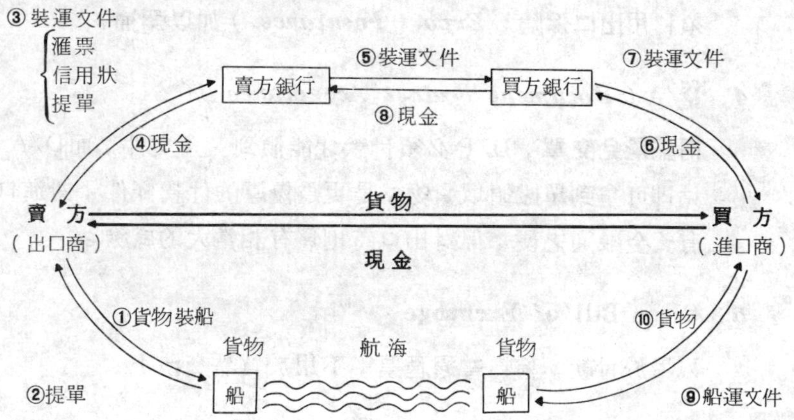

最終目的是中央的兩道線，即賣方以貨物交換買方的現金。爲達到這個目的，實務步驟如下：

① 貨物交由船公司裝船。

② 領取船公司簽發之提單（B/L）作爲收據。

③ 以此提單及買方銀行發行的信用狀，開立以買方銀行爲付款人的跟單滙票（這時所有證件稱爲裝運文件，其中最重要的是提單）。

④ 然後到銀行辦理押滙，領取現金。

⑤ 本國銀行再向買方銀行提出這些文件。

⑥ 買方銀行將款項寄給賣方銀行。

⑦ 買主持著裝運文件，可待船駁進港，憑單據提貨。

** 這種信用狀跟單滙票是正規的付款方式，若不用信用狀，可用條件較利於買方的D/P滙票或D/A滙票。

3. D/P（ ***Documents against Payment*** ）

稱爲**付款交單**，當銀行向進口商提出跟單滙票時，進口商應立即付款，然後才能取得裝運文件辦理提貨，但是銀行對於一切支付不知情，也沒有保證。因此，信用上的風險較大，用D/P，D/A方式時，因無銀行信用介入，出口商之交易銀行大多不願承購，所以必須利用**出口保險**（ ***Export Insurance*** ）加以彌補。

4. D/A（ ***Document against Acceptance*** ）

稱爲**承兌交單**，D/P必須付款才能領到裝運文件，而D/A只要承兌即可拿到單據領取貨物，是更爲優厚的付款條件。對進口商而言，有資金融通之便，但對出口商則負有相當大的風險。

5. **Clean Bill of Exchange**

只用於付款，稱爲**普通滙票**，不用於貿易交涉上。

6. **Open Account**

此爲**記帳交易**，和國內交易一樣，約定在一定期限內，不必逐筆付款，只須在截止日期清算，送交盈餘。今日的貿易已幾乎不採用這種方式。

*　　*　　*

✦信用狀Letter of Credit（L/C）

信用狀乃貿易上不可或缺的付款保證文件，於契約成立後，由出口商要求進口商開設信用狀。以下是簡單的開設過程，按數字順序來發行:

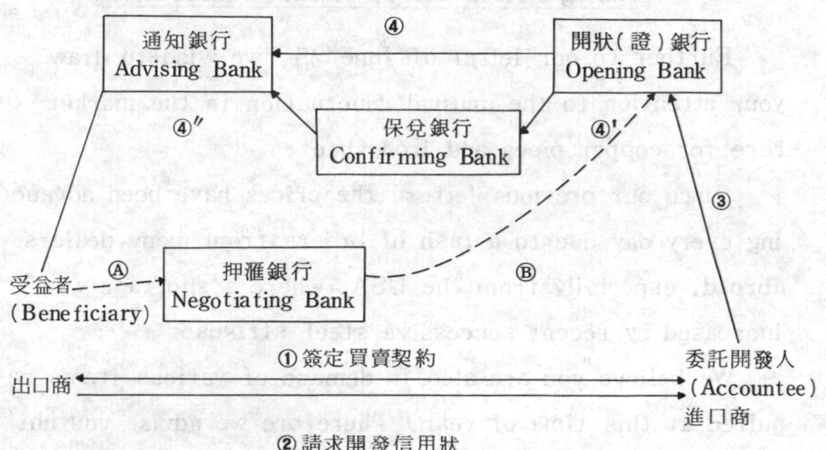

Confirm L/C「**保兌信用狀**」是將開狀銀行發行的信用狀，再由國際上有信用的銀行雙重保證。押滙時要由押滙銀行將文件送交開狀銀行，押滙銀行可以是通知銀行或另一家銀行。

1 追踪函 Follow-up Letter

【實務須知】

- ***further to*** ⇨進一步補充
- ***draw your attention*** ⇨促請您注意
- ***prices have been advancing*** ⇨價格節節上漲
- ***in demand of*** ⇨需求

<實 例>

Dear Sirs,

Rising Prices due to Market Fluctuations

Further to our letter of June 25, we wish to draw your attention to the unusual fluctuation in the market here for copper pipes and iron sheet.

Since our previous letter, the prices have been advancing every day due to a rush of orders from many dealers abroad, especially from the USA, where a shortage was increased by recent successive steel strikes.

We believe you are also in demand of various items required at this time of year. Therefore we advise you not to delay in considering the quantity of demand.

Under the circumstances, we are unable to keep our prices valid for more than two weeks, so please cable us your acceptance immediately at ten per cent (10%) over last year.

Yours faithfully,

敬啓者：

由於市場變動，價格提高

進一步補充我方6月25日信函，希望促請您注意，本地銅管和鐵板的市場異常的變動。

自從我方上封信以來，由於外國許多貿易商蜂擁而至的訂單，價格每天節節上漲，尤其是從美國，當地鋼鐵工人最近接連的罷工，使得短缺增加。

相信在一年這個時機需求的各種項目，貴公司也同樣需要。因此，我方勸您不要遲延考慮需要量。

在這種情形下，本公司無法保持價格超過兩星期仍然有效，所以請立刻以電報告知您願意接受比去年高百分之十的價格。

** ______________________

fluctuation〔ˌflʌktʃʊˈeʃən〕*n.* 變動；波動

copper〔ˈkɑpɚ〕*n.* 銅

rush〔rʌʃ〕*n.* 蜂擁而至；搶購

circumstance〔ˈsɝkəmˌstæns〕*n.*（*pl.*）情形；情況

valid〔ˈvælɪd〕*adj.* 有效的

2 針對詢價報價 Offer against Inquiry

【實務須知】

- ***market is enjoying an upward trend*** ⇨市場行情看漲
- ***no further stock available to offer*** ⇨可供應的存貨不多
- ***not to overlook this opportunity*** ⇨勿忽視此機會，此爲勿失良機之意

＜實 例＞

Dear Sirs,

Thank you very much for your inquiry of June 18 requesting us to quote the prices for our first class tweed and black serge.

Concerning the above, we have just cabled you the following firm offer:

> 50,000 yds. sample No. 235 black serge @ Stg. £29-96p and No. 685 tweed @ Stg. £32-75p per yd. CIF Keelung shipment August subject to reply received here by June 20.

We are sure you will find our prices very reasonable. The market here is enjoying an upward trend, and we have no further stock available to offer at the same price.

We advise you not to overlook this opportunity and hope to receive your prompt order by cable.

Yours faithfully,

敬啓者：

非常感謝貴公司6月18日的詢價函，要求本公司對高級斜紋軟呢和黑色斜紋嗶嘰布料報價。

有關上述事情，本公司剛剛以電報告知確定報價如下：

> 五萬碼 到基隆運費、保險費在內價，様品號 235號黑色斜紋嗶嘰布料，每碼二十九英鎊九十六辨士，而第 685號斜紋軟呢，每碼三十二英鎊七十五辨士，船期八月，本報價以6月 20日接到回覆爲條件。

確信貴公司將發現價格非常合理。本地市場行情看漲，且同一價格可供應的存貨不多。

敬請勿失良機，希望立刻接獲貴公司電報訂單。

** ——————————

tweed〔twid〕*n.* 斜紋軟呢

serge〔sɝdʒ〕*n.* 斜紋嗶嘰布料

3 確定報價 Firm Offer

【實務須知】

- ***automatic exposure meter & range meter*** ⇨自動測光表和測距儀器
- ***Banker's Irrevocable L/C*** ⇨銀行的不可撤銷信用狀
- ***production ration*** ⇨生產配額
- ***with the approach of the leisure season*** ⇨由於休閑季節來臨

<實 例>

Gentlemen:

Thank you for your inquiry of June 25, against which we have quoted the price as shown in the following firm offer cabled today subject to your reply here by the 15th.

Commodity: Model FAU-150 Full-automatic tube camera equipped with automatic exposure meter & range meter

Quantity: 500 sets

Quality: Specified in the attached specification sheets

Price: $250.00 C.I.F. Los Angeles in US dollars per unit on Banker's Irrevocable L/C, under which we draw a draft at 30 d/s.

Shipment : July 30

With the approach of the leisure season, the demand for high quality cameras is increasing. The compact styling and superb quality will certainly present excellent sales as shown by our production ration.

We trust you will take advantage of this seasonal opportunity and favor us with an early reply.

Very truly yours,

敬啓者:

感謝貴公司6月25日之詢價函,對此我方今天已用電報告知如下的確定報價,但須以貴公司的回覆於15日抵達爲條件。

商品:FAU-150型 全自動35mm照相機,並有自動測光表和測距儀器的設備

數量:五百台

品質:詳細說明如附寄的明細表

價格:到舊金山的運費、保險費在內價,每台美金二百五十元,以銀行的不可撤銷信用狀爲條件,憑此本公司可以開立見票三十天後付款滙票

船期:7月30日

由於休閑季節的來臨,對高品質照相機的需求逐漸增加。依本公司生產配額所示,精緻的樣式及優越的品質必定會呈現極佳的銷售額。

相信貴公司會利用此季節性良機,並早日惠予答覆。

** ———————————————

full-automatic tube camera 全自動35mm照相機

take advantage of 利用

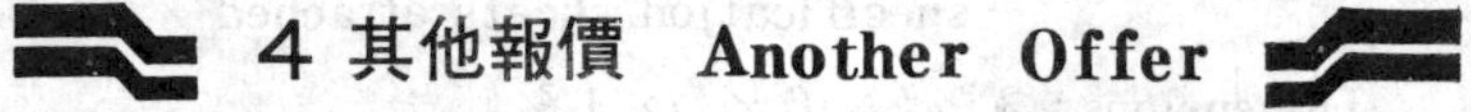

4 其他報價 Another Offer

【實務須知】

- ***July production*** ⇨7月生產量
- ***schedule suitable for you request*** ⇨適合貴公司要求的時間表
- ***A.A.R.*** = *Against All Risks* ⇨擔保全險；一切險
- ***W.A.*** = *With Average* ⇨水漬險；單獨海損賠償險

<實 例>

Dear Sirs,

Thank you very much for your inquiry on 5th July cabled as follows:

LT
TAIPEI MAO YUAN
CABLE QUOTATION CIF SYDNEY PORTABLE RADIO
FX-503 5000 SETS AUGUST SHIPMENT STRONG
FM DEMAND ADD ABOVE JULY PRODUCTION
PHILIP

We have arranged to insert your added order into our July production. Fortunately we had made a schedule suitable for your request and components, but please note this was an exception. Generally we need two months prior notice to commencing production.

In response to your cable we have just cabled the following subject to the same price as your last order.

Article: Model FX-503 portable transistor radio

Specification: 3-band FM/AM/SW Detailed in the specification sheets attached

Dimensions: $3\frac{3}{4}'' \times 6\frac{1}{8}'' \times 1\frac{3}{4}''$

Price: Aust. $12.35 CIF Sydney per unit (Same as your original order)

Quantity: 5,000 sets

Shipment: August 25

Insurance: A. A. R. including W. A.

Payment: Banker's Irrevocable L/C, under which we draw you a draft at sight

Packing: Usual cardboard box for each unit and 50 sets packed in wooden case

With the advent of FM broadcasting, orders are rushing from many parts of Asia and Africa. We expect you will also extend your marketing activities to take advantage of this wonderful opportunity.

Yours faithfully,

敬啓者：

感謝貴公司7月5日詢價，電文如下：

LT

台北懋源

請電報報價，FX-503型手提收音機五千台到雪梨的CIF價格。

船期8月。需求强烈。請加入7月生產量。　　菲力普

本公司已經安排，將貴公司續購訂單加入7月生產量中。很幸運地，能就您的要求及成分作了適當的時間表，但是請注意，這是一次例外。通常我們必須在兩個月前收到通知方能開始生產。

爲答覆貴公司的電報，本公司剛剛發出電報通知下列與貴公司上次訂單相同的價格。

物品：FX-503型手提電晶體收音機

品種、規格說明：FM/AM/SW三波段　詳細說明請見所附明細表

尺寸：$3\frac{3}{4}'' \times 6\frac{1}{8}'' \times 1\frac{3}{4}''$

價格：每台到雪梨運費、保險費在內價澳幣十二元三十五分（和原來訂單相同）

數量：五千台

船期：8月25日

保險：擔保全險，包括水漬險

付款：銀行的不可撤銷信用狀，本公司可憑以開立即期滙票

包裝：每台用普通紙板盒包裝，每五十台用木箱包裝

由於調頻廣播的來臨，訂單從亞洲、非洲許多地方湧進。期望貴公司也利用這次大好機會，擴展市場活動。

** ———

transistor radio 電晶體收音機

advent〔ˈædvɛnt〕*n.* 來臨；到來

cardboard〔ˈkɑrdˌbord〕*n.* 紙板

實用例句

【必備詞彙】

- ***subject to being unsold*** ⇨以尚未售出爲條件，即先到先售之意
- ***for your information*** ⇨供您參考
- ***subject to prior sale*** ⇨有權先售，即以先到先售爲條件

※ ※ ※

1. We are glad to offer you firm the silk blouse as cabled below:

   300 doz. S/# 1302 Silk Blouse @ US $30.50 per doz.

   C. I. F. New York shipment October subject to your reply here by morning of the 5th.

   樂意向貴公司提出絲衫的確定報價，電文如下：

   樣品號1302 絲衫三百打，到紐約的運費、保險費在內價，每打美金三十元五十分，船期10月，但須以貴公司的回覆於本月5日早晨送達爲條件。

   * blouse〔blauz〕*n.* 罩衫；短上衣

2. We are pleased to make an offer for this lot ***subject to being unsold***, since it is our final stock now out of production. It is especially marketable for its superb design and quality and offered at the lowest prices.

   以尚未售出爲條件，本公司樂意對此批貨品報價，因爲該貨是本公司最後一批存貨，現已不再生產。以其優越的設計及品質，加上以最低價格報價，尤其具有適銷性。

3. ***For your information***, the market here has been rising steadily, approximately $50 to $100 in a week.

供您參考，本地市場持續穩定上漲，一星期大約從五十元漲到一百元。

4. Although our prices are slightly higher than others', orders have been rushing in owing to the fine quality of our products. You will surely be satisfied at marketing our commodity.

   雖然本公司的價格比其他公司稍微高一點，但是因爲產品品質優良，訂單紛至。貴公司在銷售本公司產品時，必定會感到滿意。

5. If acceptance is received by the 15th, we will be able to rush the goods to Keelung for loading before the ship leaves on the 20th.

   若於本月 15 日前接到承諾，本公司將能夠在 20 日船離開前，火速將貨物送抵基隆裝運。

6. We offer these goods ***subject to prior sale*** because the market is exciting now and we cannot keep it open too long. Therefore please cable your acceptance immediately upon receiving this cable.

   本公司對這些貨品的報價，有權先售，因爲市場目前非常活躍，我方無法使此價有效太久。因此，請接獲此電報後，立即以電報承諾。

※ ※ ※

第4章 答覆報價

Reply to Offer

接到 Offer 時，要立刻斟酌，是完全無條件接受，予以**承諾**(**Acceptance**)呢？還是提出**還價**(**Counter Offer**)，表達自己的條件？對 Offer 置之不理的作法，是交易上極不禮貌的行爲，即使對方條件與我方相距太遠，也應該坦誠說明我方的立場，或許對方會有意想不到的讓步，縱然買賣做不成，卻留有良好印象。切記眞誠是獲致非常有利的 Offer 或 News 的主要因素。答覆報價時，須注意以下各種內容：

1. Acceptance

所謂承諾，即是在 Firm Offer（確定報價）的期限內完全接受對方的條件。其內容不外乎表達自己願意接受的意思，並附上契約書及訂單，當然亦可附寄對契約條件範圍內的希望事項。爲了便利對方充裕地籌備貨品、裝船等，即使是 Free Offer （不限定期限報價），最好也能儘速回覆。

2. Counter Offer

還價時不僅是修正不同意的條件，也是重新申報，通常一宗買賣，大多要經過買賣雙方多次往返磋商，方能成交。但是在反覆磋商過程中，務必清楚明晰地表達意見，以免反招誤解。在磋商期間，難免市場情況有所變動，故應多加留意，適切下判斷。

*　　　*　　　*

✦ C.I.F. 價格的計算

C.I.F. 及 F.O.B. 的計算，往往需要相當熟悉的概念，絕不可等閒視之。現舉收音機爲例，詳述如下：

1. 向工廠採購交貨之原價　　$ 5,000.00

2. 包裝費一紙箱裝一台　　$ 10.00

　　　一木箱裝一百台　　$ 8,000.00

3. 工廠到船上運費、搬運費　　$ 5,000.00

4. 簽發品檢證明書手續費一台　　$ 2.00

5. 利潤 10%，電報費、其它雜費　　$10,000.00

6. 裝船各項費用、搬運費　　$ 2,000.00

7. 結滙換算率　　U.S. 1$ = NT$27.00

8. 假定一台 2 Kg，一木箱 200 Kg，而一木箱容量 5 才（一材積容量 40 才 = 40 *cu.ft.*），據此計算一百台，以一個木箱裝運的 F.O.B. 價格：

(a) 以原價買入　　@ 5,000 × 100 = $500,000 …根據 1

(b) 利潤 10%　　$500,000 × 0.1 = $ 50,000 …根據 5

(c) 電報費、雜費　　$ 10,000 …根據 5

(d) 國內運費　　$@ 5,000 \times \frac{5才}{40才} = \$ \quad 625$ …根據 3

(e) 貨物包裝費　　@ 10 × 100 + 8,000 = $ 9,000 …根據 2

(f) 品檢費用　　@ 2 × 100 = $ 200 …根據 4

(g) 裝船各項費用 @ 2,000 × $\frac{5}{40}$ = $ 250 …根據 6

合計 $570,075

(h) 換算爲美元 $570,075 ÷ 27 = US$21,113.85

(i) 單價(每台) US $14,251.88 ÷ 100 = US$211.14

故F.O.B.單價US $211.14

估計C.I.F.單價時要另外加上運費、保險費

(j) 到進口港之海上運費、搬運費 US$50.00

(k) 海上保險 0.5%,預定利潤 10%。

C & F (Cost & Freight)價是

F.O.B.總價=$21,113.85=Cost US$21,113.85

海上運費Freight @ 50 × $\frac{5}{40}$ = US$ 6.25

C & F US$21,120.10

C.I.F.尚須增加10%做爲保險額,I(Insurance)的計算方式如下:

$$I = (x + 0.1x)\frac{0.5}{100}$$ (假設C.I.F.=x)

$$CIF(x) = C + F + I$$

$$x = 2,112,010 + (1.1x)\frac{0.5}{100}$$

$$100x = 2,112,010 + 0.55x$$

$$99.45x = 2,112,010$$

$$x = 21,236.90$$

故C.I.F.總價爲US$21,236.90

1 接受報價 Offer Accepted

【實務須知】

- ***purchase note*** ⇨購買確認書。如不另開購買確認書，而將各項交易條款扼要列入信函中，即成 purchase confirmation 。
- ***shipping instructions*** ⇨裝運指示
- ***open L/C in your favor*** ⇨開立以貴公司爲受款人的信用狀
- ***to ensure prompt execution*** ⇨爲確定使貴公司立即執行

<實 例>

Dear Sirs,

We are pleased to accept your cable of July 15 offering 300 dozens Silk Blouse S/# 1302 at US$30.50 per doz. CIF New York for immediate shipment.

In reply we have just cabled you as follows:

YOURS 15TH ACCEPT IMMEDIATE SHIPMENT REQUESTED AS USUAL CORNWELL.

To confirm this order, we are enclosing our purchase note No. 1002 including shipping instructions. To ensure prompt execution, we have instructed our bankers to open an irrevocable L/C in your favor by cable, which you will receive within a few days.

Though small in quantity, the order is very important for us. We ask, therefore, that you give your very best attention in completing it as soon as possible.

Yours very truly,

敬啓者：

很高興接到您7月15日電報報價，S/# 1302絲衫三百打，到紐約運費、保險費在內價每打美金三十元五十分，即刻裝運。

本公司剛剛以電報答覆如下：

對貴公司15日函，願接受即刻裝運，要求照往常一樣　康威爾。

爲了確認本訂單，茲隨函附寄第1002號購買確認書，包括裝運指示。爲確定使貴公司立即執行，本公司已指示交易銀行，以電報開立貴公司爲受款人的不可撤銷信用狀，貴公司將可於近日內收到。

雖然數量很少，但是對我方而言，本訂單非常重要。因此，懇請貴公司就此事給予最深的關切，儘速履行。

2 購買確認書 Purchase Note

【實務須知】

- ***confirm purchase acceptance*** ⇨ 確認採購承諾
- mark〔mɑrk〕*n.* 嘜頭
- ***for full invoice amount plus*** 10% ⇨ 以發票全額加百分之十
- ***design and assortment*** ⇨ 式樣及配色
- ◇CRN◇ ⇨ 此嘜頭，亦可用英文CRN in diamond over New York with numbers one to three. 表示。

New York

#1—3

＜實　例＞

(LETTERHEAD)

September 15, 19—

PURCHASE NOTE

No. 1002

Messrs. Fu I Textile Co., Ltd.
48 Heng Yeng Rd., Taipei
Taiwan, R.O.C.

We have the pleasure to confirm our purchase acceptance of the following merchandise from you on the terms and conditions specified below:

Article: Silk Blouse, S/# No. 1302
Embroidered in flower design

Quantity: 300 (three hundred) dozens

Price: at US$30.50 per dozen CIF New York

Shipment: By October 20

Terms: Draft at sight under Irrevocable L/C

Packing: One dozen in a carton and one hundred (100) dozens in a wooden case

Marks: ◇CRN with numbers 1 to 3
New York

Insurance: W.A. with Against All Risks for full invoice amount plus 10%

Cables: Yours of 10th and ours of 8th

Remarks: Design and assortment same as your sample No. 1302

Yours sincerely,

Cornwell Textile Co., Ltd.

F. R. Steven

Import Manager

（信　頭）　　19—9月15日

採購單

第1002號

富億紡織品有限公司

中華民國台灣台北市衡陽路48號

茲樂意確認本公司的採購，依下列詳述的條件，願接受貴公司下列的貨品：

貨品：絲衫，S/# 1302號
繡花的設計

數量：三百打

價格：到紐約運費、保險費在內價，每打美金三十元五十分

船期：10月20日前

條件：憑不可撤銷信用狀開立即期滙票

包裝：一打裝一紙箱，一百打裝一木箱

嘜頭：<CRN> 編號從1到3

紐約

保險：發票全額加百分之十的水漬險及擔保全險

電報：貴公司10日，我方8日

備註：式樣及配色與貴公司第1302號樣品相同

康威爾紡織品有限公司

F. R. Steven

進口部經理　　敬上

** ———————————

embroider〔ɪm'brɔɪdɚ〕*v*. 刺繡於

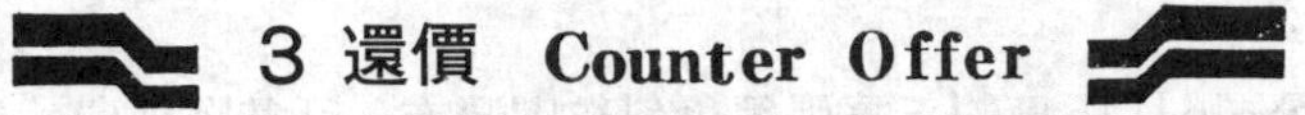

3 還價 Counter Offer

【實務須知】

- ***yds.*** = *yards* ⇨碼
- **@ *Stg.*** = *at Sterling Pound* ⇨以英鎊價格
- ***counter offer*** ⇨還價
- ***a July shipment*** = *a shipment during July* ⇨7月的船期

＜實 例＞

Dear Sirs,

We have received your offer of June 15 on 50,000 yds. black serge @Stg. £29-96p and tweed @Stg. £32-75p CIF Keelung, against which we have cabled you our counter offer as follows:

YOURS 15TH ACCEPTABLE IF JULY

Your offer meets our requirement both in price and quality. However, we need the shipped goods at latest by the end of August. Therefore, a July shipment is the latest. Please cable your acceptance by the morning of the 20th.

We trust that you will be able to accommodate us and give your prompt acceptance by return letter soon.

Thank you for your kind co-operation.

Yours faithfully,

敬啓者：

貴公司6月15日對五萬碼黑色斜紋嗶嘰布，以基隆運費、保險費在內價，每碼報價二十九英鎊九十六辨士，斜紋軟呢每碼報價三十二英鎊七十五辨士，已經收到，並對此將本公司的還價以電報告知貴公司如下：

貴公司15日報價若在7月，則可接受

貴公司的報價在價格及品質方面，皆符合我方要求。然而，本公司至遲在8月底以前需要該批船貨。因此，7月的船期是最遲的。請於20日早上前以電報告知您的承諾。

相信貴公司將能給予本公司方便，並在接到信後以回郵立即承諾。

感謝您親切的合作。

** ______________________

accommodate〔ə'kɑmə,det〕*v.* 給予方便；幫助

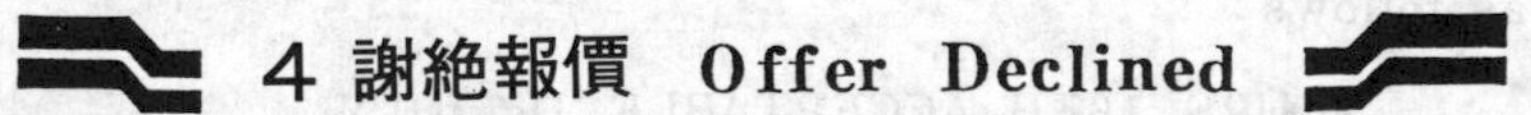

4 謝絕報價 Offer Declined

【實務須知】

- ***commanding a fine reputation*** ⇨博得極佳的聲譽
- retail stores ⇨零售商
- ***would like to refrain*** ⇨只好謝絕
- ***in the light of present market considerations*** ⇨鑑於目前市場的考慮
- marketable price ⇨適銷的價格
- ***induce a proper countermeasure*** ⇨勸使採取適宜的對策

<實 例>

Gentlemen:

Full-Automatic Tube Camera

Thank you for cabling us an offer for your high quality tube camera. However, we have to point out the following:

Although you emphasized the wonderful production record shown for this set, we have on hand a very powerfully competitive camera of German make which is also commanding a fine reputation over here.

Moreover the German make is lower in price by $20 to $50 and the design and style are excellent.

Our retail stores report that yours will be competing with other best selling cameras if the price is reduced by $30. But we think this is too large a discount for you, so we would like to refrain from placing an order with you.

Please accept the decline of your offer in the light of present market considerations and assist us with a more marketable price in the future.

We hope this will meet your prompt attention and induce a proper countermeasure.

Very truly yours,

敬啓者：

全自動35mm照相機

感謝貴公司以電報告知品質優良的35mm照相機的報價。然而，本公司必須指陳如下：

雖然貴公司强調這台相機優越的生產記錄，然而本公司現有一台價格非常具有競爭性的德國製相機，該貨在本地也博得極佳的聲譽。

況且，該德國製品價格低約二十元到五十元，而設計和樣式均極優越。

據本公司零售商報告,若貴公司價格降低三十元，則能與其它銷售最佳的照相機相競爭。但是我方認爲此折扣對貴公司而言太大了，所以只好謝絕向貴公司訂購。

鑑於目前市場的考慮，無法接受貴公司的報價,未來請以更適銷的價格協助本公司。

希望此事能引起貴公司即刻的關切，並勸您採取適宜的對策。

** ――――――――

on hand 現有

【必備詞彙】

- ***in view of the prevailing prices*** ⇨ 鑑於盛行的價格
- ***unless approved*** ⇨ 除非得到贊同
- ***upon examining the cost*** ⇨ 經過檢視成本
- ***regret our inability～*** ⇨ 抱歉難以～

⁂ ⁂ ⁂

1. We confirm our acceptance for your cable offer of May 23 on 100 bales cotton S/# 316 @Stg. £11-33p per 100 lbs. CIF Keelung.

   本公司確認接受貴公司5月23日，對樣品號316一百包棉花的電報報價，到基隆的運費、保險費在內價，每一百磅十一英鎊三十三辨士。

2. ***In view of the prevailing prices*** in this market, your quotation is a little expensive. We have just cabled you a counter offer asking for a large discount. ***Unless approved*** we regret that a business agreement will not be acceptable.

   鑑於本地市場盛行的價格，貴公司的報價稍微貴了一點。是故剛剛以電報告知還價，要求大打折扣。除非貴公司贊同，否則此次交易契約恕難接受。

* prevailing〔prɪ'velɪŋ〕*adj.* 盛行的；流行的

3. We are glad to confirm acceptance of your counter offer of August 11 on our portable transistor radio Model BX-153. ***Upon examining the cost***, we have found some discountable charges and determined to make a 10% discount despite a small loss.

   很樂意確認接到貴公司8月11日，對本公司BX-153型手提電晶體收音機的還價。經過檢視成本，發現有些費用可以打折，雖然有輕微損失，我方決定打百分之十的折扣。

4. Thank you for considering this matter, but we regret that we are not in a position to meet your requirement since the prices you have quoted are much higher than those quoted from our usual suppliers.

   感謝貴公司考慮此事，但是因為貴公司的報價較本公司平常的供應商之報價高出甚多，故無法答應貴公司要求，至感抱歉。

5. The prevailing low prices in this market are nearly 19% higher than yours and therefore we ***regret our inability to*** accept the counter offer mentioned in your letter.

   本地市場盛行的低廉價格,幾乎較貴公司的價格高出百分之十九，因此歉難接受貴公司信中提及的還價。

6. Thank you for your kind cooperation in meeting our demands. We hope you will furnish us with further mutually profitable offers in the future.

   感謝貴公司親切合作,迎合本公司的要求。希望未來能以更多互相有利的報價提供給本公司。

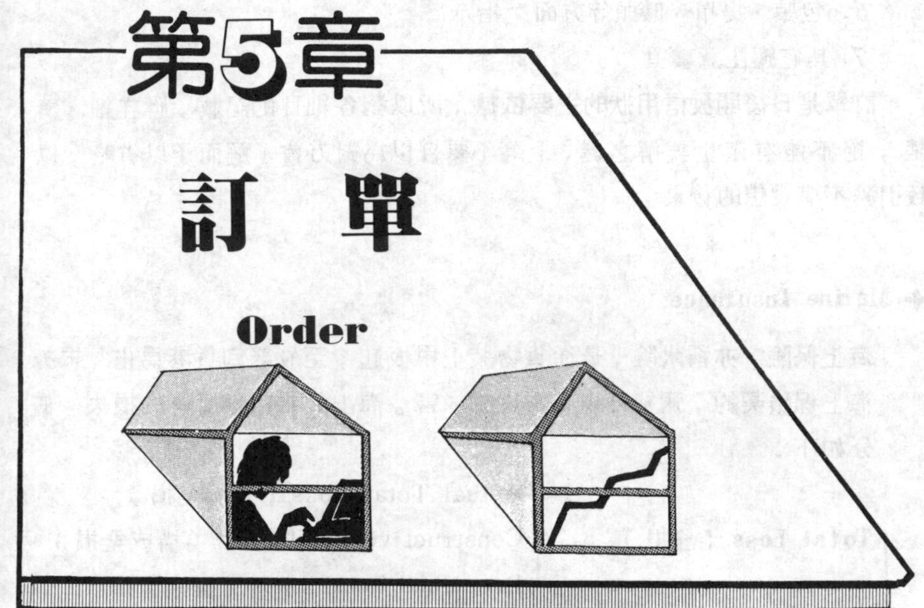

買賣雙方除了藉由Offer及Counter Offer 的往返，達成協議，接受對方開出的條件，而下訂單（ **Order** ）之外，有時買方可能只憑賣方寄來的樣品、目錄及價目表，在指定交貨期的條件下，直接訂購。此時賣方若接受（ acknowledge ），就可成立買賣契約 。當然這種情形下，買方大都對以往交易的賣主之品質、價格及交貨期已有充份的了解，只要說明清楚，把訂單寄出即可 。訂單內容務必包含所有基本交易條件的細目 。茲條例如下：

1. 貨品（需註明樣品編號、目錄編號、貨品名稱、價目表編號、日期等）
2. 數量
3. 價格 、付款條件
4. 裝船日期
5. 運送、保險等條件

6. 包裝、提單、嘜頭等方面之指示

7. 其它應注意事項

訂單是日後開發信用狀的主要依據，所以對各細目的記載，應詳細、清楚，絕不能有產生誤解之處，千萬不要自以為對方會了解而予以省略，以致引發不堪設想的後果。

* * *

✦ Marine Insurance

海上保險，亦稱水險，是從貨物裝上甲板起，至最終卸貨港為止，根據海上保險契約，彌補可能有的貨物損害。海上貨物保險所稱的損失，概分如下：

- **Total Loss**（全損）
  - Actual Total Loss（實際全損）
  - Constructive Total Loss（構成全損）
  - Presumed Total Loss（推定全損）
- **Particular Loss**（分損）
  - General Average（共同海損）
  - Particular Average（單獨海損）

全損是契約部分記載的貨物，全部滅失的情況，若是實際完全滅失，就稱為**實際全損**；若雖非實際全損，但依規定可視為全損者，稱為**構成全損**；若為船舶行蹤不明，已逾規定期限，而推定為全損者，稱為**推定全損**。分損又稱為Average（**海損**），指部分貨物遭受損害的情形，於海上碰到特殊情況時，船長為顧及船舶安全，被迫採取投棄或故意擱淺等非常措施，若投棄之物品是全體損失，需由所有裝船關係者負擔時，稱為**共同海損**；若只有自已本身的貨物部分單獨受到損害，稱為**單獨海損**。為彌補這些損失的保險契約計有：

1. Total Loss Only（T.L.O. = F.A.A.）全損險

   又稱為Free From All Average（F.A.A.）只擔保全損的情況，因此保險費最低。

2. Free from Particular Average (F.P.A.) 單獨海損不賠險

單獨海損不保，單獨海損以外者才保，俗稱平安險。

3. With Average (W.A.) 單獨海損賠償險

單獨海損保，擔保特約事項之外的所有損害。在某種程度以下的損害(一般保險金額的3～5％以下)，依Franchise Clause (免費率)而不賠償，俗稱水漬險。

4. Against All Risks (A.A.R.) 全險

全險擔保，擔保單獨海險及輸送期間偶發的損害。不擔保遲到及由貨物特有性質產生的損害、戰爭危險、及罷工等所遭受的損失，保險費最高。

5. Special Clause 特殊條款(特殊險)

特殊條款是擔保全險以外的一些特殊條款，包括：

Warehouse to Warehouse Clause (W/W) 倉至倉條款

Perils Clause 危險條款

Risks on Deck Cargo 甲板堆積貨物險

Theft, Pilferage and Non-Delivery (TPND) 偷竊及短卸

Sweat Damage Risk 汗濡險

Shortage 短少

Rain and Fresh Water Damage (RFWD) 雨及淡水損失

Strikes, Riots, Civil Commotion 罷工、暴動、內亂

Leakage & Breakage Clause 漏損及破裂條款

其餘免賠事項依各國、各保險公司而異，往往解釋、規定上有所差別，因此，應該調查清楚再定契約。

✦ Marine Insurance Policy

海上保險保單證明保險契約的成立，可應損失程度而據單索賠。保險金額(Insurance Amount)是將貨物的原價加上10％～15％的預估利潤來計算的。締結保險契約時，若對貨品、船名、及保險金額尚不清楚，則不能締

結肯定契約（Definite Insurance），而應締結個別的臨時保險契約（Provisional Insurance），如船名未定時，應該締結流動保單（Floating Policy），交易金額未定時，須締結不定值保險單（Unvalued Policy）。

數種商品不限發送地點之不同，一併向保險公司投保，所有貨物皆投保的情況，稱爲開口保險或預定保險（Open Cover）。其保單稱爲開口保險單（Open Policy），各種貨物都可據此保險單證明投保。

* * *

✦嘜頭（**Shipping Mark**）

爲使裝、卸貨物時，易於辨認卸貨港、貨主、及數量，以方便各項作業起見，在包裝外表標明各種記號，俗稱嘜頭。下圖①②③項乃絕對必要者，其餘則視情況而定，配合貨主、進口國的指示而增加。

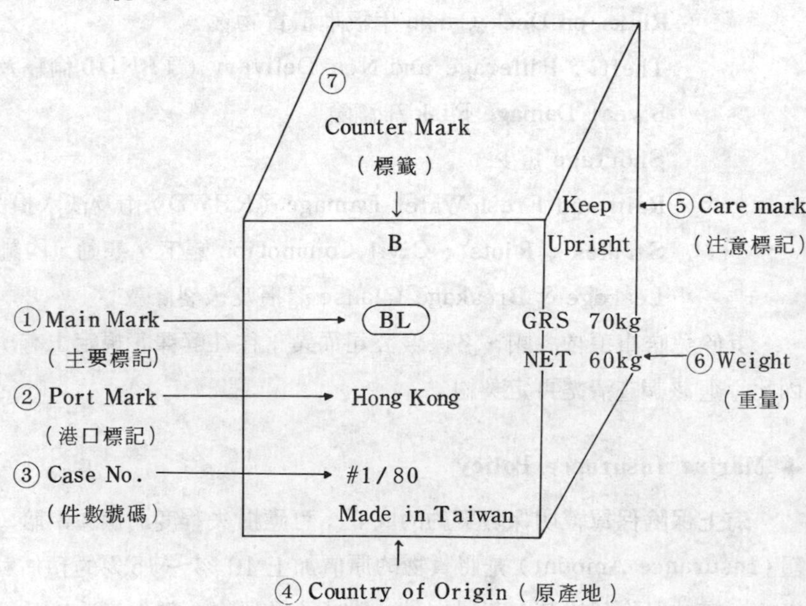

1. Main Mark 主要標記

△S 像S in Triangle over Seals 通常在標記中間和周圍註上 Seals

貨主名字的第一個字母。

除了三角形之外，常用的主要標記形狀有：

◇ Diamond	× Cross
◇ Upright Diamond	Circle in Square
□ Square	Triangle in Circle
▭ Rectangle	⬭ Oval
Cross in Diamond	⬠ Pentagon
♡ Heart	⬡ Hexagon
△ Triangle	Diamond with Cross Ends
✡ Cross Triangle	Cross Circle
Three Triangle	○ Circle

2. Port Mark 港口標記

位於Main Mark之下，說明目的港名稱。例如：New York, Chicago via San Francisco, Venice via Suez, etc.

3. Number

通常表示爲NOS.1/40, NOS. 30/45, #120/123

4. Care Mark 注意標記

標於需要特別處理的貨物上，以提醒裝卸工人小心注意。

Keep Cool 保持涼爽	Keep Flat 平放
Keep Dry 保持乾燥	Keep Upright 直放
Poison 有毒	Porcelain 瓷器
Dangerous Goods 危險物品	On Deck 置於甲板
Fragile 易碎	Don't Throw Down 不可投擲
Handle with Care 小心搬運	No Hooks 不准用鈎

✦ 品名、數量的表示方法

a. 白色襯衫一百疋，樣品號 150 ，每疋四百三十元 。

100 pcs. White Shirting S/#150 @ $ 430 per pc.

b. Tiger 商標鋅白罐一百噸，淨重三十磅，每罐五百元 。

100 tons Zinc White "Tiger" in drums, ea. cont'g 30 lbs. net, @ $ 500 per drum (ea. = each, cont'g = containing)

c. 3/8 英吋螺絲帽樣品號 30 號一百籮，每籮一英鎊三十二辨士，基隆運費、保險費在內價

100 gross ⅜″ nut S/#30 @£1-32p per gross C.I.F. Keelung

d. 膠鞋尺寸樣品號 40 ，一千打，每打二千元 。

1,000 dozs. Rubber Shoes Size No. 40, @ $ 2,000 per doz.

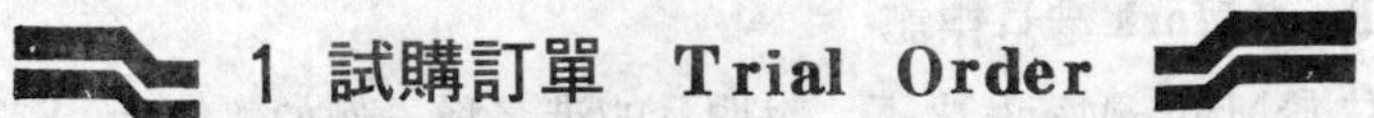

1 試購訂單 Trial Order

【實務須知】

· ***in accordance with*** ⇨ 依據；按照
· particular 〔 pə′tɪkjələ˞ 〕 *n*. 細節；詳細說明
· ***Order Sheet*** ⇨ 訂單
· ***be in a hurry to*** ⇨ 著急～
· ***upon receipt of which*** ⇨ 一俟接獲～

〈實 例〉

Dear Sirs,

Thank you for your samples and price list of 10th September. We are pleased to find that your materials appear to be of fine quality.

As a trial we are delighted to give you a small order for 100 pcs., white shirting S/#235. Please note that the goods are to be supplied in accordance with your samples.

The particulars are detailed in the enclosed Order Sheet No. 123. We are in a hurry to obtain the goods, so please cable your acceptance, upon receipt of which we will open an irrevocable L/C through Bank of Taiwan, Taipei.

If this initial order turns out satisfactory, we shall be able to give you a large order in the near future.

Yours faithfully,

敬啓者：

感謝貴公司9月10日的樣品和價目表。很高興發現貴公司的質料顯然品質優良。

茲樂意下一百疋樣品號235號白襯衫衣料的小額訂單，作爲試購。敬請注意，貨品須照貴公司的樣品供應。

細節詳列於附寄的第123號訂單中。本公司急於得到該批貨品，所以請以電報告知貴公司的承諾，一俟接獲，我方會經由台北的台灣銀行，開立不可撤銷信用狀。

若初次訂單結果令人滿意，不久的將來本公司將會大量訂購。

** ——————————

initial 〔ɪ'nɪʃəl〕 *adj*. 最初的；開始的

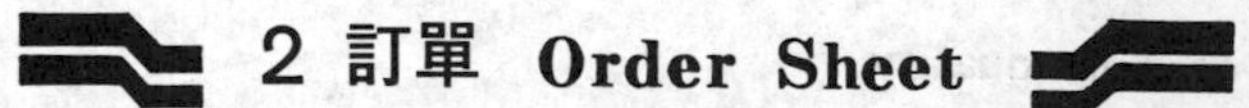

2 訂單 Order Sheet

【實務須知】

- ***exactly as shown in the sample*** ⇨完全如樣品所示
- ***per piece*** ⇨每件
- 10 pcs. in Hessian bale ⇨每十疋以粗麻布綑包
- 50 pcs. in wooden case ⇨每五十疋以木箱包裝
- ***A.A.R.*** = *Against All Risks* ⇨擔保全險
- ***certificate of quality inspection*** ⇨品質檢驗證明書
- shipment samples ⇨裝運樣品
- ***prior to shipment*** ⇨在裝運之前

＜實 例＞

23rd September, 19 —

Messrs. Jefferson & Co., Ltd.
4 Hall Street, Calcutta
India

We have the pleasure of placing the following order with you.

Quantity	Description	Unit Price	Amount
100 pcs. (2 cases)	Cotton White Shirting Sample No. 253 Exactly as shown in the sample	C.I.F. Keelung in Pound Sterling @ £ 4 - 33p per piece	£ 672-00

Shipment : During October

Packing : 10 pcs. in Hessian bale

50 pcs. in one wooden case

Marks : △OTK with number 1 and 2 under port mark stating the country of origin

C/#1-2

Keelung

Made in India

Insurance : A.A.R. for full invoice amount plus 10%

Terms : Draft at 30d/s under an irrevocable L/C

Remarks : Certificate of quality inspection & shipment samples to be sent by air mail prior to shipment

ABC Trading Co., Ltd.,

Jim Chen

Import Manager.

19 — 年 9 月 23 日

傑佛森有限公司公啓

印度加爾各答海爾街 4 號

茲樂意向貴公司訂購如下：

數量	品質、規格說明	單　價	總　價
一百疋 （二箱）	白色棉襯衣料 樣品編號 253 完全如樣品所示	到基隆運費、保險費在內價 以英鎊計 每疋四英鎊 三十三辨士	六百七十 二英鎊正

船期：在 10 月間

包裝：每十疋以粗麻布綑包

每五十疋以木箱包裝

嘜頭：OTK 編號從一到二，下面爲港口符號，說明原產地

C/#1-2

基隆

印度製

保險：發票全額加百分之十的擔保全險

條件：憑不可撤銷信用狀開立見票三十天後付款滙票

備註：品質檢驗證明書和裝運樣品須在裝運前，空運寄來

3 訂購確認書 Order Confirmation

【實務須知】

· ***cable order dispatched this morning*** ⇨ 今天早上拍發的電報訂單

· ***stock news*** ⇨ 存貨訊息。廠商藉存貨一覽表告知門市部、代理店庫存狀況，以便順利收、發訂單。需花費較多時間交貨者，尤其需要。

· ***these items available by the date*** ⇨ 這些貨品在此日期前可以到手

· ***usual careful execution*** ⇨ 往常的愼重履行

〈實 例〉

Dear Sirs,

We are glad to confirm our cable order dispatched this morning as follows :

LT
TAIPEI MAO YUAN EADER
ARRANGE SHIPMENT BX 157 600 TRC 418 800
BOTH DURING AUGUST PV 123 1200 BY
SEPTEMBER

ELECTROLEADER

Article	Model	Quantity	Shipment
Transistor Radio	BX-157	600 sets	August
Tape Recorder	TRC-418	800 sets	August
Portable TV	PV-123	1,200 sets	September

In your stock news we found these items available by the date mentioned above. We would like you to arrange shipment accordingly.

We will cable the shipping instructions and the credit immediately upon receiving your acceptance by cable.

We hope that you will promptly accept our order and make your usual careful execution.

Yours faithfully,

敬啓者：

茲樂意確認今天早上拍發的電報訂單如下：

台北懋源

BX157 型六百台、TRC418 型八百台，船期請安排在8月間，PV123 型一千二百台在9月前。

領先電子公司

品目	機型	數量	船期
電晶體收音機	BX-157	600 台	8 月
錄音機	TRC-418	800 台	8 月
手提電視機	PV-123	1,200 台	9 月

本公司從貴公司存貨訊息中發現，這些項目在上述日期以前可以到手。故請如期安排船運。

一俟接獲貴公司的電報承諾，本公司將即刻以電報告知裝運指示和開出信用狀。

盼貴公司儘速接受本公司訂單，並如往常慎重履行。

** ______

transistor 〔træn'zɪstɚ〕 *n.* 電晶體（用以代替無線電中眞空管之細小器材）

portable 〔'portəbl̩〕 *adj.* 可攜帶的；手提的

【必備詞彙】

· ***seasonal demand*** ⇨ 季節性需求
· ***referring to your cable*** ⇨ 參照貴公司的電報
· ***Rotary Printing Press*** ⇨ 輪轉印刷機
· ***have your acknowledgement*** ⇨ 得到貴公司的承諾

⁂ ⁂ ⁂

1. Thank you very much for your sample of June 25 , on which we would like to place an order with you for Model FAX-223. Our stocks are running short by a high ***seasonal demand***

but as winter approaches it will decrease accordingly. Therefore, we will need the goods in time so as to take advantage of present demand and request the complete shipment within the stipulated date.

非常感謝貴公司6月25日寄來的樣品，茲樂意訂購 FAX-223型貨品。由於高度的季節性需求，本公司存貨即將短缺，但是當冬天迫近，需求也將因而減少。所以我方需要此貨品，以來得及利用目前的需求，懇請於規定日期內全部裝運。

* approach〔ə'protʃ〕*n.* 接近；迫近

2. ***Referring to your cable*** offer No. 113 dated August 11, we are pleased to place an order for ***Rotary Printing Press*** Model RPR-411. Please notify your acceptance by return cable.

參照貴公司8月11日第113號電報報價，茲樂意訂購 RPR-411型輪轉印刷機。請立刻以電報告知承諾。

3. We have just received your letter of the 28th September and confirm an order for 500 sets of the Electronic Desk-top calculator.

已收到貴公司9月28日來函，在此確認桌上型電子計算機五百台的訂單。

* calculator〔'kælkjə,letɚ〕*n.* 計算機

4. Please let us ***have your acknowledgement*** of these orders by cable no later than the morning of the 20th, otherwise we shall have to place them elsewhere.

懇請於20日早上以前，以電報告知對這些訂單的承諾，否則我方將必須向別處訂購。

* acknowledgement〔ək'nɑlɪdʒmənt〕*n.* 承諾；承認書

5. Please pay special attention to the execution of this order. If ***inferior goods are inserted*** and an unfavorable impression is established among the customers, we will be unable to remedy it under the present situation.

請特別注意本訂單的履行事宜。若雜有劣品，造成客戶不良的印象，在這種情況下，我方將無法補救。

* inferior 〔ɪnˈfɪrɪɚ〕 *adj*. 劣等的；較低的

⁂ ⁂ ⁂

接到訂單後，務必儘速作答，以利對方順利得到進口貨物，實施其銷售計畫。若庫存有限而不得不加以拒絕時，也要從速辦理，以免對方要求代替品時，措手不及。若收到的是**電報訂單**（***Cable Order***），則應以電報答覆，再以書信確認，表示愼重。接受訂單時，須明示各種交易條件之細目，其要點如下：

1. 表示接受之意，並感謝對方。

2. 重覆訂單內容（貨品名稱、數量、裝運、價格、包裝、保險、付款條件等）。

3. 引述訂單號碼、日期、買賣契約應注意事項。

4. 特別註明預定裝船日期。

5. 確保履行出貨，並希望能再予訂購。

訂單是交易的第一步，賣方務必表示站在對方的立場，願全力給予協助，同時表明希望今後能有更緊密的交易關係之誠意。

*　　　*　　　*

✦ 包裝 Packing

包裝除可**保護商品**，利於裝卸外，更可藉著合適的外觀來**提高商品的價值**。雖然目前貿易上仍舊以保護商品爲重點，但精美的Carton（紙箱）及Paper box（紙箱）的圖案，顯然都是爲求提高***brand image***（**品牌形象**）而設計的。

1. 包裝常用術語：

Make-up …… 提高商品價値的包裝。

Inner Packing …… 內包裝；將商品包裝得較小而緊密。

Outer Packing …… 外包裝；將內裝之物品包裹得較大而堅實。

2. 貨物依包裝外表形態可分爲：

Casing cargo 箱裝貨物	Crating cargo 板條箱裝貨物
Baling cargo 綑包貨物	Jarred cargo 瓶裝貨物
Bagged cargo 袋裝貨物	Barrelled cargo 桶裝貨物
Canned cargo 罐裝貨物	Unpacked cargo 無包裝貨物

3. 貨物依所使用的包裝物可細分爲：

裸裝貨物Nude cargo ……Cargo in Bulk（散裝），Coil（捲），Roll（捲筒），Bundle（綑、束），Reel（捲盤筒）

包裝貨物 Packed cargo
- 紙箱……Paper box, Carton box
- 木箱
  - Wooden case（木箱）
  - Tin-lined case（錫條木箱）
  - Ply-wood（三夾板）
  - Crate case（木板條箱）
  - Skelton case（通孔箱）
- 綑包
  - Hessian Cloth（粗麻布）
  - Burlap（麻布）
  - Straw Mat（草蓆）

包裝貨物 Packed cargo

- 袋裝……Sack（棉布袋），Paper bag（紙袋），Gunny bag（痲袋）
- 桶裝……Barrel（大鐵桶），Cask（鐵桶），Keg（小鐵桶）
- 其它……Drum（鐵製油桶），Jar（陶器瓶），Pot（壺、罐），Basket（籃、簍），Iron Flask（鐵製細頭瓶）

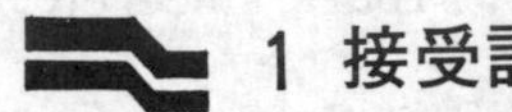

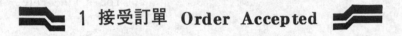

1 接受訂單 Order Accepted

【實務須知】

- ***confirm our acceptance*** ⇨確認本公司的承諾
- ***Sales Note*** ⇨售貨單；購買確認書
- ***first available ship*** ⇨第一艘適用的船隻；即下一班到該目的港的船隻
- ***be confident of handling your order with complete satisfaction*** ⇨有自信能將訂單處理得令貴公司完全滿意
- ***initial business*** ⇨初次交易

＜實　例＞

Dear Sirs,

Thank you very much for your order of June 20 on 30,000 yds. white shirting. We are pleased to confirm our acceptance as shown in the enclosed Sales Note, together with the copy of our cable dispatched today.

We have arranged for immediate shipment as requested. Please open your L/C by telegram by the end of June upon accepting our requirement by cable.

The first available ship is scheduled for departure on the 10th July. We are confident of handling your order with complete satisfaction, providing your L/C reaches us by the end of June.

We hope that this initial business will lead to a pleasant business relationship and further orders in the future.

Yours sincerely,

敬啓者：

非常感謝貴公司於6月20日訂購三萬碼白色襯衣料。茲樂意確認我方的承諾，如附寄的購買確認書及今天拍發的電報副本所示。

本公司已按照要求安排立即裝運。一俟接受我方電報要求，敬請在6月底以前以電報開立信用狀。

第一艘適用的船預定於7月10日離開。倘若貴公司的信用狀能在6月底以前抵達，我方有自信能將本訂單處理得令您完全滿意。

希望初次交易將導至愉快的交易關係，並盼將來有更多訂單。

**

shirting〔ˈʃɝtɪŋ〕*n.* 襯衣料；襯衣布

providing〔prəˈvaɪdɪŋ〕*conj.* 假使；倘若

 2 售貨單 Sales Note 

【實務須知】

- ***country of origin*** ⇨原產地

  <比較> ***certificate of country of origin*** ⇨原產地證明書

- packing〔'pækɪŋ〕*n.* 包裝
- ***in Hessian bale*** ⇨以粗麻布綑包
- ***subject to the agreement*** ⇨以合同爲條件
- ***unless otherwise specified*** ⇨除非另有聲明

<實 例>

August 21, 19-

Dear Sirs,

Sales Note

We are pleased to confirm our sale of the following commodity on terms and conditions set forth below:

Commodity:	Cotton White Shirting Sample No. 253
Quantity:	100 pieces (One Hundred Pieces)
Price:	@ £4-33 p (Four pounds thirty-three pence) CIF Keelung in Sterling Pound
Amount:	£672-00 (Six Hundred and seventy two pounds only) in Sterling Pound CIF Keelung
Terms:	Draft at 30 d/s under an irrevocable L/C
Shipment:	During July

Packing: 10 pcs. in Hessian bale and 50 pcs. in wooden case

Marks: OTK with numbers 1 and up under port

Keelung mark stating the country of origin

Made in India

Insurance: A.A.R. for full invoice amount plus 10%

Remarks: 1. Certificate of Quality Inspection & Shipment Samples to be sent prior to shipment

2. Unless otherwise specified in this Sales Note, all matters not mentioned here are subject to the agreement of the general terms and conditions of business concluded between both parties.

Jefferson & Co., Ltd.
Roderick Jefferson
Sales Manager

19－年8月21日

敬啓者：

售貨單

樂意確認下列貨品的銷售，其條件敍述如下：

貨品：白色棉襯衣料樣品號第253號

數量：一百疋

價格：四英鎊三十三辨士

以英鎊計到基隆之運費、保險費在內價

總價：六百七十二英鎊正，以英鎊計到基隆之運費、保險費在內價

條件：憑不可撤銷信用狀開立見票三十天後付款滙票

船期：7月間

包裝：每十疋用粗麻布綑包，每五十疋用木箱包裝

嘜頭：OTK　編號從1開始，港口符號下面述明原產地

基隆

印度製造

保險：發票全額再加百分之十的擔保全險

備註：1. 品質檢驗證明書和船運樣品於裝運前寄出

2. 除非本售貨單另有聲明，所有這裏未提到的事情，皆以雙方締結的商務合同之一般條款及情況爲條件。

傑佛森有限公司

羅德里克・傑佛森

銷售部經理

**

pence〔pɛns〕*n.*〔英〕 *pl. penny* 辨士

sterling〔'stɝlɪŋ〕*adj.* 英國貨幣的（通常寫於金額之後，略作 *stg.*）

prior to 在…之前

3 推薦代替品

Substitute Recommendation

【實務須知】

- book〔bʊk〕*v*. 接受訂購
- ***mechanical redesigning*** ⇨機械的重新設計
- ***considering your inconvenience*** ⇨考慮您的不便
- ***upon finishing the redesigning*** ⇨一俟完成重新設計
- ***discount price*** ⇨折扣價
- ***meet your immediate acceptance*** ⇨得到貴公司立即承諾

<實 例>

Dear Sirs,

Thank you very much for your cable order of 18th September requesting a Rotary Printing Press Model PM-600, PM-800 and PM-1600. We are pleased to book all except the first one which is now under mechanical redesigning.

As you requested us to ship them by November end, we have just cabled you two alternatives concerning Model PM-600 as shown in the enclosed cable:

1. As an excellent substitute for PM-600 we recommend PM-630. This is our latest model and much superior in printing speed, 90 revolutions per minute. Considering your inconvenience, we will make a special price discount to Stg. £1500-00. If this is acceptable, please cable us "Accept" and we will dispatch all items in November.

2. We may ship PM-800 and PM-1600 during November and PM-600 during January next year upon finishing the redesigning, providing you prefer to import PM-600.

We are very sorry for the inconvenience. However, please note our wish to offer an alternative, especially our special discount price.

We hope this will meet your immediate acceptance so that we can execute the order in a most satisfactory manner.

Yours faithfully,

敬啓者：

非常感謝貴公司9月18日的電報訂單，該訂單要的是 PM-600、PM-800、PM-1600 型輪轉印刷機。除了第一型因爲目前正在重新設計機器以外，玆樂意接受所有訂購。

因爲貴公司要求於11月底以前裝運，本公司剛剛已經以電報告知有關 PM-600 型的兩種代替品，如附寄的電文所示：

1. 我方推薦 PM-630 作爲 PM-600 的極佳代替品。這是本公司最新型產品，印刷速度更優越，每分鐘旋轉九十次。考慮到您的不便，我方將打特別折扣到一千五百英鎊正。若可以接受此價，請以電報告知「接受」，本公司將於11月發送所有項目的貨品。
2. 若貴公司寧可進口PM-600，本公司可能於11月間裝運PM-800和 PM-1600，PM-600 則在完成重新設計後，於明年1月間裝運。

對此不便，本公司至感抱歉。然而，請注意我方對提供代替品的願望，尤其請注意特別的折扣價。

希望此事能得到貴公司立即承諾，以便本公司能以最令貴公司滿意的方式，履行訂單。

** ______________________

rotary〔ˈrotərɪ〕*adj.* 旋轉的；輪轉的

alternative〔ɔlˈtɝnətɪv〕*n.* 可取代之物；代替品

revolution〔ˌrɛvəˈluʃən〕*n.* 旋轉；循環一周

實用例句

【實務須知】

- ***ensure immediate shipment*** ⇨確保立即裝運
- ***out of stock*** ⇨沒有存貨
- ***established policy*** ⇨既定的方針
- ***be compelled to*** ⇨不得不

※ ※ ※

1. Thank you for your order. We are pleased to ***ensure immediate shipment*** as requested despite shipping and manufacturing difficulties.

   感謝貴公司的訂單。雖然裝運和生產上有困難，茲樂意確保按照要求，立即裝運。

2. The goods ordered are now ***out of stock***. We suggest you substitute No. 28, which is excellent value for the price. Shall we ship the substitute, or would you prefer to wait until we obtain the goods?

訂購的貨品目前已無存貨。建議貴公司以第 28 號代替，該貨以此價格而言，非常有價值。要我方裝運代替品嗎？或是貴公司寧可等到本公司得到該批貨品？

3. We have just received your order with many thanks. However, you state very different terms from the general terms and conditions previously agreed to. Instead of accepting D/A, we have to ask you to open an irrevocable L/C according to our ***established policy.***

剛接獲貴公司訂單,萬分感激。然而,貴公司指述的條件與先前同意的一般條件，差異甚大。本公司不願接受承兌交單，懇請貴公司依據我方既定的方針，開立不可撤銷信用狀。

＊ D/A = *documents against acceptance* 承兌交單

4. As the goods you ordered are now in stock, we will ship them ***without fail*** by the M/S "President" leaving Keelung on 23rd October.

因為貴公司訂購的貨品目前有存貨,本公司必定由 10 月 23 日離開基隆的總統號柴油輪裝運。

＊ ***without fail*** 必定；無誤

5. We deeply regret that we are not in a position to accept your order at the old prices. As stated in our last letter, all raw materials have risen considerably as well as labor expenses, and we ***are compelled to*** increase the price of all our products.

本公司無法以舊價接受貴公司訂單,深感遺憾。如上封信所載，所有原料和工資皆大幅上漲，本公司不得不提高所有產品的價格。

＊ raw〔rɔ〕*adj.* 未加工的；天然的

⚘ ⚘ ⚘

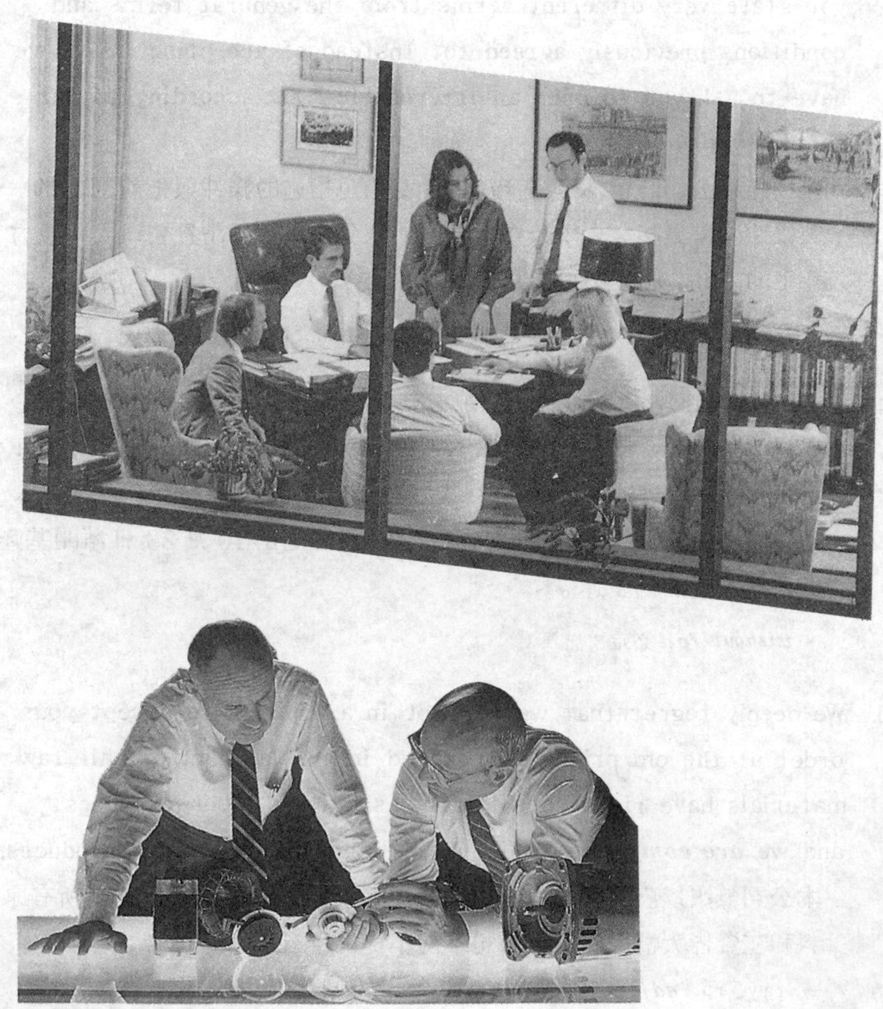

PART Ⅳ

Execution of Sales Contract

買賣契約的履行

✦ 買賣契約之履行

一旦確定訂單、締結交易，買賣雙方就必須共同履行契約，以下簡單介紹此後雙方各自的業務。

A.賣方的業務

賣方必須按契約規定將貨品送交買方，故需在裝船期限內，完成貨品之製造、籌備事宜。接近裝船日期時，應按照船公司訂定的船期表（Shipping Schedule），安排開航日期，最遲需在開航前四至六天，完成包裝、檢查之準備工作，再將貨物運往船公司的倉庫。商品在製造、運送完成後，仍需妥善包裝，並接受出口檢驗、品質檢驗等必經的檢查。

若需要政府發給出口許可證（Export Licence），應到國貿局申請。在向船公司洽訂船艙（Booking Ship's Space）的時候，還得考慮到達進口港的日期，及運費之差異。（加入海運同盟之船公司，運費皆相同。運費依W／M之原則，不論就重量或材積計算，都是船公司吃香。）再下一步是向船公司索取船長簽名的裝運單（Shipping Order : S/O）。

當輸出契約費用規定以外幣計算時，換算成台幣則會和預定的金額有所差異（因為外滙市場之變動），故最好先預備一份有固定滙率的購買契約（Buying Contract，由銀行的觀點來看，稱為購買契約）。再將銀行之出口申報書（Export Report）提呈海關，以取得輸出許可證(Export Permit)。

以**CIF**條款所訂立的契約，得向保險公司支付保險金（Premium），領取保險單。貨物在搬入船公司的倉庫後，需經過公證行（Sworn Measurer）會同報關人員檢驗數量、重量、品質及材積，並把結果記載於裝運單（S／O）上，以領取材積重量證明單（Certificate and List of Measurement and／or Weight），並依此計算運費。出口申報是把貨物搬入保稅地區（保稅庫房Bonded Shed、保稅倉庫Bonded Warehouse、指定保稅地區Designated Bonded Area、保稅工廠Bonded Factory、保稅展示廳Bonded Exhibit Hall），同時附上

1. 銀行出口申報書及海關用出口申報書
2. 商業發票（Commercial Invoice）
3. 包裝明細表（Packing List）
4. 裝運單（S/O）
5. 出口許可證（Export Licence，必要時）
6. 檢驗證明書（Inspection Certificate）

貨物與這些文件經檢查後，在出口申報書上蓋印，成爲輸出許可證，再呈示給保稅地區的官員，就可由碼頭裝貨工人裝船了。此時，貨主（或委託報關行）和船公司各派數人在甲板上點貨，大副經過自行點貨，並據此文件簽發大副收據M/R（Mate's Receipt）。貨品無不良情況時，發給Clean M/R，繳交運費後，向船公司換取提單（Bill of Lading；B/L）。（如果是不潔提單Foul B/L時，只要加上賠償保證書Letter of Indemnity，就可發給Clean B/L）。

以提單爲主，備齊以下之裝運文件

1. 發票（Invoice）
2. 原產地證明書（Certificate of Origin）
3. 保險單（Marine Insurance Policy）
4. 領事簽證發票（Consular Invoice）
5. 海關發票（Customs Invoice）
6. 檢驗證明書（Inspection Certificate）
7. 包裝明細表（Packing List）

再連同跟單滙票（Documentary Bill of Exchange），若有信用狀則亦附帶請銀行購入（押滙Negotiation），以當日外滙市場之滙率領取貨款。裝船後，應立即以電報發出裝運通知（Shipping Advice），並附寄相關文件之副本給買方，一方面通知其貨物已裝船，另一方面也期待貨物安然抵達，滿足對方之條件。如此，賣方義務已盡，也履行了買賣契約。以下將賣方業務流程以簡圖表出：

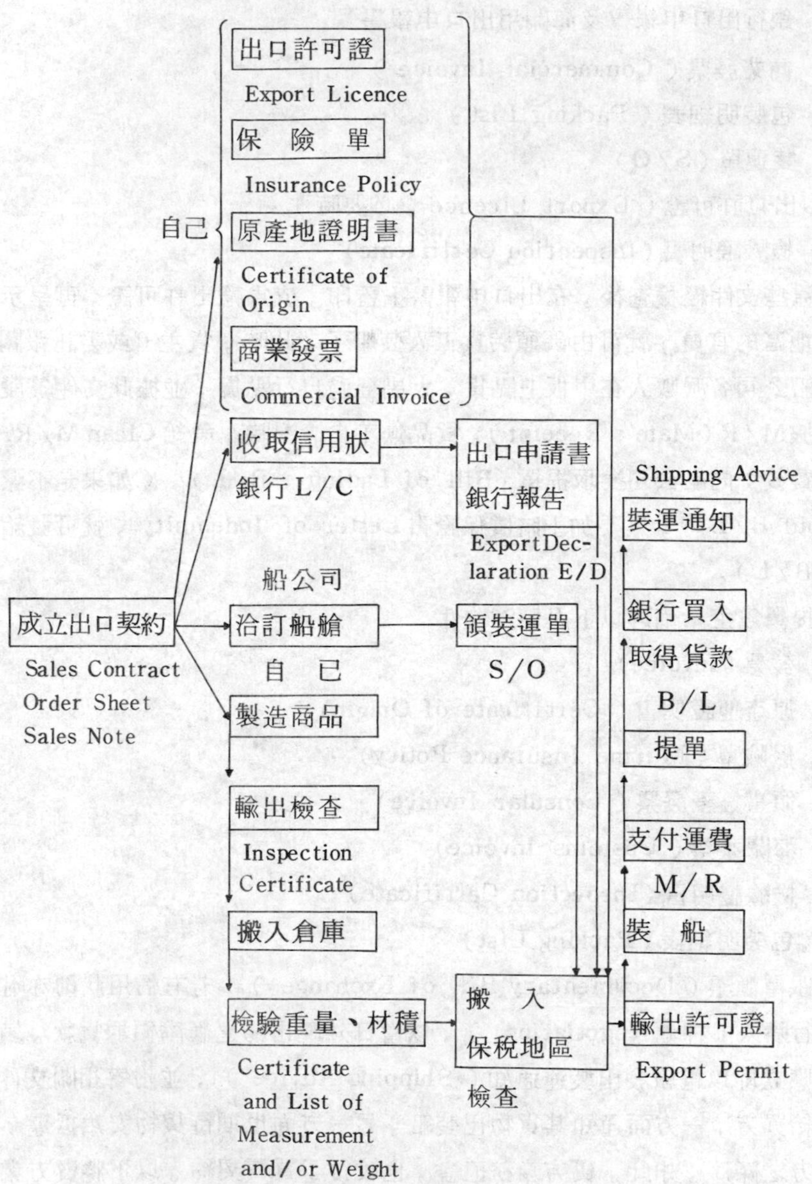
出口許可證
Export Licence
保 險 單
Insurance Policy
自己
原產地證明書
Certificate of Origin
商業發票
Commercial Invoice
收取信用狀
銀行 L/C
出口申請書
銀行報告
Export Declaration E/D
Shipping Advice
裝運通知
船公司
成立出口契約
Sales Contract
Order Sheet
Sales Note
洽訂船艙
自 已
領裝運單
S/O
銀行買入
取得貨款
B/L
提單
製造商品
輸出檢查
Inspection Certificate
支付運費
M/R
裝 船
搬入倉庫
檢驗重量、材積
Certificate and List of Measurement and/or Weight
搬 入
保稅地區
檢查
輸出許可證
Export Permit

B.買方的業務

與賣方出口相對的買方是進口人。輸入和輸出相反，必須在達成契約之前完成進口申報(Import Report)。

若需押滙則要向政府代理人的外滙銀行，一併提出進口申報書(五份)及保證金，才能獲得認可。達成契約後即向外滙銀行支付手續費，請求開發以賣方爲收件人的信用狀。寄送裝運指示,等待貨品及提單的到來。然後會收到船公司寄來的**到貨通知**(**Arrival Note**)。當提單到達開狀銀行時，若爲見票即付條款，就得立刻交款，若爲D/A terms (Documents against Acceptance terms ,承兌後交單據條款)，只要承兌，若爲D/P terms (Documents against Payment terms, 付款後交單據)，則以付款、或送交信託收據(T/R, Trust Receipt)給銀行的方式，以取得提單。

若提單未到而貨物已送達，可以用形式發票(Proforma Invoice)行假通關，將銀行保證書(L/G， Letter of Guarantee)交給船公司，若有提單，則需與保證書一併交給船公司，以領取提貨單(D/O , Delivery Order)。由理貨員(Stevedore)辦理卸貨，卸下來的貨要搬入保稅地區。

買方須備妥下列文件，提呈給海關，並繳付進口稅(Import Duty)，才能領到輸入許可證(Import Permit)

1. 進口許可證(Import Licence)
2. 發票(Invoice)
3. 包裝明細表(Packing List)
4. 重量材積證明書(Certificate and List of Measurement and/or Weight)
5. 原產地證明書(Certificate of Origin)
6. 進口申報書(Import Declaration ,五份)

再向保稅官員呈示提貨單(D/O)和輸入許可證，以領取貨物。這時，貨物若有損傷，可請有關單位驗明損傷程度及事實，並開發驗證單，依照損壞程度向保險公司、船公司或賣方提出索賠(Claim)的要求。

若爲D/A terms（承兌後交單據條款），期滿得付清貨款；若是預繳保證書，則提單到達時，須換成信託收據，期滿時以支票付款。以下將進口貿易流程，以簡圖表示：

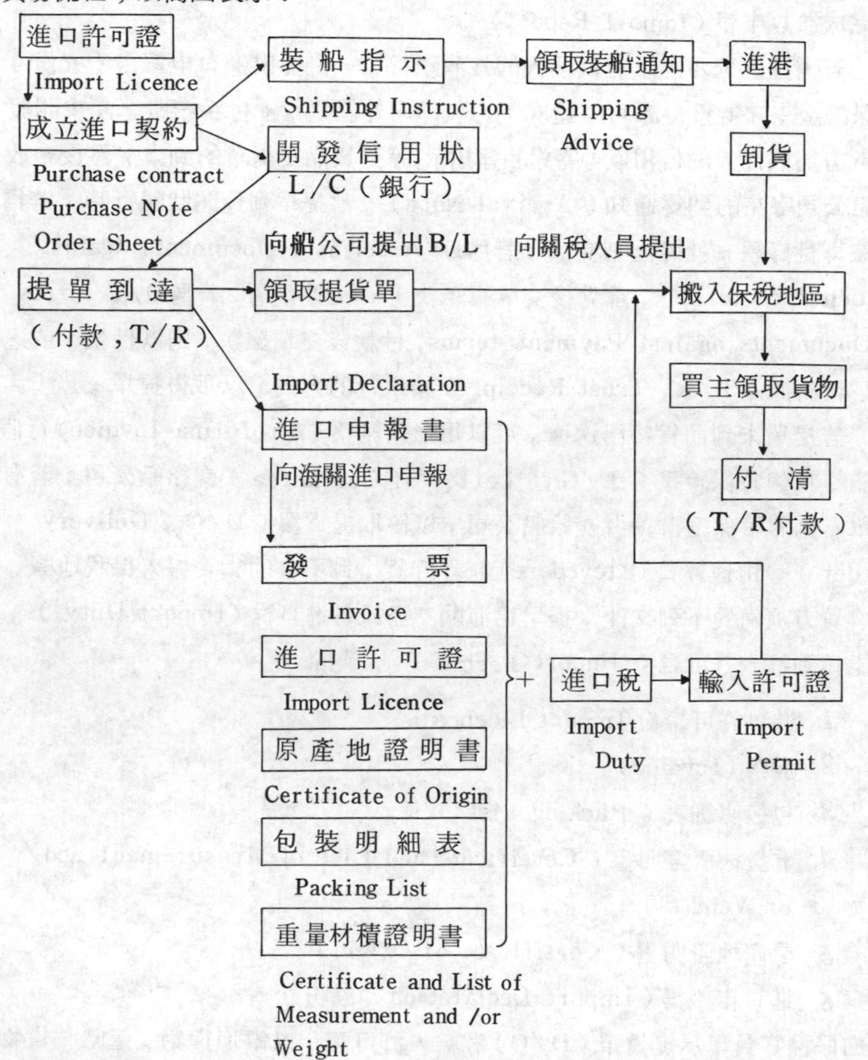

第1章

信用狀

Letter of Credit

進出口貿易，最常用的付款方式就是**押滙票據**（滙票），因為這是**附有信用狀**的買賣，即使進口商拒絕付款，開設信用狀的銀行也保證會付起這個責任，所以對出口商而言非常安全。通知銀行也能安心買下賣方開出的滙票。

若成立買賣契約，進口商有義務以L／C作為付款條件的時候，得委託某外滙銀行，經過一定的程序，開發一張以出口商為受益人的信用狀。由於以信用狀交易是最確實的方式，出口商越早收到信用狀越有保障，也可以趕快進行裝船的準備。以下談的是以信用狀為中心的貿易函件。

1. 督促進口商開發信用狀。
2. 可依狀況之變化，請求修改信用狀，並應確實把握裝船日期。
3. 信用狀若有文字上的錯誤，必須修正使不產生購買及其他方面的障礙。

*　　*　　*

✦ 信用狀（**Letter of Credit**）的關係人：

1. Accredited Buyer

委託開發信用狀人，即進口商，信用狀是由進口商委託銀行開立的。

2. Opening Bank（Issuing Bank）（開狀銀行）

與進口商來往的外滙銀行。開發信用狀的銀行。有最終付款責任，是進口地的銀行。

3. Beneficiary（受益人）

信用狀的受益人。即出口商，信用狀乃根據此出口商所提出之條件而開立的，爲交易上的受益人。

4. Advising Bank（Notifying Bank, Informing Bank）（通知銀行）

接受海外信用狀發行銀行之委託，通知並交付信用狀給賣方，謂之通知銀行。

5. Negotiating Bank（押滙銀行）

裝船之後，買入提單併其他裝運文件及滙票，把貨款交給出口商。和通知銀行有別，但也可以是同一銀行。通常是與出口商來往的外滙銀行。

✦ 信用狀的種類（**Type of Credit**）如下：

1. Traveller's L/C（旅行信用狀）

2. Commercial L/C（商業信用狀）
- Clean L/C（無擔保信用狀）
- Documentary L/C（跟單信用狀）

其中跟單信用狀又可細分如下：

- Irrevocable L/C（不可撤銷信用狀）
- Revocable L/C（可撤銷信用狀）

- Confirmed L/C（保兌信用狀）
- Unconfirmed L/C（不保兌信用狀）

Straight L/C（指定押滙銀行的信用狀，Special L/C，
Restricted L/C）
Open L/C（不指定押滙銀行的信用狀，General L/C）

With Recourse L/C（可追索信用狀）
Without Recourse L/C（不可追索信用狀）

Original L/C（原信用狀）
Local L/C（國內信用狀）

Transferable L/C（可轉讓信用狀）

Banker's L/C（銀行信用狀）

Escrow L/C（記帳易貨信用狀）

Back to Back L/C（對開信用狀）

Revolving L/C（循環信用狀）

London Acceptance L/C（倫敦銀行承兌信用狀）

New York Acceptance L/C（紐約銀行承兌信用狀）

信用狀大致分爲以上所列各種，其中最常用的是 Irrevocable confirmed L/C ，但組合使用的信用狀也不少，因此有必要說明各項信用狀的內容：

1. Traveller's L/C

其結構是在本國外滙銀行存入現金，領取這種旅行信用狀，在國外時可到與這銀行有協定的銀行，簽名即可兌換現金。主要是爲安全計，出國時可免帶現金，不涉及貿易。

2. Commercial L/C（Clean L/C & Documentary L/C）

商業信用狀用於一般之交易活動，但無擔保信用狀（Clean L/C）和貨物並非一體，所以只用在以現金付款的情形下，諸如滙款、運費、保險金等貿易以外的支付。跟單信用狀（Documentary L/C）是取得貨款的保證，一般貿易大多採用這種信用狀。以下是這類信用狀的說明。

a. Irrevocable L/C, Revocable L/C

一旦開發不可撤銷信用狀(Irrevocable L/C),若無買方、賣方、開狀銀行、通知銀行的同意,不可以撤銷,開狀銀行以滙票之承兌來確定付款。而可撤銷信用狀(Revocable L/C)即使在限定的期間內,也可以由買方予以撤銷。

b. Confirmed L/C, Unconfirmed L/C

保兌信用狀(Confirmed L/C)除了開狀銀行以外,還需另一有國際信用的銀行予以雙重保證。無這種保證的就稱為不保兌信用狀(Unconfirmed L/C)。

c. Straight L/C, Open L/C

有指定押滙銀行者,稱爲指定押滙銀行信用狀(Straight L/C),反之則爲不指定押滙銀行信用狀(Open L/C)。不指定者對出口商較方便。

d. With Recourse L/C, Without Recourse L/C

若開發滙票的人負有請求償還權的信用狀,稱爲可追索信用狀(With Recourse L/C),若不負償還責任的信用狀,就是不可追索信用狀(Without Recourse L/C)。

e. Original L/C, Local L/C

由國外銀行原始開出的信用狀稱爲原信用狀(Original L/C),若把這信用狀抵押給銀行,由其開立給製造商或批發商的信用狀,稱爲國內信用狀(Local L/C)。

f. Transferable L/C

信用狀的受益人可以將信用狀金額的一部或全部轉讓給第三者,就稱爲可轉讓信用狀。

g. Banker's L/C

押滙票據的擡頭人(即負責兌付的人)非進口商,而爲信用狀的開狀銀行,或其託收銀行者,稱爲銀行信用狀。

h. Escrow L/C

記帳易貨信用狀（Escrow L/C）是用來連結出口與進口的個別交易。買方不將貨款付給賣方，而將其寄存於銀行的賣方帳戶中，當賣方反過來向買方購入商品時，由賣方請求以此存款當做抵押品，開立以買方爲受益人的信用狀，以付清款項。

i. Revolving L/C

爲免每次買貨，而逐次開發信用狀之麻煩，規定在滙票付清之後，就自動對同一個交易對象開立的信用狀稱爲循環信用狀。

j. London Acceptance L/C, New York Acceptance L/C

需向開狀銀行的倫敦分行、紐約分行提呈滙票，加以承兌，再由開狀銀行根據分行的通知，向進口商開出同額的票據，讓進口商承兌。期滿之日，再將貨款滙交紐約或倫敦分行。

k. Back to Back L/C

買方與賣方都開出信用狀，進出口互相抵銷。稱爲同時開發信用狀，多用於索賠貿易時。

✤ 與信用狀有關的公司：

1. Confirming House

確認公司是經進口商之委託確認訂單，代付貨款，日後再向進口商催收這些款項，目前在西非，南非極爲流行。出口商開出以Confirming House爲擡頭人的滙票，回收款項。

有London Confirming House等等。

2. Acceptance House, Discount House

承兌公司（Acceptance House），票據貼現公司（Discount House）。前者是接受進口商的委託開出以本身爲擡頭的滙票，做爲開立信用狀的依據。後者是當有託收滙票時，委託其貼現的。

*　　　*　　　*

以下特就信用狀中最常被使用的不可撤銷信用狀，舉出幾個實例。務請熟讀信用狀之內容。讓關係者對各項條件一目了然，是寫狀人最重要的工作，更要防範因一時疏忽導致裝船的失誤。

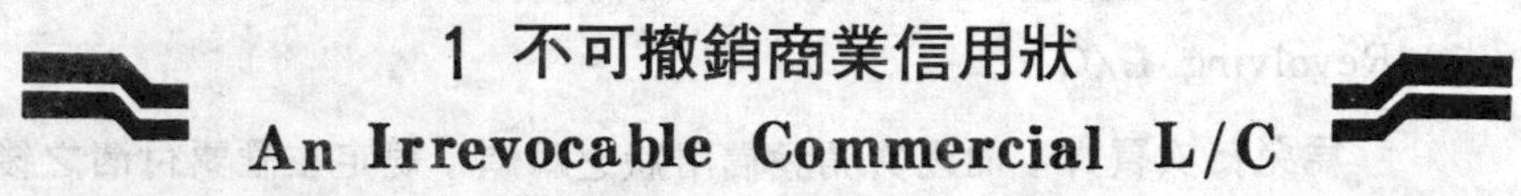

1 不可撤銷商業信用狀
An Irrevocable Commercial L/C

【實務須知】

- irrevocable commercial letter of credit ⇨不可撤銷商業信用狀
- ***authorize you to value on～*** ⇨授權給貴公司向～請款
- ***for account of ～*** ⇨以～的帳戶，即由～付款之意
- ***up to an aggregate amount of～*** ⇨總額可達～
- ***at sight*** ⇨見票付款
- commercial invoice ⇨商業發票
- marine insurance policy ⇨海險保單
- the Institute War Clauses ⇨倫敦學會戰爭險條款
- the Institute Cargo Clauses All Risks ⇨倫敦學會貨運全險條款
- the Institute Strike Clauses ⇨倫敦學會罷工險條款
- Packing List ⇨包裝明細表
- Consular Invoice ⇨領事簽證發票
- Clean on board bill of lading ⇨清潔裝艙提單
- ***made out to order and blank endorsed*** ⇨收貨欄註明 to order 及空白背書
- Partial Shipment ⇨分批裝運
- ***draft must be negotiated*** ⇨滙票須經過押滙
- ***endorsed by the negotiating bank*** ⇨由押滙銀行背書
- the drawee bank ⇨付款銀行

- drawers, endorsers, bona fide holders ⇨出票人、背書人、善意持票人
- ***duly honoured*** ⇨如期付款

<實 例>

23rd June, 19—

IRREVOCABLE COMMERCIAL LETTER OF CREDIT

INDIAN COMMERCIAL BANK, LTD.

33A MARINE LINES, BOMBAY 1.

No. 32648

The Mao Yuan Electric Co., Ltd.

Taipei, Taiwan

Dear Sirs,

We hereby authorize you to value on Indian Commercial Bank, Ltd., Bombay, for account of The Pravatak Commercial Corporation, Bombay up to an aggregate amount of (One Thousand Five Hundred Pounds Sterling Only) Stg. £1500-00 available by your drafts at sight for 100% invoice cost accompanied by

Signed commercial invoice in triplicate

Marine insurance policy or certificate, endorsed in blank for 110% of the invoice cost including: The Institute War Clauses, and the Institute Cargo Clauses All Risks and the Institute Strike Clauses

Packing List in triplicate

Consular Invoice in duplicate

Full set of clean on board ocean bill of lading made out

to order and blank endorsed, and marked "Freight Prepaid" and "Notify" The Pravatak Commercial Corporation, Bombay,

evidencing shipment from Keelung port to Bombay, of Cassette Tape Recorder Model CRT-508 one hundred sets (100 sets) @ Stg. £1500 CIF Bombay.

Partial shipments are not allowed. Transhipment is not allowed. Bills of lading must be dated not later than 31st August, 19—. Drafts must be negotiated not later than 20th September.

Special Instructions: All cargoes must be packed in strong wooden cases.

All drafts must be marked "Drawn under Indian Commercial Bank, Ltd. Irrevocable Letter of Credit No. 32648 dated 23rd June, 19—."

The amount of any draft drawn under this credit must be endorsed by the negotiating bank on the reverse hereof and the presentation of each draft, if negotiated, shall be a warranty by the negotiating bank that such endorsement has been made. If the draft is not negotiated this letter of credit must be presented, together with the draft and all relative documents, to the drawee bank on or before the above mentioned expiration date, and the amount of any draft drawn under this credit must be endorsed by the drawee bank on the reverse hereof.

We hereby agree with the drawers, endorsers and bona fide holders of drafts drawn under and in compliance with the term of this credit that such drafts will be duly honoured on due presentation and on delivery of documents as specified to the drawee bank.

Subject to uniform customs and practice for documentary credits (1962 revision) international chamber of commerce brochure No. 222

Yours faithfully,
Indian Commercial Bank, Ltd., Bombay
Kimler Assingham
Manager

Via Airmail thru:
Bank of Taiwan, Ltd.
Taipei, Taiwan.

19一年6月23日

不可撤銷商業信用狀

印度商業銀行

孟買1海線33A （此爲信用狀開狀銀行）

編號：32648

懋源電氣有限公司 （此爲信用狀受益人）

台灣台北市

敬啓者：

茲藉此授權給貴公司,向孟買的印度商業銀行請款，由孟買的帕瓦達商業公司付款，總額可達一千五百英鎊正,須檢附貴公司開立發票全額的即期滙票，及

簽名的商業發票一式三份

包括倫敦學會戰爭險條款、倫敦學會貨運全險條款、和倫敦學會罷

工險條款，以發票額110％投保，空白背書的海險保單或證明書

包裝明細表一式三份

領事簽證發票一式兩份

全套清潔海洋裝艙提單，收貨欄註明 to order ，空白背書，並註明「運費已付」和孟買帕瓦達商業公司爲到貨通知人，

以上各種單據載明從基隆港到孟買，裝運 CRT-508 型卡式錄音機一百台，到孟買運費、保險費在內價十五英鎊。

不可分批裝運。不可轉運。提單日期不可遲於 19－年 8 月31 日。匯票須於 9 月 20 日前押匯。

特殊指示：所有貨物須用堅固木箱包裝。

所有滙票須註明「憑印度商業銀行 19－年6月23日第32648號不可撤銷信用狀開立」。

憑本信用狀開立的任何滙票金額，須由押滙銀行就此點在反面背書，若經押滙，則每張滙票之提呈須由押滙銀行擔保，背書乃因此而設。若滙票未經押滙，本信用狀須於上述期限內（當天包括在內），連同滙票及所有相關文件，提呈給付款銀行，且任何憑本信用狀開立的滙票金額，須由付款銀行就此點在反面背書。

茲藉此對憑著並依照本信用狀條款而開立滙票之出票人、背書人及善意持票人承諾，這種滙票若依照付款銀行的規定，如期提呈並交付單據，則將如期付款。

以國際商會第 222 號手册的

商業信用狀統一慣例（1962 年修訂）

爲條件

孟買印度商業銀行

經理Kimler Assingham敬上

以航空郵遞，經由：

台灣台北市的台灣銀行轉知

**

aggregate〔ˈæɡrɪɡɪt, -ˌget〕*adj*. 合計的

hereby〔hɪrˈbaɪ〕*adv*. 藉此　triplicate〔ˈtrɪpləkɪt〕*n*. 一式三份的文件

duplicate〔ˈdjupləkɪt〕*n*. 一式二份；副本

reverse〔rɪˈvɝs〕*n*. 反面；顚倒　in compliance with 依從

 2 要求開立信用狀 Request for L/C 

【實務須知】

- ***you will meet with approval*** ⇨ 貴公司將會贊同
- ***we may be forced to cancel*** ⇨ 我方或許不得不取消

〈實　例〉

Dear Sirs,

We invite your attention to the fact that the letter of credit covering your order No. 105 has not reached us in spite of our repeated requests.

We urged our suppliers to execute an early delivery of products at higher prices to suit your requirements, which we trust you will meet with approval.

As we have not received your L/C we may be forced to cancel your order. However, we would prefer you to establish your L/C by the end of August so that we can continue our usual friendly business relations.

Yours faithfully,

敬啓者：

懇請惠予注意,貴公司第105號訂單的信用狀，雖經本公司一再要求，仍未送達。

爲配合貴公司的需求,本公司以較高的價格，促請供應商早日履行交貨，相信必能符合貴公司要求，並予以贊同。

因爲尚未接到信用狀，我方或許不得不取消您的訂單。然而，本公司寧可貴公司於8月底前開立信用狀，以便能持續雙方往常友好的交易關係。

3 修改信用狀 L/C Amendment

【實務須知】

- ***negotiate the draft to our banker*** ⇨將滙票交由我方交易銀行押滙
- ***amend the L/C*** ⇨修改信用狀
- ***extend the validity*** ⇨延長有效期限。因錯誤或其它各種情勢之變化，常常有不得不請求修改信用狀文字的情形，此時必須以鄭重的口氣請求對方。

〈實 例〉

Dear Sirs,

Thank you very much for your letter of credit No. CU-12083 covering your order No. 145 for copper plates.

Upon checking, however, we found that the name of the commodity was incorrectly described as "Iron Plate", and the shipment date expires on 20th September.

The first available ship will leave here around 25th

September . Also we will be unable to negotiate the draft to our banker since they were not informed of the different commodity on L/C prior to negotiating the draft.

We have asked you, therefore, to amend the L/C within a couple of days with the name of merchandise changed to "Copper Sheets" and extend the validity and shipping date to the end of September.

If acceptable, please amend the L/C by cable.

Yours faithfully,

敬啓者：

非常感激貴公司編號CU-12083的信用狀，以承保您第145號訂單訂購的銅製餐具。

然而，一經檢查，本公司發現貨品名稱被誤爲「鐵製餐具」，而船期於9月20日期滿。

第一艘適用的船隻將於9月25日左右離開本地。而且，本公司也無法將滙票交由交易銀行押滙，因爲在押滙前，他們尙未接獲信用狀商品名稱改變之通知。

因此,要求貴公司在幾天內修改信用狀，將貨品名稱改爲「銅器」，並將有效期限及船期延至9月底。

如果可以接受，請以電報修改信用狀。

實用例句

【必備詞彙】

- ***expiration of L/C*** ⇨ 信用狀的期限
- ***establish L/C = open L/C*** ⇨ 開立信用狀
- ***L/C number*** ⇨ 信用狀號碼
- ***D/P without L/C*** ⇨ 不須信用狀的付款交單

※ ※ ※

1. Due to the Chinese New Year's holidays it is difficult for us to dispatch your order goods by the date stipulated. We are very sorry for your inconvenience, but please accept our request for an ***extension of L/C*** to February 30.

   由於春節假期的關係，要在規定的日期前發送訂貨是很難的。爲貴公司帶來不便，至感抱歉，但請接受本公司的要求，將信用狀期限展延至2月30日。

2. We are pleased to confirm our cable dispatched today asking you to amend the terms as stipulated in the general terms and conditions of business concluded between us.

   茲樂意確認今天拍發的電報,那是要求貴公司照雙方締結的一般商務條件及情況，修改條件。

3. The ***expiration of your L/C*** is so near that we cannot possibly execute the shipment requested. Therefore, please extend the date two weeks more.

   貴公司信用狀的期限太近,本公司不可能照要求履行裝船。因此，請再延期兩週。

4. Though you informed us that you had already ***established the L/C*** we have not as yet received it. Please inform us of the ***L/C number*** by cable.

   雖經貴公司通知已開立信用狀，但到現在尚未接到。請以電報通知信用狀號碼。

5. We need an extension of your L/C immediately in order to execute the order as requested. Please cable us to that effect by the 10th.

   急需貴公司展延信用狀期限，以便依照要求履行訂單。請在 10 日前以電報告知此意。

6. We usually do business on an Irrevocable Letter of Credit. However, if necessary we may be able to reach terms ***D/P without L/C***.

   本公司通常以不可撤銷信用狀交易。不過，必要時或許能夠接受不須信用狀的付款交單的條件。

※ ※ ※

貨品完成製造、調配之後，即可陸續裝船。裝船前必須備妥前章所述的各項文件，此外最重要的是先洽訂船艙（*Booking Ship's Space*）、申請船隻（*Shipping Application*）。然後才可以取得裝運指示（*S/O, Shipping Order*）。

裝船必備文件已載明於契約、訂單和信用狀中，必須依此妥善準備完整的文件。完成裝船之後，立刻以電報拍發裝運通知（Shipping Advice），然後再以信件確認。裝運通知不只是通知買方已完成裝船，也是通知貨到請對方準備付款事宜。其他相關文件副本也應隨裝運通知附寄，因為有必要依此預先通知買方裝運文件的內容。

裝運通知應詳載之內容如下：

1. 訂單編號、契約編號、訂購日期。
2. 品名、數量、品質、其他。
3. 嘜頭、貨物數量。
4. 船名、開航日期、裝貨港、船公司名稱。

5. 滙票之買入通知，裝運文件的副本。

裝船須按照信用狀的指示辦理，無論裝船日期、貨物之轉運（transshipment），分批裝運（partial shipment）等都應確實辦理。若未依信用狀履行契約時，買方不但可以拒絕收貨，甚至可以拒絕付款，不能不特別小心。

* * *

✦ Shipping Documents 裝運文件

裝運文件是通關、裝船時必備的文件，須依照信用狀、訂單來確定其構成要素，茲分別條述如下：

1. 必備文件

a. Commercial Invoice 商業發票

b. B/L (Bill of Lading) 提單

c. Insurance Policy or Certificate 保險單或證明書

2. 一般附寄文件

a. Certificate and List of Measurement and/or Weight 重量材積證明書

b. Packing List 包裝明細表

c. Certificate of Origin 原產地證明書

3. 進口國家要求的文件

a. Customs Invoice 海關發票

b. Consular Invoice 領事簽證發票

前者是出口商對進口商海關保證進口貨物的眞實性而簽發。後者則是出口地領事館爲防止營運費及僞造發票導致逃稅而簽發，以使進口海關行事便捷。

4. 依商品而必備之文件

a. Inspection Certificate 檢驗證明書

b. Certificate of Health 衛生證明書

✦ **Bill of Lading（B/L）提單**

提單是貨物的領取證；除了象徵所有權的有價證券外，也可藉由背書（Endorsement）轉讓，將所有權轉讓給善意持票人的流通證券；也是船公司和貨主之間交換的運輸契約書。

✦ **提單的種類（Type of B/L）如下：**

1. ***Shipped B/L***（On Board B/L）；***Received B/L***

   裝運提單（Shipped B/L）和**備運提單**（Received B/L）之不同在於，前者是在出口港租船甲板上，貨物已裝船後再簽發的 B/L；而後者是貨物未裝船，但已搬入船公司的倉庫，對領到的貨物所簽發的。

2. ***Order B/L***；***Straight B/L***

   指示提單（Order B/L）和**記名提單**（Straight B/L）不同。指示提單不指定收貨人（Consignee），僅以 to order 表示指定，具有流通性（negotiable），可依背書（Endorsement）轉讓的提單。而記名提單乃直接註明指定的收貨人，是非流通性（non-negotiable）不可轉讓的提單。指示提單爲流通提單（Negotiable B/L），可依正本之正當背書而轉讓船貨。其收貨人可因指定而分爲：

   a. To Order（指定）
   b. To Order of *Shipper*（由託運人指定）
   c. To Order of *Negotiating Bank*（由押滙銀行指定）
   d. To Order of *Collecting Bank*（由託收銀行指定）
   e. To Order of *Agent of Shipper*（由託運代理人指定）
   f. To Order of *Buyer*（由買方指定）

   a、b兩種情況下，出口商須在證券背面打上公司名稱，作爲署名，向外滙銀行提出，這種署名稱爲空白背書（Blank Endorsement）。完全背書（Full Endorsement），則是由託運人指定被背書人。c、d、e、f 等情況則不必背書。

3. *Clean B/L ; Foul B/L*

清潔提單(Clean B/L),是指貨物完全沒有包裝破損或包裝不安全者。**不潔提單**(Foul B/L),又稱瑕疵提單,是指船公司職員認爲貨物有包裝破損、或包裝不安全的情況。不潔提單可以藉著賠償保證書(Letter of Indemnity),而更正爲清潔提單。

4. *Through B/L ; Optional B/L*

聯運提單(Through B/L)是由兩家承運人共同完成承運的提單,貨物在送達目的港之前,不需再辦任何手續,而使用同一提單轉運。**可選擇卸貨港提單**(Optional B/L),其上載有數個港口,可在進港前決定卸貨港的權利。

5. *Stale B/L ; Air Way Bill*

過期提單(Stale B/L)是裝船之後,經過10~15天,才向外滙銀行提出的提單,爲了避免產生爭執,最好附上保證書(L/G)。**空運提單**(Air Way Bill)是向航空公司領取航運貨物的憑證,因爲是記名式,故流通性不大。

1 裝運申請書 Shipping Application

【實務須知】

- ***shipping application*** ⇨ 裝運申請書；貨主致船公司的船位申請函，是於委託運輸時提出的運送契約明細。
- cft.＝cubic foot 立方英呎
- ***shipping order*** ⇨ 裝運通知
- ***weight & measurement*** ⇨ 重量和材積

〈實 例〉

Taipei, 18th July, 19—

Shipping Application

No. 2378
The Evergreen Shipping Co., Ltd.
24 Chung Cheng Rd., Keelung

Dear Sirs,

Please grant us Shipping Order for the undermentioned goods for the M/S "President" which will set sail on the 19th August, 19— from Keelung to Calcutta.

Marks & Nos.	Packing	Weight & Measurement	Description
CPW (in triangle) Calcutta C/# 1-3	Wooden cases	240 kgs. 320 cft.	1-band portable transistor radio 600 sets Model BX-256

Yours faithfully,

Product Wholesale Corporation

....

Manager

台北，19—年7月18日

裝運申請書

第2378號
長榮航運有限公司
基隆中正路24號

敬啓者：

請惠賜下列貨品由總統號柴油輪載運的裝貨單，該船將於19—年8月19日從基隆駛往加爾各答。

嘜頭及編號	包裝	重量和材積	品種、規格說明
CPW（三角形） 加爾各答 箱號1-3	木箱	240公斤 320立方英呎	單波段手提電晶體收音機　600台 BX-256型

產品批發公司

經理……　敬上

2 裝貨單 Shipping Order

【實務須知】

- receive on board ⇨ 在船上接收
- apparent good order and condition ⇨ 外表完整無缺
- grant accompanying Receipt ⇨ 簽發附帶收據
- shipping order ⇨ 裝運單

<實 例>

Shipping Order

To the Commanding Officer, Evergreen Shipping Company's

Steamer : M/S "President" Voy. No. CE-55-A

Loading Port : Keelung Destination : Calcutta

With transshipment at ………

From Product Wholesale Corporation

Please receive on board the undermentioned Goods in apparent good order and condition, and grant accompanying Receipt :

(Particulars Furnished by Shipper of Goods)

Marks & Nos.	Packings	Description	Weight and Measurement
CPW (in triangle) Calcutta No. 1/3 Made in Taiwan	3	Wooden cased 1-band transistor radio 600 sets	240 kgs. 320 cft.

Remarks : ______________________

Evergreen Shipping Co., Ltd.

裝貨單

致長榮海運公司指揮官

輪船：總統號柴油輪，航行編號CE-55-A

裝貨港：基隆　目的港：加爾各答

在………轉運

產品批發公司交運

請在船上接收下列外表完整無缺的貨品，並簽發附帶收據：

（細節由貨物託運人提供）

嘜頭和編號	包　裝	品種、規格說明	重量及材積
CPW 加爾各答 No. 1/3 台灣製造	3	木箱裝載 單波段電晶體 收音機600台	 240公斤 320立方英呎

備註：

長榮海運有限公司

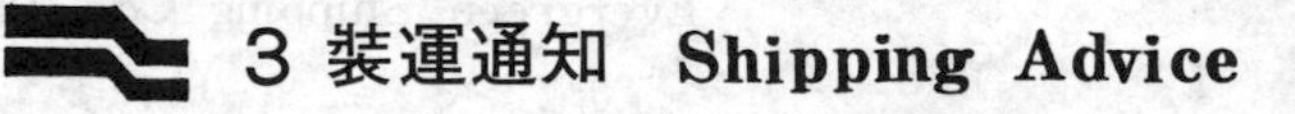

3 裝運通知 Shipping Advice

【實務須知】

- ***shipping advice*** ⇨裝運通知
- ***the relative shipping document*** ⇨相關的裝運文件
- M/S：motor ship ⇨柴油引擎船
- ***to cover this shipment*** ⇨以支付此次船貨
- ***honor the draft upon presentation*** ⇨在提出時承兌本滙票
- ***reach you in good order*** ⇨完整無缺運達

〈實　例〉

Dear Sirs,

We are pleased to confirm our cable 18th September, 19— informing you that we shipped the following good covering your order No. 4123 dated June 30 on the same day by the M/S "President" of The Evergreen Line as per enclosed copies of the relative shipping documents.

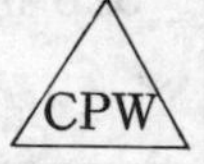

Three cases portable transistor radio

Calcutta　　Model BX-256 600 sets

C/#1-3

Made in Taiwan

To cover this shipment, we have drawn a draft at sight and negotiated it through Bank of Taiwan with the L/C, No. 2981 issued by The Indian Commercial Bank, Calcutta. We hope you would honor the draft upon presentation.

We believe that the goods will reach you in good order

and give you perfect satisfaction so that you may furnish us with further orders.

Yours faithfully,

敬啓者：

茲樂意確認本公司19一年9月18日的電報，通知貴公司6月30日第 4123 號訂單之貨物，已經在同一天由長榮海運的總統號柴油輪，按照附寄的相關裝運文件裝運下列貨物。

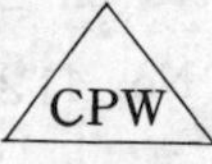

三箱的手提電晶體收音機

加爾各答　　BX-256 型六百台

箱號1-3

台灣製造

爲支付此次船貨，本公司開立一張即期滙票，並經由台灣銀行憑加爾各答印度商業銀行開立的第 2981 號信用狀押滙。希望貴公司在提示時承兌本滙票。

相信該批貨品將完整無缺運達，並令貴公司完全滿意，以使貴公司再提供訂單。

4 商業發票　Commercial Invoice

【實務須知】

- ***commercial invoice*** ⇨ 商業發票
- ***shipped per M/S "President"*** ⇨ 經由總統號柴油輪承運
- ***goods ex M/S "President"*** ⇨ 由總統號柴油輪交貨的貨物

- ***undersigned***〔ˌʌndɚˈsaɪnd〕*adj*. 下署的；此爲貨主
- ***Stg***. £1,689-30p ⇨由1563英鎊增加百分之十保險費而來

<實 例>

Date: 22nd September, 19—
No. IV 2893

Invoice of three cases of Portable Transistor Radios sold to Messrs. Pravatak Wholesale Corporation, 51 Main Street, Calcutta, shipped per M/S "President" of Evergreen Line sailing from Keelung to Calcutta on 21st September by the undersigned against Order No. 4123 of 30th June.

Marks & Nos.	Description	Unit price	Amount
	1-band	@ Stg.	Stg.
△ CPW	Portable transistor	£2-28p	£1,536-00
Calcutta	radio 600 sets	CIF Calcutta	
C/#1-3	Model BY-256	600 sets Total Stg.	
Made in Taiwan			£1,536-00

Ministry of Economic Affairs Export License No. CA-11-1145

Gross weight 240 kgs.

Net weight 225 kgs.

Measurement 320 cft.

Insured with The Taiwan Fired Marine Insurance Co., Ltd. for Stg. £1,689-30p L/C No. 2981 opened by The Indian Commercial Bank, Calcutta. Draft drawn through Bank of Taiwan, Taipei.

Taipei Trading Co., Ltd.

....

Sales Manager

日期：19一年9月22日

編號：IV 2893

本發票乃由下署公司憑6月 30 日第4123號訂單，賣給加爾各答緬因街 51 號的帕瓦達批發公司，三箱的手提電晶體收音機，由長榮海運的總統號柴油輪承運，於9月 21 日從基隆駛往加爾各答。

嘜頭及編號	品種、規格說明	單價	總價
CPW 加爾各答 箱號1-3 台灣製造	單波段 手提電晶體收音機 六百台 BY-256型	二英鎊二十八辨士	一千五百三十六英鎊整
		到加爾各答運費、保險費在內價	
		六百台總計一千五百三十六英鎊整	

經濟部輸出許可證編號CA-11-1145

毛重　240公斤

淨重　225公斤

材積　320立方英呎

投保台灣產物保險有限公司一千六百八十九英鎊三十辨士，信用狀編號2981，由加爾各答印度商業銀行開立。滙票由台北台灣銀行開發。

台北貿易有限公司

銷售部經理………敬上

5 匯票 Bill of Exchange

【實務須知】

- ***First Exchange*** ⇨第一聯滙票
- ***at*** 30 ***days after sight*** ⇨見票後三十天付款
- ***second of the same tenor and date being unpaid*** ⇨同樣要旨同日開出的第二聯不再付款
- ***pay to Bank of Taiwan*** ⇨付款給台灣銀行；此爲押滙銀行
- ***value received*** ⇨收到貨價後
- charge〔 tʃɑrdʒ 〕*v*. 轉帳；劃付～帳戶
- ***drawn under～*** ⇨憑～而開立

<實 例>

No. 200

Bill of Exchange

For Stg. £ 1536-00 *Taipei*, September 25, 19—

At 30 days after *sight of the* FIRST *Exchange* (SECOND *of the same tenor and date being unpaid*) *Pay to* Bank of Taiwan, Ltd., Taipei, *or order the sum of* one thousand five hundred thirty six only in Sterling Pounds

Value received and charge the same to the account of Pravatak Wholesale Corporation, Calcutta

Drawn under The Indian Commercial Bank, Ltd.,

Irrevocable L/C No. 2981 *Dated* 30th June, 19—

To The Indian Commercial Bank, Ltd. Calcutta

Taipei Trading Co., Ltd.

Manager

編號：200

滙 票

台北，19一年9月25日

一千五百三十六英鎊正

在第一聯滙票提出三十天後（同樣要旨同日開出的第二聯不再付款），請付款給台北的台灣銀行，一千五百三十六英鎊正的金額，收到貨價後，，並請劃付加爾各答帕瓦達批發公司之帳戶，本滙票係憑加爾各答印度商業銀行19一年6月30日之第2981號信用狀而開立。

此致加爾各答印度商業銀行

台北貿易有限公司

經理………敬上

6 船期延誤 Shipment Delayed

【實務須知】

- ***every effort is being made*** ⇨已經盡全力
- ***beyond our control*** ⇨超出我方所能控制的
- ***take every precaution*** ⇨全力預防。延期交貨很可能導致對方索賠，甚至可能發展成不履行契約，需特別注意。

<實 例>

Dear Sirs,

We are very sorry to advise you that the shipment during September covering your order No. 413 is impossible to execute within the date stipulated on account of manufacturers' labor shortage.

The Tung Chi Iron Works, Ltd. with which your order was placed is suffering a serious labour shortage by a recent rush of orders and a general shortage of young workers.

Every effort is being made to deliver the goods as requested. However, they say that a one month delay of shipment is unavoidable. We ask, therefore, that you kindly approve the situation with a 3% price discount as shown in the enclosed cable.

Although this is beyond our control, we deeply apologize for the inconvenience you have been put to.

We assure you that we will take every precaution against such trouble arising in the future.

Yours faithfully,

敬啓者：

很抱歉通知貴公司,原訂9月間裝運貴公司第413號訂單貨品的船期，由於製造商勞力缺乏，不可能在規定期限內履行。

貴公司訂單所下達的東吉鐵工廠，最近因爲大批訂單湧進，及普遍缺乏青年勞工，故勞力短缺甚爲嚴重。

他們已經盡全力照要求交貨。不過他們說船期延遲一個月是不可避免的。因此,懇求貴公司在如附表所示,價格打折百分之三的情況下,予以贊同。

雖然這件事非本公司能力所能控制,但是對於帶給貴公司的不便深感抱歉。

我方可以確保必定全力預防將來再發生這種麻煩。

實用例句

【必備詞彙】

- ***have the pleasure of ~ ing*** ⇨ 樂意~
- ***value you*** ⇨ 請貴方付款;即開立滙票請對方付款之意
- bill〔 bɪl 〕*n.* 支票;滙票
- present〔 prɪ'zɛnt 〕*v.* 提呈;提出
- ***sudden sailing cancellation*** ⇨ 突然取消航行
- ***disorganization in our business*** ⇨ 本公司營業上的混亂

⁂ ⁂ ⁂

1. We are pleased to inform you that we have shipped today 100 bales of cotton covering your order No. 50 by the S. S. " President ", for which we trust you will find all the goods in order.

   本公司今天已經由總統號輪,裝運貴公司第50 號訂單的一百包棉織品,特此奉告,相信必能完整無缺地運達。

2. We ***have the pleasure of*** informing you that the M/S " President " has arrived today and that three cases of your goods

are awaiting your delivery. We have to ask you to take delivery within three days from today.

總統號柴油輪今天已抵達,貴公司的三箱貨品正恭候查收，特此奉告，並懇求貴公司從今天起三天內取貨。

3. We have ***valued you*** at 90 d/s and the bill $340.00 will be presented to you by Bank of Taiwan.

本公司已開給貴公司見票九十天付款滙票,該票面額三百四十元，會由台灣銀行提呈給貴公司。

4. We deeply regret our inability to dispatch your order by the S.S. "Golden Gate" which was to leave Kaohsiung on 30th September due to the ***sudden sailing cancellation***.

本公司無法由金門號輪發送貴公司訂的貨,至感抱歉，該船由於突然取消航行，而預定在9月 30 日離開高雄。

5. Despite our repeated requests, your delay in giving us the L/C and shipping instructions has caused a serious ***disorganization in our business***.

雖經本公司一再要求,貴公司仍延遲給我方信用狀和裝運指示，因而引起本公司營業上的嚴重混亂。

⁂ ⁂ ⁂

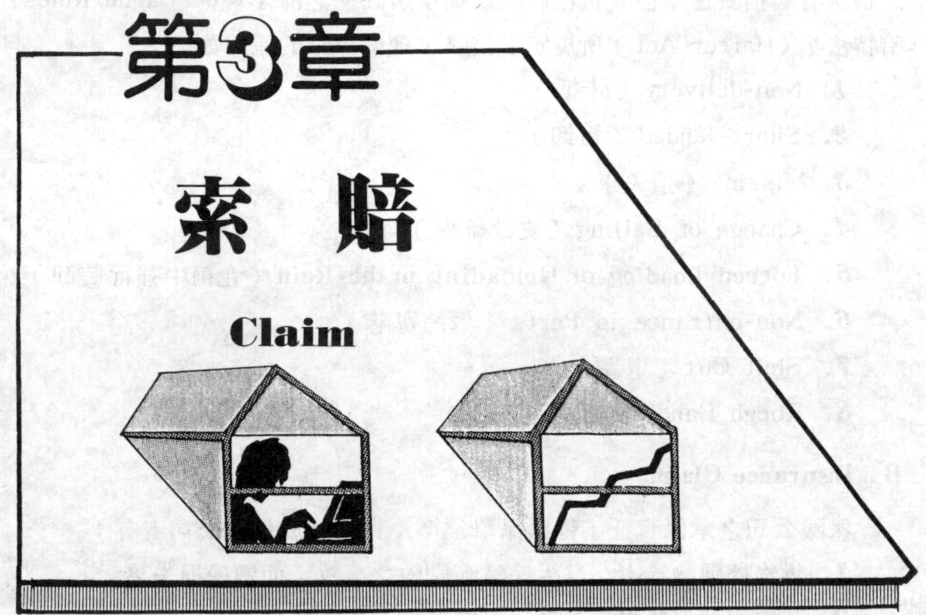

安然完成裝船之後，仍然可能因為誤解、事件、過失、故意等，產生意想不到的抱怨和糾爭。廣義的Claim包含訴怨（ complaint ）、請求賠償（ claim ）、紛爭（dispute）等等。索賠依其原因分為，因突發、自然、不可抗力因素而產生的**運輸索賠**（***Transportation Claim***）或**保險索賠**（***Insurance Claim***），以及因必然、內在因素引起的**貿易索賠**（***Trade Claim***）。前者需逕向運輸、保險公司請求賠償。而貿易索賠本質上責任歸於賣方，其解決方式影響到將來的交易，不可不慎重處理。發生索賠事件時，應避免寄望過去的交情，應該依據損失程度、內容及賠償要求等事實，客觀地處理。

與其爭執不下而徒留嚴重的不滿，倒不如依據交易基本條約，冷靜處理。有時甚至要果斷地訴求於仲裁機構，以求達到圓滿解決。

*　　　　*　　　　*

A. Transportation Claim

運輸索賠又稱為**裝運索賠**，船公司對於承運的貨物，在運送途中所遭受之損失有賠償責任，但其責任範圍以提單所註明之海牙規則(Hague Rules)哈特法案(Harter Act)所規定者爲限。運輸索賠的原因如下：

1. Non-delivery（未抵）
2. Short-landed（短卸）
3. Missing（遺失）
4. Change of Sailing（更改航程）
5. Forced Loading or Unloading in the Rain（在雨中強行裝卸）
6. Non-entrance in Ports（取消寄港）
7. Shut Out（退關）
8. Rough Handling（搬運不當）

B. Insurance Claim

保險公司之承保責任，皆以保單爲準，責任屬於保險公司者有：

1. 貨物於運輸途中，發生保險範圍內之事故，而遭受損失者。
2. 其它依據保單規定事項，可向保險公司索賠者。

C. Trade Claim

貿易索賠屬於出口商的責任，其原因爲：

1. Inferior Quality（品質不良）
2. Different Quality（品質不符）
3. Bad Packing（包裝不良）
4. Breakage（破損）
5. Shortage（短裝）
6. Different Shipment（裝運不符）
7. Delayed Shipment（延遲裝運）
8. Illegal Shipment（違法裝運）
9. Breach of Contract（未履行契約）
10. Cancellation（解約）

 1 貨品有瑕疵 Defective Goods 

【實務須知】

- ***upon unpacking*** ⇨開箱時
- ***cutting sample*** ⇨剪下的樣品
- ***strict about the quality…*** ⇨對品質要求嚴格
- ***be impatient to take delivery of goods*** ⇨急著要提貨
- ***favor us with a prompt solution*** ⇨惠告迅速的解決方案

＜實 例＞

Dear Sirs,

Our Indent No. 538: Black Serge

We should like to draw your attention to the defective goods shipped by the M/S "Sunlight" on 23rd July.

Upon unpacking the cases, we found that the quality was much inferior to the sample on which we approved the order. Moreover the length of each piece is short by approximately 5 meters.

After examining the enclosed cutting samples we sent as evidence from the Lloyd's Survey Report, we are sure you will agree to the inferiority of the goods.

We are now in a very awkward situation, because our customers, who have been very strict about the quality, are very impatient to take delivery of the goods.

We hope that you will immediately take this matter into your careful consideration and favor us with a prompt solution by return cable.

Yours faithfully,

敬啓者：

本公司第538號代購訂單：黑色斜紋布料

懇請惠予注意，於7月23日由陽光號柴油輪運來的貨品有瑕疵。

開箱時，本公司就發現貨品品質遠比我方答應訂單時的樣品差。此外，每件貨品的長度短少將近五公尺。

經檢驗剪下附寄的樣品，玆奉寄羅伊德公司的公證報告做爲證據，相信貴公司必會同意此貨品之低劣。

因爲本公司客戶向來對品質要求非常嚴格，又急著要提貨，目前我方處境非常困窘。

相信貴公司會立即審愼考慮此事，並馬上回電惠告迅速之解決方案。

** ———

indent〔ɪn'dɛnt〕*n*. 代購訂單

awkward〔'ɔkwəd〕*adj*. 不便的；尷尬的

 2 公證報告 Survey Report 

【實務須知】

- ***this is to certify*** ⇨ 本報告乃用以證明
- ***on their premises*** ⇨ 在他們的事務所（營業場所）
- ***ascertain the exact measurement*** ⇨ 確定精確的材積

- ***consignees' premises*** ⇨前述之收件人事務所
- ***silk velvet*** ⇨絲天鵝絨
- ***of the undersigned*** ⇨下署人的

<實 例>

18th September, 19—

Lloyd's Surveyor

Survey Report No. 14258

Measurement of Silk Velvet

shipped by Sanyang, Taipei

This is to certify that the undersigned surveyor performed a survey at the request of Messrs. P.W. Lindsey & Co., 502 Public Street, San Francisco, California on their premises on 5th September, 19— in order to examine the above mentioned goods and to ascertain the exact measurement of the same.

Shipment by the steamer "Sunlight" arriving San Francisco on or around 25th August and thence by track, arriving at the consignees' premises on 2nd September, 19—.

Bill of Lading: # 4325 dated Taipei, Taiwan, 23rd July, 19—. Invoice:dated Taiwan, 10th July, 19—.

Marks & Nos.	Shipment	Invoice Value
◇PWL◇ San Francisco C/ # 1/5 Made in Taiwan	Five cases 5,000 yds. silk velvet covering Order No. 347 & Sales Contract No. S-387.100 pcs. of silk velvet each 50 yds. Each US $500.00 CIF San Francisco	Total amount US $50,000.00 CIF San Francisco

S/# 518

It is the opinion of the undersigned that the length of each piece is short by 15 yards from the standard size normally marketed here and stated in the Shipper's Sales Contract No. S-387. It might be possible for the consignees to dispose of the goods as "defective goods" to retail stores and thus establish the loss. If this procedure cannot be undertaken, there is no alternative but to reship the entire goods. This report is issued without prejudice.

Lloyd's Survey Officer
Pike Willcock

19一年9月18日

羅伊德公司調查員

公證報告編號：14258

台北三陽公司運來的絲天鵝絨之材積

本報告乃用以證明下署調查員，應加利福尼亞舊金山市公共街502號P.W.林德西公司之請，於19一年9月5日，在該事務所，目的在檢驗上述貨品，並確定其精確的材積。

船貨由陽光輪於8月25日左右運抵舊金山，之後於19一年 9月2日由火車運抵前述之收件人事務所。

提單：4325號，日期爲台灣台北市19一年7月23日。發票日期：台灣19一年7月10日。

嘜頭及編號	船　　貨	發票額
PWL 舊金山 箱號　1/5 台灣製造	五箱五千碼絲天鵝絨，爲第347號訂單，及銷售契約編號：S-387之訂貨。一百匹絲天鵝絨，每匹五十碼。到舊金山的運費、保險費在內價，每匹美金五百元正。樣品號518	總金額 美金五萬元正 到舊金山運費、保險費在內價

下署人的意見爲：每匹長度較在本地正常買賣的標準尺寸，及在發送人銷售契約編號S-387內所記載的，短缺十五碼。對收件人而言，可能以「有瑕疵的貨品」處理，而賣給零售店，以彌補損失。若此措施不能採行，則不得不運回全數貨品。本報告之發佈絕不含成見。

羅伊德公司調查員
派克·威爾科克

**

procedure〔prə'sidʒɚ〕*n*. 訴訟程序；措施

alternative〔ɔl'tɝnətɪv〕*n*. 可取之道；選擇餘地

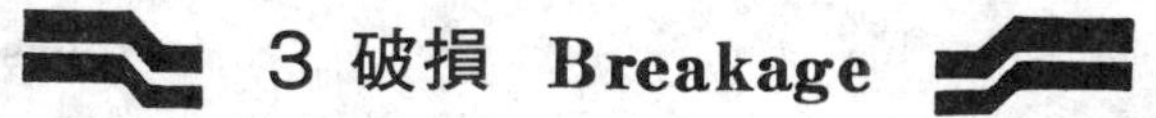

3 破損 Breakage

【實務須知】

- ***per our order*** ⇨以我方的訂單
- ***be of the opinion*** ⇨認爲
- ***import duty*** ⇨進口稅
- ***covering the loss*** ⇨抵償損失

- ***at your expense*** ⇨由貴公司付款
- ***upon arrival*** ⇨運抵時
- ***with freight forward*** ⇨運費由提貨人付款

〈實 例〉

Gentlemen：

This is to inform you that we have received 10 cases of Typewriters shipped by the S.S. "President" of The Evergreen Line per our order No. 203, but have found cases No.5 and No.9 badly damaged.

We are of the opinion that the cases were too fragile and the packing was not sufficient for export.

We enclose a survey report showing damage to be the result of faulty packing. We ask you therefore to send us a check for US $60.00 covering the loss we paid for the import duty and survey report including the charge for repair or to reship the new items at your expense. Upon arrival we will return the cargo with freight forward.

Your prompt attention of this matter is urgently requested.

Yours truly,

敬啓者：

已接到由長榮海運總統號輪承運的、我方第203號訂單之十箱打字機，特此奉告。但是我們發現第五箱和第九箱嚴重損壞。

本公司認爲箱子太脆弱，且包裝對出口而言，不夠堅固。

茲隨函附寄公證報告，證明破損乃因包裝不良所致。因此懇請您寄來六十美元支票，以抵償本公司支付進口稅、公證報告（包括修理費用）的損失,或者由貴公司付款再運來新貨品。運抵時，本公司會以運費由提貨人付款方式寄回貨品。

急切懇求貴公司儘速處理此事。

** ______

fragile〔'frædʒəl〕*adj.* 脆的；易碎的

faulty〔'fɔltɪ〕*adj.* 有缺點的；有漏洞的

實用例句

【必備詞彙】

- ***subject to shipment by the end of July*** ⇨ 以7月底前運送爲條件
- considerable inconvenience ⇨ 極大的不便
- numerous complaints ⇨ 許多怨言
- ***F.A.Q.* ＝ *Fair Average Quality*** ⇨ 良好平均品質
- ***Survey Report*** ⇨ 公證報告
- ***not in accordance with the specifications*** ⇨ 與品質、規格說明書不相符合
- ***offset the damage*** ⇨ 補償損失

⁂ ⁂ ⁂

1. As these orders were accepted ***subject to shipment by the end of July***, the goods should have reached us three weeks ago. As we have been put to ***considerable inconvenience*** from the delay,

please cable if you can execute the order within a week. If not, we shall have to cancel the order.

因爲當初接受這些訂購貨品的條件爲在7月底前運送，貨品應該在三星期以前送達。這次遲延帶給本公司極大的不便,若貴公司能在一週內履行訂單，請以電報告知。如不能，本公司勢必得取消訂單。

2. We regret having to inform you that we had ***numerous complaints*** concerning your mechanial toys. We did not take the trouble to examine the goods as we believed them to be reliable, but the greater part of the goods have been returned by customers who are dissatisfied with them.

必須告知貴公司,本公司接獲許多有關機械玩具的怨言，至感遺憾。因爲相信這些貨品很可靠，故未費心加以檢驗，但是大部分貨品已被不滿意的客戶退回。

3. From the Survey Report which was held on our premises, you will readily admit that the goods are much inferior in quality to ***F.A.Q.*** and short of the weight agreed to in the contract.

從在我方事務所做的公證報告，您會欣然承認，這批貨品質較良好平均品質差得多，且較契約中同意的重量爲輕。

4. Although this is considerably inferior to your sample, we will accept it if your list price can be reduced 20 per cent.

雖然貨品遠較樣品爲差,若貴公司價錢可降低百分之二十，本公司願意接受。

5. The 100 cartons of cameras covering our order No.100 shipped by M/S "Sunlight" reached us in an unsatisfactory condition. They are ***not in accordance with the specifications*** of the order. We hope you will immediately propose a settlement to

offset the damage.

本公司第100號訂單的一百盒照相機，由陽光號柴油輪承運，已抵達，但品質非常令人不滿。該貨與訂單的品質、規格說明書不相符合。希望貴公司立即提出解決之道，以補償損失。

* carton〔'kɑrtn̩〕*n.* 紙板盒

⁂ ⁂ ⁂

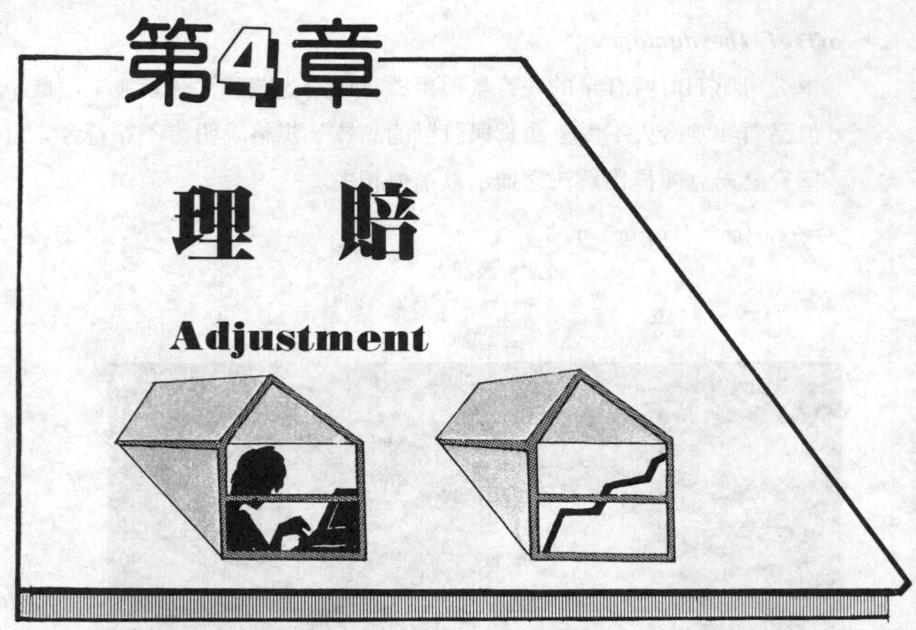

第4章

理　賠

Adjustment

對方提出索賠時，必須立即調查事實。調查清楚並確定責任所在之後，再據以採行**減價、換貨**或**修理**等步驟。當索賠款額不高時，可以藉著當事人之間的協議，圓滿解決，應該把握時效，迅速完成。若金額龐大，無法以雙方協商來解決的時候，就要選擇國際商務仲裁所（The International Arbitration）等公平的仲裁機構來解決。若**裁定**（ **Award** ）不成立時；就得考慮利用法院的職權達成和解。如果實在找不到解決的途徑時，最後只有走向**訴訟**（**Litigation**）一途，但是訴訟曠時費財，缺乏實效。

碰到索賠事件，首先，應該依據契約書，基於雙方共識的基礎上，明白表示具體的理賠，並要迅速、冷靜地處理。能夠考慮對方立場，以坦誠的態度來處理，必然是最有效的。當對方想盡辦法，以品質不夠標準或瑕疵要求折價時，賣方應力陳己方的正當理由，並表示不惜解除契約或對簿公堂的強硬態度。要注意處理索賠事件不要涉及感情，**冷靜、客觀**地解決方爲上策。提昇對貿易習慣、實務的了解，萬無一失地履行契約，才是防止此類事件發生的根本方法。

*　　　　*　　　　*

1 同意索賠 Claim Settled

【實務須知】

- ***filter in*** ⇨滲入
- ***despite rigorous inspection*** ⇨雖然經過嚴格檢查
- ***as a settlement*** ⇨做爲賠償
- ***maximum care and efficiency*** ⇨最大的細心及效率

＜實 例＞

Dear Sirs,

We are very sorry to learn from your letter of 25th August that our shipment covering your order No. 167 was found defective.

Upon investigation we have discovered that defective goods sometimes filter in despite rigorous inspection prior to shipment. We protested very severely to the manufacturer with whom your order was placed.

They deeply apologize for the matter and assure that they shall never allow such carelessness to happen in future shipments. As a settlement we have arranged to reship the whole goods by the first available ship, with a special discount of 3% off the invoice amount.

We add our apology for your trouble and promise to execute your orders in the coming future with maximum care and efficiency.

Very truly yours,

敬啓者：

從貴公司8月25日來函,得知運給貴公司第167號訂單的貨品有瑕疵,至感抱歉。

經過調查後發現，雖然在運出前本公司曾嚴格檢查，但有瑕疵的貨品有時仍會滲入。我方已向您訂單所下達的製造商提出嚴重抗議。

他們對此事深感抱歉，並確保將不容許今後的船貨再發生同樣的疏忽。本公司已安排交由第一艘適用的船隻，重運全部貨品，並給予發票額百分之三的特別折扣，作爲賠償。

謹爲貴公司的麻煩致上歉意,並保證今後以最大的細心、及效率履行貴公司的訂單。

** ____________________

apologize 〔ə'pɑlə,dʒaɪz〕 *v.* 道歉

2 不同意索賠 Claim Unadmitted

【實務須知】

- ***take every effort to fulfill～*** ⇨ 盡全力以履行～
- ***as evident from～*** ⇨ 由～可證明
- ***certificate of packing inspection*** ⇨ 包裝檢驗證明書
- ***clean B/L*** ⇨ 清潔提單
- ***lodge a claim*** ⇨ 提出索賠
- ***wherever possible to process the claim*** ⇨ 儘可能協助進行索賠
- ***prevent such a recurrence*** ⇨ 防止類似事情再發生

<實 例>

Gentlemen :

Thank you for your letter of August 25 concerning the 100 cases of Typewriter covering your order No. 315.

After a careful investigation, we could not find any error on our part because we took every effort to fulfill your order as evident from the certificate of packing inspection enclosed. Moreover the lots were on board the ship in perfect condition which was clearly stated in the clean B/L.

We suggest, therefore, that you lodge a claim with the insurance company. We will assist you wherever possible to process the claim.

Though it was quite beyond our control, we are very sorry for the inconvenience you have suffered.

We assure you we will make every attempt to prevent such a recurrence in the future.

Yours very truly,

敬啓者：

感謝貴公司8月25日有關第315號訂單，一百台打字機的來函。

經過愼重調查，找不出我方有任何缺失，因爲由附寄的包裝檢驗證明書可以證明，本公司已盡全力履行貴公司的訂單。況且，這批貨完整無缺地上船，在清潔提單中記載得很清楚。

因此，建議貴公司向保險公司提出索賠。本公司願儘可能協助貴公司進行索賠。

雖然非本公司能力所能控制,對於貴公司所遭遇的不便,至感抱歉。

我方向您確保，將盡力防止未來再發生類似事情。

實用例句

【必備詞彙】

- ***upon investigation*** = ***upon tracing the case*** ⇨ 經過追查
- ***make a claim*** ⇨ 提出索賠
- ***shipping clerk*** ⇨ 負責船務的職員
- ***balance of your order*** ⇨ 貴公司訂單的餘額
- ***familiarly connected plants*** ⇨ 密切關連的工廠
- ***debit us*** ⇨ 記入我方借項
- ***in view of*** ⇨ 鑑於
- ***meet you half way*** ⇨ 遷就貴公司

※ ※ ※

1. We have received your letter of May 10 ***making a claim*** for the shipment. ***Upon investigation***, we find that our ***shipping clerk*** shipped Sample No. 10 instead of No. 15. We are sorry for the inconvenience and have made provision not to have it happen again.

   貴公司5月10日來函對本次船貨提出索賠，業已知悉。經過追查發現，本公司負責船務職員將樣品號第 15 號寄成第 10 號。對此不便至感抱歉，並已規定不可再發生這種錯失。

* provision 〔prəˈvɪʒən〕 *n*. 規定；條款

2. We are sorry for the delay in shipping the ***balance of your order*** No. 122. However, we are not entirely responsible because of a serious labor shortage which occured at one of our ***familiarly connected plants***.

   延遲運送貴公司第122號訂單的餘額,至感抱歉。然而，並非全應由我方負責，因為一家與本公司關係密切的工廠，發生嚴重的勞工短缺。

3. Please ***debit us*** with any expenses and accept our apology for the inconvenience. We assure you of our best attention in subsequent orders.

   請將一切費用記入我方借項，對此不便也請接受本公司道歉。我方確保隨後的訂單將特別小心注意。

   * subsequent 〔ˈsʌbsɪˌkwɛnt〕 *adj*. 隨後的；後來的

4. This is the first complaint we have ever received in our long business relations with you. Please understand that this is really an exception, and we will do our utmost to correct it.

   這是與貴公司長久的交易關係中,第一次接到的抱怨。請予諒解，這實在是一次例外，本公司會盡全力改正。

5. We are not responsible for the difference of quality between our shipping samples and your counter sample because you okayed it prior to shipment. However, ***in view of*** our long and pleasant relations, we will ***meet you half way*** by offering a discount of 10%.

   有關運去的樣品與您的相對樣品品質不同，不應由本公司負責，因為在運送前已徵得貴公司認可。不過,鑑於雙方長期愉快的關係，本公司將提供百分之十的折扣，以遷就貴公司。

第5章

帳款之解決

Account Settlement

貿易上，有用付款與貨物無直接關連的付款方式，作爲雙方金錢往來的情況，譬如**記帳交易**（***Open Account***）、**清潔滙票**（無擔保滙票，***Clean Bill of Exchange***）等。但是，一般的付款方式還是以**跟單滙票**爲主，這是指出口商開立滙票，以貼現的方式讓予外滙銀行，同時以裝運文件(Shipping Documents）做抵押或擔保。

跟單滙票若有信用狀，由銀行保證付款是最穩當安全的，稱爲**附信用狀跟單滙票**（***Documentary Bill of Exchange with L/C***），又因信用狀規定爲不可撤銷信用狀，是標準的付款方式。無信用狀的D/A、D/P滙票，規定見票五個月內，或裝船後六個月內付款，也是一種標準的付款方式。但是，由於沒有信用狀保證付款，所以必需由國家經營的輸出保險制度來擔保風險。輸出保險的種類如下：

1. 輸出融資保險

2. 託收方式（D/P、D/A）輸出保險

3. 中長期延付輸出保險

4. 海外工程輸出保險

這些保險不僅為保證輸出費用的回收，更是為了拓展輸出貿易而設立的。

*　　　　*　　　　*

除了以上所談的，依據付款的時間，又可分為預付（payment in advance）、交貨付款（cash on delivery）、後付（on credit）及分期付款（installment）等，跟單滙票付款屬於交貨付款（cash on delivery）。預付方式有 Bank Bill（銀行滙票），T.T.（電滙，Telegraphic Transfer），定貨付款（C.W.O.: cash with order）等。其他如 part payment in advance（部分預付），cash on shipment（裝運付款）等屬於 Open Account，Clean Bill 之外。但這些都必須以無外幣限制，自由使用外幣為前提，不是當前貿易的主流。

*　　　　*　　　　*

現在讓我們簡單地介紹賒售（Credit Letter）時的結算清單（Statement of Account）、託收函（Collection Letter）、滙款（Remittance）及收據（Receipt）等範例。

隨著貿易而產生的英語，和日常生活使用的英語幾乎屬於同一範疇，由於受到篇幅的限制，無法全部收錄在本書中。因此，只把與貿易最有關的英語列在下面，提供讀者參考。

1 寄銷清單 Account Sales

【實務須知】

- ***dispose of*** ⇨ 賣掉
- ***Account Sales*** ⇨ 寄銷清單
- ***net proceeds*** ⇨ 淨收益
- ***draw against our account*** ⇨ 憑我方帳戶開立

<實 例>

Dear Sirs,

Your Consignment : S/# 215

We are pleased to inform you that your consignment of 100 dozen fountain pen S/# 215 received by M/S "Phoenix" were profitably disposed of.

We are sending you the enclosed Account Sales from which you will find that the goods were sold out at higher prices than listed. We are glad to give you such a favorable report.

The net proceeds due to you will be paid immediately upon presentation of your draft. Please draw against our account as usual.

Yours faithfully,

敬啓者．

貴公司的託售貨品：樣品號 215

由鳳凰號柴油輪承收，貴公司樣品號 215 號鋼筆一百打的託售貨品，已獲利售出。

茲隨函附寄寄銷清單，貴公司將發現這批貨以比表列價格高的售價賣出。本公司很高興向貴公司提出這種有利的報告。

貴公司應得之淨收益，在滙票提呈時將立即付淸。請如往例憑我方帳戶開立滙票。

**

consignment〔kən'saɪnmənt〕*n.* 託售貨品

profitably〔'prɑfɪtəblɪ〕*adv*. 獲利地；有益地

favorable〔'fevərəbl̩〕*adj*. 有利的；良好的

2 寄銷清單 Account Sales 

【實務須知】

- ***ex M/S "Phoenix"*** ⇨由鳳凰號柴油輪交貨
- ***by order and for the account of～*** ⇨基於～的命令及利益
- ***payable at sight*** ⇨見票即付

<實 例>

16th September, 19—

Account Sales

Account sales of 100 dozen fountain pens S/# 215 ex M/S "Phoenix" marketed by Peter Williamson & Co., Ltd. by order and for the account of Ta Ming Soundries Co., Ltd., Taipei, Taiwan.

100 doz. S/# 215 Fountain pens @ 8/6		£ 86-00p
	Charges	£ 7-00p
Cape Town No. 1	Commission 10%	£ 8-30p
	Stg.	£ 71-20p

Payable at sight

Cape Town, 10th September

Peter Williamson & Co., Ltd.

....

President

19一年9月16日

寄銷清單

樣品號215號 的鋼筆一百打之寄銷清單，由鳳凰號柴油輪交貨，彼得•威廉森有限公司，基於台灣台北市大明雜貨有限公司之命令及利益承銷。

PW	一百打樣品號215號的鋼筆每打8.6鎊	八十六英鎊正
	費用	七英鎊正
開普敦	百分之十的傭金	八英鎊三十辨士
第1號		七十一英鎊二十辨士

見票即付

開普敦，9月10日

彼得•威廉森有限公司

董事長……… 敬上

**

market〔ˈmɑrkɪt〕*v.* 出售　charge〔tʃɑrdʒ〕*n.* 費用；索價

commission〔kəˈmɪʃən〕*n.* 傭金；委託

3 託收信函 Collection Letter

【實務須知】

• ***statement*** ⇨報告書；借貸表

• ***rendered up to the*** 30***th September*** ⇨提出至9月30日結算

的

- ***monthly account*** ⇨每月清單
- ***found in order*** ⇨查核無誤
- ***your remittance*** ⇨貴公司的滙款

＜實 例＞

Dear Sirs,

We are sending herewith our statement of account on 30,000 yards white shirting S/# 1014 shipped by the S/S "Phoenix" rendered up to the 30th September.

According to the terms and conditions of the monthly account agreed upon, we should like to receive settlement by 20th October.

If found in order, please favor us with your remittance within the period stipulated.

Yours faithfully,

敬啓者：

茲隨函附寄由鳳凰號輪承運、樣品號 1014 號 、三萬碼的白色襯衣料，提出至 9 月 30 日的結算清單 。

依照每月清單同意的條款與狀況，本公司願於 10 月 20 日前接獲清償款項。

若查核無誤，請在規定期間內賜予滙款 。

**

statement〔'stetmənt〕*n.*〔商〕報告書；借貸表

settlement〔ˈsɛtl̩mənt〕*n.* 清償

4 付款通知 Payment Advice

【實務須知】

- ***in full settlement*** ⇨以全數結清帳款
- ***in the credit of our account*** ⇨記入我方帳戶的貸項
- ***upon arrival of the cheque*** ⇨支票送達時

＜實 例＞

Dear Sirs,

We have received your letter of 18th September requesting us to send you the remittance by 20th September.

Upon checking your statement of accounts, we found it quite in order and are sending herewith a cheque on the South Africa Bank, Ltd. for Stg. £116-00 in full settlement for this month, which amount please put in the credit of our account.

We shall appreciate it if you will send us your receipt upon arrival of the cheque.

Yours faithfully,

敬啓者：

貴公司9月18日來函，要求在9月20日前滙款給貴公司，業已知悉。在檢視貴公司結算清單時，發現查核無誤，茲隨函附寄一張南非銀行所開發，總額一百一十六英鎊的支票，以全數結清本月的帳款，請將該金額記入我方帳戶的貸項。

支票送達時，若蒙寄來收據，將不勝感激。

** ______________________

herewith〔hɪrˈwɪθ, -ˈwɪð〕*adv.* 附此；同此

receipt〔rɪˈsit〕*n.* 收據

5 收據 Receipt

【實務須知】

- ***a further request for an order*** ⇨再次要求訂單
- ***received of～*** ⇨茲收到～
- ***in settlement of commission*** ⇨結算傭金；此爲大明有限公司以 Funk & Buck Co., Ltd. 的代理店身分，銷售商品，進行協調，領取傭金，開立收據。

<實 例>

5th October, 19—

Funk & Buck Co., Ltd.
16 Public Street,
Cape Town

Dear Sirs,

Thank you very much for your cheque for Stg. £116-00 on The South Africa Bank, Ltd. in settlement of your account for commission of agent during September, for which we are sending herewith a receipt.

We deeply appreciate your past business relations with us and hope that you will furnish us with a further request for an order in the future.

Yours faithfully,

....

Import Manager

5th October, 19—

Ta Ming Co., Ltd.

Received of Messrs. Funk & Buck Co., Ltd., Cape Town, South Africa the sum of One Hundred and Sixteen Pounds Only in settlement of Commission Account.

Stg. £116-00

Ta Ming Co., Ltd.

....

Accounting Manager

19—年10月5日

芬克及巴克有限公司

開普敦公共街16號

敬啓者：

非常感謝貴公司總額一百一十六英鎊正，南非銀行所開發的支票，以結算9月的代理傭金帳款，茲隨函附寄收據一張。

對於貴公司和本公司過去的交易關係，深爲感激，希望將來能再次向我方索求訂單。

進口部經理………敬上

19一年10月5日

大明有限公司

收到南非開普敦芬克及巴克有限公司，一百一十六英鎊正的金額，以結算傭金帳款。

大明有限公司

會計部經理………敬上

實用 例句

【必備詞彙】

- ***remittance of payment*** ⇨ 付帳滙款
- ***take legal steps*** ⇨ 採取法律途徑
- forthcoming〔'forθ'kʌmɪŋ〕*adj.* 即將到來的；即將出現的
- ***such unpleasant steps as legal procedures*** ⇨ 像法律訴訟這類不愉快的途徑
- ***imposed by～*** ⇨ ～採取緊縮政策
- ***goods consigned*** ⇨ 委託的貨品

※ ※ ※

1. We are wondering why your ***remittance of payment for*** 100 dozen handkerchiefs does not reach us despite our repeated requests. Please let us have your remittance immediately. If not, we will be obliged to ***take legal steps.***

   我方想知道爲什麼貴公司對支付一百打手帕的滙款，雖經一再催討仍未送達。懇請立卽滙款，若再不滙出，本公司將不得不採取法律途徑。

2. We heard that the general recession in business has made it difficult for you to collect the stipulated sum from your customers. However, we ask you to understand that we do business only on commission, and if your remittance is not ***forth-coming,*** we will fall into an extremely difficult situation.

   聽說普遍性商業不景氣,使貴公司向客戶收集規定的金額，變得很不容易。不過,請貴公司了解,您我雙方交易乃基於委託關係,若貴公司滙款不到，本公司將落入極端困難的處境。

   * recession〔rɪˈsɛʃən〕*n.* 商業暫時衰弱現象；蕭條

3. Your unusual delay in payment contrary to the terms of our agreement puts us into a very awkward situation. We sincerely hope we can avoid ***such unpleasant steps as legal procedures.***

   貴方付款異常的遲延，違背契約的條款，致使本公司處於非常困窘的境地。誠摯地希望我方能避免採用，像法律訴訟這類不愉快的途徑。

4. Owing to a tight monetary situation ***imposed by*** the government, it is difficult to let you have a cheque at once. We shall appreciate it, therefore, if you will give us an another fortnight to settle your account due September 30.

   由於政府採取緊縮政策，銀根很緊，很不容易立即給貴公司支票。因此若蒙再寬限兩星期，以清償貴公司9月30日到期的帳款，則不勝感激。

   * monetary〔ˈmɑnə,tɛrɪ〕*adj.* 金融的；財政的
   fortnight〔ˈfɔrt,naɪt〕*n.* 兩星期；十四天

5. Your letter of October 18 has just been received, and we are sending herewith an account for the ***goods consigned*** to us on August 25. We are pleased to enclose our cheque for US$ 1,600.45 on Bank of Taiwan.

剛收到貴公司10月18日來信，茲隨函奉寄8月 25 日委託本公司的貨品之帳單。並樂意附寄台灣銀行的美金一千六百元四十五分支票一張。

※ ※ ※

PART V

Miscellaneous in Foreign Trade

外貿附帶事項

第5章

通函、報告和社交電文

Circulars, Report & Social Message

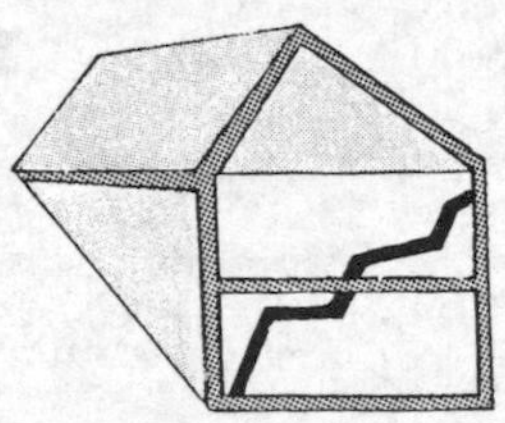

Circulars（通函）是一種充作通知函的印刷品，具有對顧客連絡**開張、遷址、設立分公司、人事變動、結構變動等事宜**的功能，一方面也具有展示營業項目、營業內容的廣告作用。可以算是一種 Sales Letter，向衆多顧客推銷產品，近來更藉著電腦打字機，同時打出多封同樣內容的信文，宛如是特地打給某人的信函，更發揮了引起對方興趣的 Sales Letter 的功能。通函大致可以分爲三類：

A. Market Report

市場報告乃是告知對方市場動向與趨勢，在貿易上具有重要地位，爲了使其不辱既定使命，在信文當中，務必對特定商品及一般市場，提供絕對可靠的資料。交易量大的綜合貿易公司或是專門貿易公司，更可藉著週刊、月刊，印製市場狀況，分送給顧客，做爲重要的交易資料。各龐大的貿易機構，更不時直接派員到海外搜集資料。

B. New Product Report

爲了推銷新產品，印刷各種 PR（Public Relations）用資料，分發給客戶，做爲介紹新產品的工具。衆所週知的，這類資料藉著適切的說明與設計書，刊載於報章雜誌，對於海外代理商的銷售聲勢，新產品的宣傳推銷，都具有極大的功用。

C. Social Message

貿易畢竟還是要靠人與人的接觸方能成立。而人與人的關係，必然伴隨著各種問候與社交，所以勢必要籌措各式問候函、邀請函、通知函。這類函件沒有固定形式，本章特舉數例以供參考。

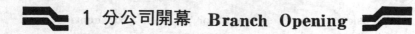

1 分公司開幕 Branch Opening

【實務須知】

- ***with a half century of pioneering research*** ⇨ 本著半世紀的領先研究
- ***manage affairs of the branch*** ⇨ 經辦分公司的業務
- ***branch manager*** ⇨ 分公司經理
- ***to favor us with your continued patronage*** ⇨ 繼續惠顧

<實 例>

Gentlemen:

Our New Branch

We are pleased to inform you that we will open our new branch on April 21 at the following address to meet the rapidly increasing demand for our electronic & electric instruments.

International Building Room No. 15-18
70702 ***Peacock Street, Chicago, U.S.A.***

With a half century of pioneering research in the manufacture and sale of our goods, we are confident we can serve you more conveniently and promptly than before.

As a branch manager, we have appointed Mr. Jim Wu who has been the sales manager of our head office for five years. He has a deep understanding and experience in the US market, and will manage affairs of the branch from its opening.

We ask you sincerely to favor us with your continued patronage.

Yours faithfully,

敬啓者：

開設新分公司

本公司將於 4 月 21 日，在下列地址開設新分公司，以滿足對本公司電子、電氣儀器快速增加的需求，特此奉告。

美國芝加哥畢卡克街70702號國際大廈 15-18 室

本著半世紀以來，在產品製造及銷售上的領先研究，本公司有信心能提供比以前更方便、快速的服務。

本公司已指派吳吉姆先生爲分公司經理，他曾做過五年總公司的業務部經理，對美國市場有深刻的了解和經驗，將從分公司開幕起經辦該處業務。

誠摯地懇求貴公司繼續惠顧。

實用例句

【必備詞彙】

- ***establish ourselves*** ⇨開業
- ***under the auspices of ～*** ⇨在～的贊助下
- ***commence business under the title of ～*** ⇨以～名稱開始營業
- ***avail ourselves of*** ⇨利用
- ***favors and commands*** ⇨惠顧與訂購
- ***transferred our business*** ⇨將本公司業務易手
- ***be payable to and by them*** ⇨ 由他們收款或付款
- ***attached table*** ⇨附表

⁂ ⁂ ⁂

1. We have the pleasure of informing you that we have ***established ourselves under the auspices of*** our customers at the above address as an exporter of textile goods. We are sure that more than 20 years' business experience will assist you in a most satisfactory manner.
在客戶的贊助下，我方已於上述地址開業，成爲紡織品外銷商，特此奉告。本公司確定二十多年的交易經驗，必能以最令人滿意的做法，協助貴公司。

2. We should like to inform you that the two Iron Works Co., Ltd., The Tung Ch'eng Co., Ltd. and Min Ch'eng Iron Works, Ltd. will be amalgamated on April 1, and ***commence business under the title of*** Tung Min Iron Works, Ltd.

東昌有限公司和敏成鋼鐵有限公司，兩家鋼鐵公司將於4月1日合併，並以東敏鋼鐵有限公司之名稱開始營業，特此奉告。

* amalgamate〔ə'mælgə,met〕*v.* 合併

3. In view of your constant orders, we have decided to establish a branch office for your convenience at the following address. We ***avail ourselves of*** this opportunity to return you our sincere thanks for your past favors.

   鑑於貴公司經常訂購，爲了您的方便，本公司決定在下列地址開設分行。利用這次機會，以誠摯的謝意，回報貴公司過去的惠顧。

   * ***for** one's **convenience*** 爲了～的方便

4. Under the ***favors and commands*** of your continued relationship with us, we have the pleasure of informing you that Mr. Paul Fu, the former branch manager will soon be replaced after completing his three years' service with Mr. Peter Wang.

   在貴公司持續惠顧與訂購的關係下，茲樂意敬告貴公司，前任分公司經理傅保羅先生，不久將三年服務期滿，由王彼得先生接替。

5. Due to an unfavorable financial situation during these years, we have decided to retire from the export business. We have ***transferred our business*** to The Chia Sheng Trading Co., Ltd. All debts and liabilities have been taken over by the above firms and will ***be payable to and by them.***

   由於近年來財政狀況不佳，本公司已決定退出外銷商務，並將業務易手給嘉昇貿易有限公司。所有的債務皆移轉給上述公司，由他們收款或付款。

   * liability〔,laɪə'bɪlətɪ〕*n.*(*pl.*) 債務

6. We are pleased to inform you that owing to the constant lots of orders, we have decided to expand our branch activities. On this occasion, we are moving our branch to the address below and are offering an opportunity to dispose of our entire stock listed in the ***attached table*** at production cost.
由於許多穩定的訂單，本公司已決定擴展分公司業務，特此奉告。趁此機會，我方將把分公司遷移至下述地址，並提供機會將列於附表的全部存貨，以生產成本賣出。

* * *

2 市場報告 Market Report

【實務須知】

· ***market this week*** ⇨本週市場
· ***tight monetary control*** ⇨嚴格的貨幣管制
· textiles and sundries ⇨紡織品和雜貨
· ***keen buying demand*** ⇨強烈的購買需求
· favorable prospects ⇨有利的展望
· ***car market remains quiet*** ⇨汽車市場持續平穩
· spot〔spɑt〕*n.* 現貨；現金交易之物
· ***home prices*** ⇨國內價格
· ***outlet levels constant*** ⇨穩定的銷售水準
· ***scrap market*** ⇨鐵屑市場
· ***opportunity for a good purchase*** ⇨便宜購買的機會。

<實 例>

General Trading Co., Ltd.

Market This Week

No. 118

(During September 15-22, 19 —)

U.S.A.

General

Despite a tight monetary control, the general trend of business for Taiwanese goods, except Textiles and Sundries, has been maintaining a keen buying demand. Reliable information reports that the government will relieve the monetary situation toward the year end. Strengthened by the demand for Christmas season and favorable prospects of business next year, prices for all Taiwanese goods are showing a general rising tendency.

Export

Iron & Steel

The car market remains quiet at present, but sales are gradually advancing. Three big motor-car manufacturers will need more iron & steel. Iron exports seem to be rising, though there were no large sales contracts concluded during last week.

Prices

Iron per ton	Spot	US $238.00
	October	US $237.00
	November	US $236.00
	December	US $236.00

Import

Home prices have fallen to low levels due to large-sized expansion of supply facilities among the big iron manufac-turers. But imports are active and keep the new outlet levels constant. The US scrap market is expected to be dull at least for the coming several weeks. This may be, therefore, the last opportunity for a good purchase.

通用貿易有限公司

本週市場

118 號

（19—年9月15—22日期間）

美國

一般性

雖然貨幣管制嚴格，除了紡織品和雜貨外，台灣貨品一般情勢一直維持強烈的購買需求。可靠的消息報告，在年末時政府將放鬆貨幣情勢。由於被耶誕季節的需求和對明年交易的有利展望所強化，所有台灣貨品的價格正顯示普遍上漲的趨勢。

外銷

鋼鐵

目前汽車市場持續平穩，但是銷售額逐漸增加。三大汽車製造廠商將需要更多的鋼鐵。雖然上週並未締結任何大銷售額的契約，鐵出口額似乎正在上漲。

價格

鐵每噸	現貨交貨價	美金238元正
	10月交貨價	美金237元正
	11月交貨價	美金236元正
	12月交貨價	美金236元正

進口

由於大鐵器製造商間，大規模地擴展供應設備，國內價格跌落到很低的水準。但是進口很活躍，並保持穩定的新銷售水準。預料美國鐵屑市場未來數週會呈現蕭條。因此，這或許是便宜購買的最後機會。

** ———

relieve〔rɪ′liv〕*v.* 放鬆；減輕

facility〔fə′sɪlətɪ〕*n.*（*pl.*）設備

dull〔dʌl〕*adj.* 蕭條的；滯銷的

※ ※ ※

Market vocabulary

1. 市場情況：

market condition　　state of market

trend of market　　tone of market

2. money market　貨幣市場　　stock market　存貨市場

rice market　米糧市場　　wheat market　小麥市場

cotton yarn market　棉紗市場　　stock change market　存貨變動市場

spot trading　現貨交易

3. strong market　強勁市場 ↔ easy market　鬆散市場

steady market　穩定市場 ↔ unsteady market　不穩定市場

calm market　平穩市場 ↔ wild market　狂亂市場

※ ※ ※

3 新產品報告 New Product Report

【實務須知】

· ***new product report*** ⇨新產品報導。廠商寄給代理店、零售商的銷售宣傳資料。

· ***cushion of air*** ⇨空氣墊

· ***fully loaded appliance*** ⇨完全裝滿的電氣製品

· ***Frigidaire attachment*** ⇨「富吉德」的附屬品；Frigidaire 爲電冰箱商標名

· ***with finger pressure*** ⇨以手指施壓

· ***flotation pad*** ⇨漂浮墊

〈實　例〉

New Product Report

A refrigerator that floats on a cushion of air is being marketed by our company. Why float a refrigerator ? Any housewife who has struggled to move a fully loaded appliance to clean behind it, or any husband who has moved one when painting walls can supply the answer.

The new Frigidaire attachment makes it possible to move the refrigerator with finger pressure and without marring floors. The special air flotation pad, which fits beneath the base, is connected to the blower on a household vacuum cleaner via the cleaner hose; air, discharged evenly through holes, in the flotation pad, lifts the refrigerator clear of the floor. Frigidaire expects to adapt the device to other heavy equipment.

新產品報導

本公司銷售一種漂浮在空氣墊上的電冰箱。電冰箱爲什麼要漂浮呢?任何一位曾經掙扎著移動完全裝滿的電氣製品，以清洗其背後的家庭主婦，或者任何一位油漆牆壁時，曾經移過這類製品的丈夫，都知道答案。

「富吉德」新型附屬品，只要手指施壓就能移動電冰箱，且不磨損地板。特殊的空氣漂浮墊，安裝在底座下，經由吸塵器的塑膠管和家庭用眞空吸塵器的風箱連接；漂浮墊的空氣，從洞孔均勻地釋出，將電冰箱舉起，離開地板。「富吉德」預料可以將此方法應用於其他重型設備。

** ______

Frigidaire〔,frɪdʒɪ'dɛr〕〔商標名〕電冰箱

mar〔mɑr〕*v.* 損毀；損傷

blower〔'bloɚ〕*n.* 風箱

【必備詞彙】

· ***cotton yarn*** ⇨ 棉紗
· ***scanty harvest*** ⇨ 歉收
· steady〔'stɛdɪ〕*adj.* 穩定的
· design〔dɪ'zaɪn〕*n.* 花樣
· ***hold off*** ⇨ 延緩
· ***approach him with a sale*** ⇨ 和他洽談買賣
· ***a promise for a purchase from us*** ⇨ 允諾向本公司採購

⁂ ⁂ ⁂

1. ***Cotton yarn*** has advanced to 760 Indian Rupees per 100 bales due to a ***scanty harvest*** this year.

   由於今年歉收，棉紗已漲到每一百包七百六十印度盧比。

   * Indian Rupee 印度盧比（＝100 *naye paise*）

2. The market remains ***steady***, which means that prices will not be lower. We think it advisable for you to make a purchase now because if demand rises, they are very likely to advance sharply.

   市場持續穩定，意即價格不會下跌。本公司認爲貴公司現在購買乃明智之舉，因爲若需求增加，價格很可能急速上漲。

3. Competition has been so serious this year that your ***designs*** and prices are hard to sell. But with a 10% discount it may be possible to push your goods.

   今年競爭如此厲害，致以貴公司的花樣和價格難以售出。但是打九折，或許可以促銷貨品。

4. Due to a policy alteration, there has been a great drop in prices. Consequently, we request you to ***hold off our*** order until favorable tone is noticed.

   由於政策變更，價格大幅下降了。因此，本公司要求貴公司將我方的訂貨延緩，直到通知您情況有利時。

5. Further to our last report which I sent from New Jersey on April 1, I am writing this in the office of Messrs. Roderick Assingham & Bros., where I have been furnished with the news that Mr. Blueneck Hope, the vice president of TRC will visit Taiwan next month for the purchase of the newest cassette tape recorder. I have ***approached him with a sale*** and received

a promise for a purchase from us.

繼續我方4月1日從紐澤西寄去的上封報告，我寫此信時，人在羅德利克·亞辛罕和布魯斯公司，我從那兒得到消息，TRC公司副董事長布魯尼克·哈普先生，下個月將前往台灣，採購最新型卡式錄音機。我已經和他洽談買賣，並得其允諾向本公司採購。

⁂ ⁂ ⁂

4 社交電文 Social Messages

【實務須知】

- ***branch staff*** ⇨分公司全體職員
- ***request the honor of your presence*** ⇨恭請貴公司蒞臨
- ***R.S.V.P.*** = *Répondez s'il vous plaît* ⇨敬請回覆
- ***a full measure*** ⇨全盤性

<實 例>

a. The newly appointed branch manager, Mr. David Wu and his branch staff of Taiwan Electric Co., Ltd. request the honor of your presence at dinner Monday, the lst of April at five o'clock, P.M.
The Madison Square Garden Hotel
R.S.V.P.

b. The president and directors of The Oriental Trading Co., Ltd. offer their hearty congratulations for the Christmas season and best wishes for a Happy New Year.

c. The president and directors of Far Eastern Co., Ltd.

wish you a prosperous future and all good luck with your new branch.

Best wishes for your grand opening and success for your new branch.

d. Congratulations on winning the Award for Services to British Industry. You richly deserve the high honor.

e. Best wishes for a happy and prosperous New Year. May the new year bring you and yours a full measure of success and prosperity.

a. 新近指派的分公司經理—吳大衞先生，和台灣電氣有限公司的分公司全體職員，恭請貴公司蒞臨4月1日，星期一下午五點鐘，在梅德森廣場花園旅館舉行的晚宴，敬請回覆。

b. 東方貿易有限公司董事長及全體董事，誠心恭賀聖誕佳節，並祝新年快樂。

c. 遠東有限公司董事長及全體董事，祝福貴公司未來昌隆,並祝新分公司一切好運。

祝福貴公司新分公司堂皇開幕，並祝成功。

d. 恭喜贏得英國工業服務獎，貴公司得此殊榮，實至名歸。

e. 祝福新年快樂、昌隆。願新的一年帶給您和貴公司全盤成功和昌盛。

第2章 介紹和推薦

Introduction & Recommendation

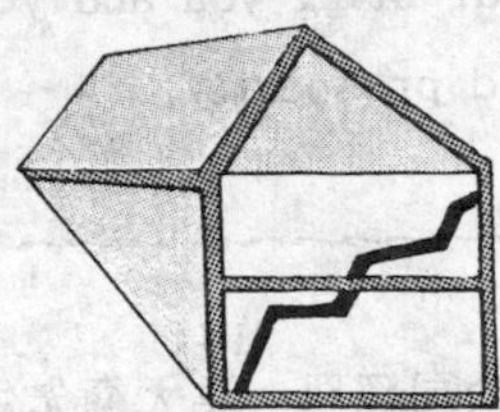

與重視資歷的我國所不同的，歐美人士相當重視介紹信。介紹人與被介紹人受到同等重視，賦予介紹、推薦以權威。貿易公司在派駐國外代表時，經常函請國外客戶及銀行寫介紹信，據說頗具效果，因此，我想國內人士也不妨考慮加以利用。還有，若是您被委託寫介紹或推薦信函時，不要只是因爲情面或形式而寫，應該正確而客觀地陳述。因爲您對被介紹人的品格和能力都有責任，所以，諸如您與被介紹人的關係、介紹的目的及其能力、爲人都應確實述及。

通常介紹函交予委託人的時候都是不封口的，以示介紹的眞正精神。最具體的是在名片或信封左下角，寫上 Introducing Mr. Smith 之類。那麼，委託人即可帶著這封信或事先寄送，而後前往面談。

以下爲名片介紹的例子：

Introducing Mr. H. Bake Williams,
who is an importer in
"Electronic Goods."
David Wang
President
AB & C Trading Co., Ltd.

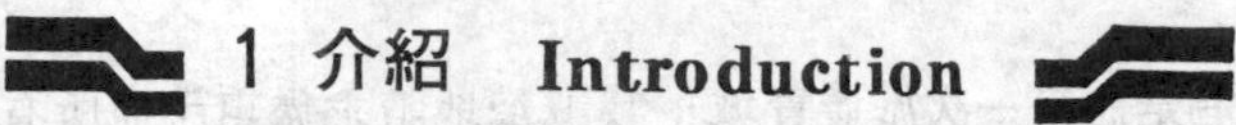

1 介紹 Introduction

【實務須知】

- ***the bearer of this letter*** ⇨持有此信的人
- ***get acquainted with～*** ⇨熟知～；熟悉～
- ***render him all the assistance*** ⇨給予他所有的協助

＜實 例＞

Please permit me to introduce Mr. David Wu the bearer of this letter, Manager of Hong Kong branch of The Oriental Trading Co., Ltd., with whom we have had business relations for many years and is believed to be one of the most trustworthy firms in our city.

He is going to visit your city for the purpose of getting acquainted with the general business customs and conditions in order to organize a new branch there.

As this is his first trip to your city, I sincerely ask you to render him all the assistance possible and facilitate the purpose of his trip.

Yours faithfully,

請容許我介紹持有此信的人—吳大衞先生，他是東方貿易有限公司香港分公司的經理。本公司和該公司有多年的交易關係，彼並被公認爲本市最值得信賴的公司之一。

他拜訪貴城，是爲了熟知一般的商務慣例和情況，以便在那兒組織新分公司。

因爲這是他第一次旅遊貴城，我誠摯地請求您惠予他所有可能的協助，並助其完成此行之目的。

**

trustworthy〔ˈtrʌst,wɝðɪ〕*adj.* 可靠的；可信賴

facilitate〔fəˈsɪlə,tet〕*v.* 幫助

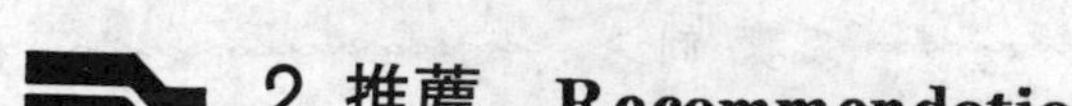

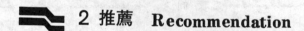

2 推薦 Recommendation

【實務須知】

- ***to whom it may concern*** ⇨ 敬致關係當事人；寫於證明文件起首做一般稱呼，有如中文的敬啓者
- ***in the employment of*** ⇨ 受雇於
- ***confidently recommend*** ⇨ 有信心地推薦
- ***conduct business*** ⇨ 經營商務
- chief manager ⇨ 主管
- ***be highly appreciated by me*** ⇨ 我會感激不盡

<實 例>

To whom it may concern:

Mr. David Wu, the bearer of this letter, has been engaged in the export of general cotton & rayon piece goods since 1971 in the employment of The International Trading Co., Ltd., Taipei.

He is a most reliable person and also an active businessman with profound knowledge of foreign trade, whom I can confidently recommend to anybody requiring his service.

As I have been conducting business with him for more than ten years as the chief manager of his department, I know him very well. Anything you may be in a position to do for him will be highly appreciated by me.

Yours faithfully

敬致關係當事人：

送此信者─吳大衞先生，自從1971年受雇於台北的國際貿易有限公司，一直從事一般棉織品和縲縈布匹的出口。

他是個最可靠的人，也是個活躍的生意人，深具對外貿易知識，我有信心把他推薦給任何需要他服務的人。

因爲身爲他那部門的主管，我曾經和他一同經營商務十多年，對他非常了解。若蒙您幫忙他任何事，我將感激不盡。

**

rayon〔ˈrean〕*n.* 縲縈　profound〔prəˈfaʊnd〕*adj.* 深奧的

實用例句

【必備詞彙】

- ***to assist him in the matter*** ⇨為了支助他這件事
- ***favor and attention*** ⇨支持與關照
- ***to prove his worth*** ⇨證明他的才幹
- ***take the liberty of～*** ⇨冒昧～
- correspondent〔ˌkɔrəˈspɑndənt〕*n.* 商務關係人
- bookkeeper〔ˈbʊkˌkipɚ〕*n.* 記帳員
- intimate〔ˈɪntəmɪt〕*adj.* 熟稔的；精湛的

⁂ ⁂ ⁂

1. We are pleased to introduce Mr. Stephen Wang, who is very eager to extend his export trade to your city. ***To assist him in the matter***, we recommend him to your kind favor and attention.

   茲樂意向貴公司介紹王史蒂芬先生,他非常渴望將出口業務擴展到貴城。為了協助他這件事，我方向他推薦貴公司,請惠予支持與關照。

2. We have the pleasure of recommending Mr. David Wu, a most trustworthy and reliable agent, with whom we have been doing business for many years.

   茲樂意向貴公司推薦吳大衞先生,他是一個最值得信賴、最可靠的代理商，本公司已經和彼有好幾年生意來往。

3. This is to certify that Mr. Paul Li has entered the Yu Tah Commercial School in September, 19— and finished the three year course in June, 19—. We cordially recommend him to

anybody who is looking for a young man willing and able to ***prove his worth.***

此乃證明李保羅先生於19一年9月就讀於育達職校，並於19一年六月完成三年的課程。謹把他推薦給任何欲徵求年青人，願意並且能夠證明其才幹的人。

* certify〔ˈsɝtə͵faɪ〕*v.* 證明（合格）

cordially〔ˈkɔrdʒəlɪ〕*adv.* 眞誠地；謹

4. During college life he showed excellence both in study and sport. He was especially good at English composition. I recommend him as a diligent, healthy, capable, and reliable young man.

在大學期間，他在學業和運動兩方面的表現都很優異，尤其精專英文作文。我推薦他這個勤勉、健康、能幹、又可靠的年青人。

5. I take the liberty of introducing Mr. John Chen, representative of the New York Times. You would greatly oblige me if you would assist him during his stay in your city.

玆冒昧向貴公司介紹紐約時報的代表——陳約翰先生。在他停留貴城期間，若蒙貴公司支助，我會非常感激的。

6. He is an excellent correspondent, bookkeeper, and rapid typist. He is not only able to speak excellent English but has an intimate knowledge of general office work.

他是個優秀的商務關係人、記帳員，打字速度也很快。他不僅能說流利的英文，而且對一般辦公室業務十分熟悉。

⁂ ⁂ ⁂

第3章

應徵就業

Employment Application

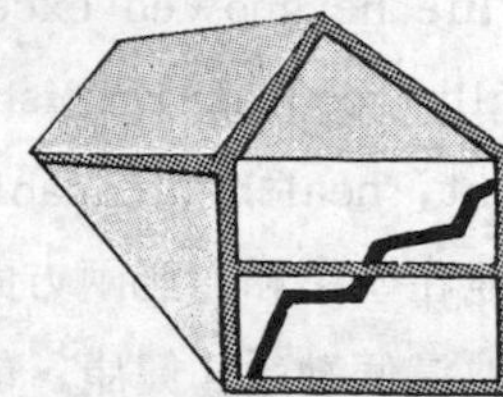

有意從事貿易工作者，當然都應該具備書寫求職函的能力。如果在純國內性質的公司，也許只要用國語，即能應付裕如了。但是如果想要在外商、外貿公司工作，英文是絕對必要的工具。尤其目前，與國外生意往來，而必須在國外設立合併公司、新公司、分公司的趨勢越來越高，英文能力已經成爲決定商務成功與否的重要關鍵。求職時，無論是看報紙的求職欄，或是經人介紹，都可發現雇主的最大要求無非是形式、內容明快流暢的優秀英文。申請函須說明：

1. 來此求職的經過。
2. 詳細明晰地說明自己的學歷、經驗。
3. 申訴熱衷這份工作的理由。
4. 能夠查詢本人人格、能力的地方。
5. 希望接獲面談通知。

通常履歷表都採文章形式，但是，教育經歷部份可兼而採用條例法。最重要的是正確認識自己的人格、能力、經驗等，加以客觀、具體、明確地表達。所以，自己的優點、特長都須詳細記載。此外，履歷表的標題可用

Curriculum Vitae **,** ***Personal History*** **,** ***Life Sketch*** 等等。

*　　*　　*

✦ **開頭部分**可以採用：

1. In response to your advertisement, I wish to apply for the position …
2. Having learned that, please consider me an applicant for (I should like to apply for)……
3. I learn from Mr. — that …

✦ **學歷部分**

在學歷方面務請明確表示，受過這份工作的相關教育，更要具體完全地敍述工作經驗，最好能附寄推薦函或證明書。結尾辭與一般書信無異，開頭稱呼採Gentlemen 。

1 應徵 Application

【實務須知】

- ***position of clerk*** ⇨ 辦事員的職位
- ***will prove useful*** ⇨ 證明是有幫助的
- ***personal interview*** ⇨ 私人面談
- ***at your convenience*** ⇨ 在您得便時；悉聽尊便

〈實 例〉

Gentlemen:

Having found your advertisement in today's *China Times* regarding a vacancy in your office, I wish to apply for the position of clerk, which you have specified.

I feel confident that I can meet your special requirements indicating that the candidate must have a good knowledge of English, for I graduated from the Department of Foreign Languages and Literature, National Taiwan University, three years ago.

In addition to my study of English while in the university, I have worked for three years as a correspondent in the firm of International Trading Co., Ltd., Taipei.

My main reason for changing my employment is to gain more experience with a superior trading company like yours. I believe that my education and experience will prove useful for work in your office.

I enclose herewith my personal history, certificate of graduation and letter of recommendation from the chairman of the University. I shall be obliged if you will give me a personal interview at your convenience.

Yours truly,

敬啓者：

在今天的中國時報上，發現貴公司有關職位空缺的廣告，我希望應徵貴公司列出的辦事員職位。

貴公司指明應徵者必須英文程度很好，我自信能滿足此特別的要求，因為我三年以前從國立台灣大學外國語文學系畢業。

除了在大學時研讀英文外，我在台北的國際貿易有限公司做了三年商務關係人。

我換工作主要的理由，是想從像貴公司這樣優異的貿易公司，吸取更多的經驗。相信我的學歷和經驗會證明對貴公司的工作是有幫助的。

茲隨函附寄上履歷表、畢業證書、和大學系主任的推薦函。若蒙得便，給我私人面談的機會，則不勝感激。

**

vacancy〔ˈvekənsɪ〕*n.* 空職；空缺　indicate〔ˈɪndɪ,ket〕*v.* 指示；指明

correspondent〔,kɔrəˈspɑndənt〕*n.* 商務關係人

certificate〔sɚˈtɪfəkɪt〕*n.* 證書

2 求才廣告及應徵 Help Wanted & Application

【實務須知】

- ***an expert male accountant*** ⇨一名專業男性會計師
- ***salary expected*** ⇨希望待遇
- ***apply for～*** ⇨應徵～
- ***no chance of advancement*** ⇨無晉陞的機會
- ***curriculum vitae*** ⇨履歷表

＜實 例＞

Help Wanted

Large American firm requires an expert male accountant with fairly good knowledge of English. Age up to 30. Reply stating age, education, experience and salary expected. Box No. 29413, Taipei.

Taipei, March 12, 19—

Box No. 29413

Taipei

Gentlemen:

In response to your advertisement in the *China Times* of March 8, I wish to apply for the position of accountant.

I am twenty-nine years old and a graduate of Taiwan University. My experience in this line of work includes four years as an accountant of the General Commercial Co., Ltd. My reason for leaving my present employment is because they are closing their Taipei Branch and I see no chance of advancement.

I am enclosing herewith my curriculum vitae and my testimonials, and believe that they may be found satisfactory. With respect to salary, I shall require $30,000 a month. I assure you that if appointed, I will do my best to give you satisfaction.

Yours very truly,

求　才

大美商公司需要一名專業男性會計師，熟諳英文。年齡在三十歲以下。應徵函請寫明年齡、教育程度、經驗和希望待遇。請寄台北29413信箱。

台北，19—年3月12日

台北 29413 信箱

敬啓者：

答覆您 3 月 8 日在中國時報的廣告，我希望應徵會計師一職。

我現年二十九歲，畢業於台灣大學。我從事這方面的工作經歷，包括在通用商業有限公司當了四年的會計師。我離開現職的原因是因為，該公司將結束台北分公司的業務，而我覺得無晉陞的機會。

茲隨函奉寄履歷表及資格證明書，相信貴公司將會感到滿意。至於薪水，我要求一個月三萬元。若蒙錄取，我必定盡全力使貴公司滿意。

** ——————————

testimonial 〔ˌtɛstəˈmonɪəl〕 *n.*（品格、行為、資格等的）證明書

appoint 〔əˈpɔɪnt〕 任命；指派

 3 履歷表 Personal History 

Personal History

March 10, 19—

Name in Full: Pin Wu

Date of Birth: September 18, 1957

Age: 29 years

Present Address: 12 Yen Ping N. Rd., Taipei

Permanent Address: 12 Yen Ping N. Rd., Taipei

Education:

September 1963-June 1969 Tachih Primary School

September 1969-June 1972 Tachih Middle School

September 1972-June 1975 Cheng-Kung High School

October 1975-June 1979 National Taiwan University

Working Experience:

June 1981-March 1985 General Trading Co., Ltd.,
Taipei, employed as a clerk

Awards:

Was awarded scholarship of National Taiwan University, September 1976.

Won first place in the International English Oratorial Contest held on October 15, 1977.

Reference: Professor Li-yang Wang of National Taiwan University, Economics Department

I hereby declare the above to be true and correct.

Pin Wu

履歷表

全名：　吳彬　　19－年3月10日

出生日期：1957年9月18日

年齡：　二十九歲

現在住址：台北市延平北路12號

永久住址：台北市延平北路12號

學　歷：

1963年9月—1969年6月　大直國小

1969年9月—1972年6月　大直國中

1972年9月—1975年6月　成功高中

1975年10月—1979年6月　國立台灣大學

工作經驗：

1981年6月—1985年3月　台北通用貿易有限公司

受雇爲職員

曾獲得之獎賞：

於1976年9月獲頒國立台灣大學書卷獎。

於1977年10月15日舉行的國際英文演講比賽贏得第一名。

證明人：國立台灣大學經濟系王力揚教授

茲據此宣佈以上所述爲眞實及正確的。

吳　彬

【必備詞彙】

- ***at the suggestion of～*** ⇨ 經由～的建議
- post-graduate〔post'grædʒʊɪt〕*adj*. 研究學程的；畢業後繼續研究的
- official〔ə'fɪʃəl〕*n*. 職員
- ***a fair trial*** ⇨ 公平的試用

⁂　⁂　⁂

1. ***At the suggestion of*** Mr. Henry Chen, I am writing to you about the vacancy in your office.

   經由陳亨利先生的建議，我寫信應徵貴公司懸缺的職位。

2. I graduated from Ming Chuan Commercial College about two years ago. Since then I have been engaged in the business of foreign trade under the employment of The General Trading Co., Ltd.

   我於兩年前畢業於銘傳商專。自從那時起，我就一直受雇於通用貿易有限公司，從事對外貿易的業務。

3. I am now in a ***post-graduate*** course of National Chung Hsin University and have been doing research in Business Administration. I have no special experience as an ***official***, but I believe that my education has been sufficient for me to fill the position satisfactorily.

我目前在國立中興大學研究所，從事企業管理方面的研究。我沒有特殊的專業經驗，但是相信我的學歷足堪勝任這份工作。

* Business Administration 企業管理

4. English was one of my most favorite subjects at school, and I assure you, if you will give me ***a fair trial***, I will do all in my power to do an excellent job.

英文是我在學校時最喜歡的科目之一，我可以向您確保，若蒙貴公司公平試用，我將盡全力做最優秀的表現。

5. I have learned through Mr. David Wang, one of the directors of International Textile Manufacturers Co., Ltd. of Taipei, that you are in need of an office clerk who, besides having a general knowledge of your trade, should also be proficient in Business English and International law.

經由台北的國際紡織製造有限公司董事之一王大衞先生得知，貴公司正缺一位公司職員，除了要有貴公司貿易的一般知識，還須精通商用英文及國際法方面的能力。

* proficient〔prəˈfɪʃənt〕*adj.* 精通的；熟諳的

⁂ ⁂ ⁂

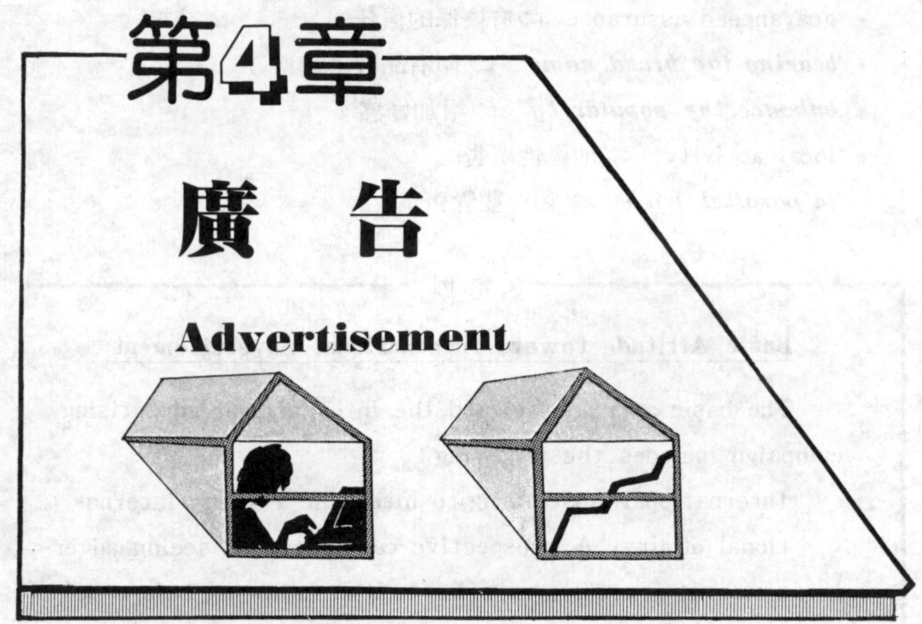

廣告分為利用直接廣告以求才或推銷商品的求才廣告、商品廣告，及欲將產品的良好印象深植於一般大衆的企業廣告。前者在報紙、雜誌上直接向相關人士廣告時，只訴求於有興趣的人，有特定目標，只要將必需的資料，簡明、清晰地刊載出來即可。至於企業廣告，是對不直接相關，又沒有興趣的大衆廣告，所以需要高度的技巧，簡而言之，要巧妙的引出人類共同關心的事，還得饒富趣味。

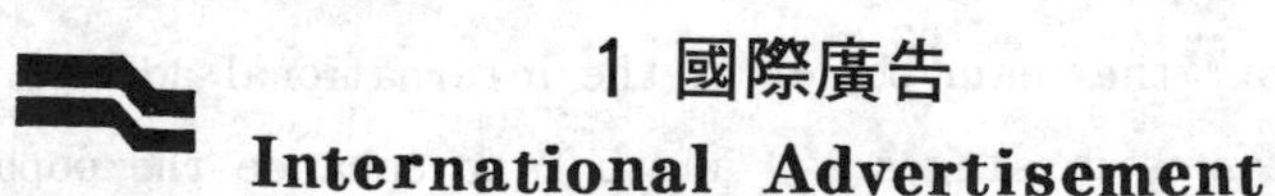

1 國際廣告 International Advertisement

【實務須知】

- ***international advertising campaign*** ⇨國際廣告活動
- ***prospective customer*** ⇨未來的顧客；可能的客戶
- quality indicative ⇨品質表示

- guaranteed assurance ⇨有擔保的信任
- ***bearing the brand name*** ⇨印有品牌（商標）
- ***enhance the popularity*** ⇨增加好感
- local activity ⇨地區性廣告
- ***in parallel with*** ⇨和…雙管齊下

〈實 例〉

Basic Attitude toward International Advertisement

The basic attitude toward the international advertising campaign includes the following:

International Advertising to meet the current international affairs. A prospective customer, on seeing advertisements, usually experiences the following before deciding to buy a product.

a. Familiarity with the brand name.

b. Understanding the brand name.

c. Guaranteed assurance of the quality indicative of the brand name.

d. Purchases of items bearing the brand name. The attitude toward advertising varies according to the particular stage the attention is focused on.

At first, the main object of the international advertisement comes in stages a) and b) to enhance the popularity of the brand name, and to have the brand name throughly understood by those who already knew it. Needless to say, the ultimate goal is to lead the customer from stage (c) to stage (d). We intend to attain this goal through local activities in parallel with our international advertising.

國際廣告基本的態度

對國際廣告活動基本的態度如下：

國際廣告迎合目前的國際事務。看廣告時，可能的顧客在決定購買某一產品之前，通常會有如下的經歷：

a. 對該品牌名稱的熟悉度。

b. 對該品牌名稱的了解度。

c. 對該品牌表示的品質有確切的信心。

d. 購買印有該品牌的貨物。對廣告的態度依注意力集中的特殊階段而不同。

首先，國際廣告主要的目的在 a 和 b 兩階段，以增強該品牌受歡迎的程度，並使那些已經認識該品牌的人，徹底了解。不用說，終極的目標是引導顧客從 c 階段進到 d 階段。我們打算經由地區性活動與國際性廣告雙管齊下，達成此一目標。

2 私人廣告 Personal Advertisement

<實 例>

Help Wanted

British Leading Firm urgently requires young male clerk with good knowledge of English. University graduate preferable. High salary. Apply with personal history to P.O.

Box 9145, Taipei.

求 才

卓越的英商公司急需熟語英文的年輕男職員。大學畢尤佳。高薪。應徵請寄上履歷表至台北郵政9145。

〈實 例〉

Land for Sale

Outstanding land beautiful landscape with mountain & seashore, Chinese garden with 150 square meters, western style house. Location Hualien commanding panoramic view. Willing to sell at one million dollars. Telephone (02)2579481 Taipei.

土地拋售

出色的土地一塊，風景秀麗，有高山、海灘、及一五〇平方公尺大的中式庭園、西式洋房。座落在花蓮，可觀賞花蓮全景。

願以一百萬元出售。請電台北(02) 2579481 。

** ———

panoramic〔,pænə'ræmɪk〕*adj.* 全景的

<實例>

Situation Wanted

Efficient in English and German, University graduate, male, 29. Seek job at large foreign trading firm. Please write to Box No. 8594. Taipei.

求 職

精通英文和德文、大學畢，男，二十九歲。願在外國大貿易公司工作。請寫信到台北郵政8594 。

3 商品廣告 Merchandise Advertisement

【實務須知】

- ***exciting gleaming finish*** ⇨最後塗上一層動人的、閃亮的色彩
- ***soft padded*** ⇨裝填柔軟的
- ***build to satisfy～*** ⇨爲滿足～而造

<實例>

Drive in spacious, beautiful comfort ……BMW.

Put yourself in a BMW.

Give your car an exciting gleaming finish.

A soft padded interior

Powerful yet economical engine

BMW has all this and more.

Built to satisfy for a long, long time. Over one million satisfied customers in more than 100 countries.

BMW…… the modern answer to modern driving.

駕駛寬敞、美麗、舒適的……BMW

置身於BMW中吧！

最後給您的車上一層動人的、閃亮的色彩

柔軟的內裝

強力卻經濟的引擎

BMW擁有這所有的特點，及其它更多優點。

這是爲了長久滿足您的需求而造的。一百多個國家，超過一百萬的顧客都感到滿意的

BMW……現代駕駛的現代答覆。

4 企業廣告 Institutional Advertisement

【實務須知】

- ***process control*** ⇨生產控制工程
- ***petroleum***〔pə'trolɪəm〕*n.* 石油
- ***specialized instruments*** ⇨專門特殊的機器

<實 例>

Who's helping to bring gas out of the sea?

Maxbuilder ……

a world leader in process control

With specialized instruments that guarantee perfect control.
From the south sea to the Arabian Desert: from Alaska to South Africa, to the Indian Gulf, Maxbuilder goes where the petroleum business is.
You will find Maxbuilder in 100 countries because that's where our business is.

誰幫人們把石油抽出海底？
馬克比德……
領先全世界的生產控制工程
以專門特殊的機器，保證控制得恰到好處。
從南海到阿拉伯沙漠：從阿拉斯加到南非、印度灣，只要哪裡有石油業，哪裡就會有馬克比德。
您可以在一百個國家發現馬克比德，因爲那是我們的業務所在。

PART Ⅵ

Telegram & Telex

電報與電傳

第1章

電報概要

Telegram Outline

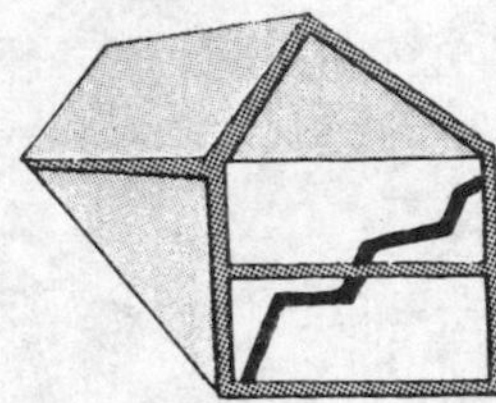

商場如戰場，時間更是致勝的重要因素，雖然對外貿易大部份仍以書信往來爲主，但是於商務洽談中發生緊急狀況時，即使限時專送也無濟於事，此時非得利用 **telecommunications**（電磁通信）不可了。telecommunications 包括 **telegram**（電報）、**telephone**（電話）、**telex**（電傳）及 **phototelegram**（傳眞電報機），貿易上以 telegram（電報）及 telex（電傳）應用最廣。拍發的資料都由國際電信局（ITA）處理，利用無線通訊及有線專用通訊系統，達到迅速通信的目的，其速度遠比使用書信爲快，需要高度技術與龐大設備，而費用也跟著昇高，所以，必須考慮異乎一般信文的電文體（Telegraphese），利用簡潔的文字以減低費用。電報可以用羅馬拼音及中文，但是從翻譯程序與文體的簡潔程度來看，還是英文通信來得經濟實惠。在此，就從 Telex 需要用到的基本知識 — 國際電報開始說明。

A. 國際電報 International Telegram

國際電報依業務區分，有公務、私務、及電信業務通訊三種，貿易使用者屬於私務電報。根據通訊速度則又可以分為L/T(書信電報，Letter telegram)，Ordinary(普通電報)和Urgent(緊急電報)。費用之計算，以字計費，包括本文、指定字(Urgent及L/T都有指定字)、收信者名稱(即Cable Address，電報掛號)、發信者名稱等。

1. ***Ordinary***(普通電報)

最低收費標準(基本費)在七字以內，按收到的先後順序拍發，發信後約五～六小時可抵達對方。若為深夜接收到，則需等到第二天早晨才拍發。可使用明語及暗語。

2. ***Urgent***(緊急電報)

最低收費標準也在七字以內，一個字的收費為普通電報的兩倍，但優先拍發，須在收報人姓名住址前加註"URGENT"的標識(指定字)，並將此指定字作一字計費。可用明語或暗語。

3. ***L/T***(書信電報)

最低收費標準在廿二字以內，一個字的費用是普通電報的一半，但必須等到Urgent及Ordinary之後才拍發，也須在收報人姓名住址前加註LT標幟(指定字)。L/T不可使用暗語。

總歸以上所述，列表如下：

種　類	指定字	費用比率	基本費字數	用　字
普通電報	不需	1	7字	明語、暗語
緊急電報	Urgent	2	7字	明語、暗語
書信電報	L/T	½	22字	明語

費用比例（以具體字數表示費用比例）

L/T（½倍）	Ordinary（1倍）Full Rate	Urgent（2倍）
—	7字（最低）	—
—	8字	—
—	9字	—
—	10字	—
22字(最低)	11字	—
23字	—	—
24字	12字	—
25字	—	—
26字	13字	—
27字	—	—
28字	14字	7字（最低）

只就費用比例來看，以 L/T 最為便宜，但是列出具體數字後，不難發現，費率最低的是 Ordinary 七字以內的基本費，一直到十字以內都以 Ordinary 最便宜。L/T 需於 Ordinary 超出十一字、L/T 超出二十二字以後，才是最便宜的。

B. 電報用字

一、電文中使用的文字、數字、記號如下：

1. 電文中使用的文字是英文 alphabet （字母）中的二十六個大寫字母。

   A, B, C, D, …, X, Y, Z

2. 數字爲 0～9 之間，共十個數字。

   1, 2, 3, …8, 9, 0

3. 記號有〔。〕〔，〕〔：〕〔？〕〔'〕〔″〕〔-〕〔（）〕〔/〕〔+〕〔“ ”〕〔×〕〔%〕〔‰〕。

獨立使用時，〔%〕以3個字母，〔‰〕以4個字母計算，相當於一個字，〔？〕也是一個字。〔“ ”〕〔（）〕一組是一個字。數字、記號、略號、暗號都以五個爲一字。15×35，50%，92/6a 各是一字，38.3%、3″×15″就分別以兩字計算了。

二、明語（*Plain Words*）

Plain Words 僅指該國國語之意，不含特別意思，是最常用者。例如 REPLY BY TENTH。明語限用中文（四碼）、英文、法文、德文、荷蘭文、西班牙文、葡萄牙文、印尼文及羅馬字、拼音日文。

三、暗語（*Code, or Secret language*）

暗語的採用無非是爲了節省費用。Code 是五個字以內的造語，有異於表面的特殊意思。即使是普通字在十五個字母以內，也算暗語，如 BEAUTIFUL = please reply within a week之類意思的話語。Code book（暗語錄）一直到最近還未普遍使用，但是，伴隨著 Telex 的發達，已漸漸引起大衆的關切。Code book 之中有 public code book（通用暗語錄）和 private code（私製暗語），通用暗語錄中，五個字母（5-letter code）的有Acme，Bentley's，三個字母（3-letter code）有Oriental 3-letter Code，Schofield's 3-letter Code，Oriental Improved Code等等。Telex 主要作爲總公司與國外分公司、合作企業、和出差地之間通信之用。所以，以各公司自製的暗語錄爲主。可是，LT 不准使用暗語，連普通字的暗語都不可以。

C. 電報的結構

以下是商用電報的結構：

<table>
<tr><td>HK 1218 NDIO 1358 ELP 1866 ← 經由路線
①NEWDELHI 22/18 20 958 ← 發報地點及發報時間</td></tr>
<tr><td>LT ← 電報等級
DAIPRINT TAIPEI ← 收報人電報掛號
②YOURS 10TH ACCEPTABLE IF 650 CABLE ← 本文
ACCEPTANCE BY 30TH HERE LICENCE
ISSUED MARKET DULL
STANDARD ← 發報人電報掛號</td></tr>
<tr><td>③COL 10 650 30 ←內容對照</td></tr>
</table>

電報必須在固定的信紙上填入①②③各項，拍發出去。①和③都是電信局的記載事項，發信人只要填具第②部分即可。參考，第①部分第一行由左端起，是爲台北電信局給最終收信局的電信通過記號或號碼。其右則爲新德里的發信局給台北電信局的通過記號與號碼，最右端是爲新德里發信局的發信號碼。第二行左端是發信地名，22／18 表最低計費字數 22，實際字數 18，20 958 指當地發信時刻爲20日9點58分。這些記號、號碼都隨著電報之不同而異。第③部分是 collation（校對），意思是說，希望您從指定電報種類到署名，尤其是有數字或數目之處，重覆檢視無誤。第②部分是發信人塡寫之處，LT是指定字，DAIPRINT TAIPEI是收報人電報掛號（Cable address）。以下的YOURS到DULL是本文，最後的 STANDARD 是發信人電報掛號。字數的計算包括以上各項目的所有字數。

D. 字數的計算

字數是按照每字多少錢的基準以算出費用的根據，但是內中細目非常複雜，本處僅就原則加以說明。

1. 明語以**十五個字母**以內爲一字計算

   by cable（2字）> telegraphically（1字）

   can accept（2字）> acceptable（1字）

2. 暗語、數字、記號、略語等，**五個字母**以內，算作一個字。

   DLP 18.25（2字）> DL/85（1字）

   2S 8d（2字）> 2S/8d（1字）

3. 將暗語做成明語，**十五個字母**以內，算作一個字。

   Christmas = please cable the order to us by 30th

   Approve = please cable by return if you can accept our proposal

   但是，若爲造語，視同記號，五個字母以內，算作一個字。如

   APDOX = In response to your proposal, we quite agree to it.

4. 辭典中有的單字、專有名詞、國名等，以連結號連結起來者，以**十五個字母**以內算作一個字。若字典上無連接號而擅自以連接號連結，亦不予承認。收件地名，是2個字，而無連接號者，仍視同一個字，如New York，San Francisco等。若將兩字合起來書寫，以十五個字母以內爲一字。

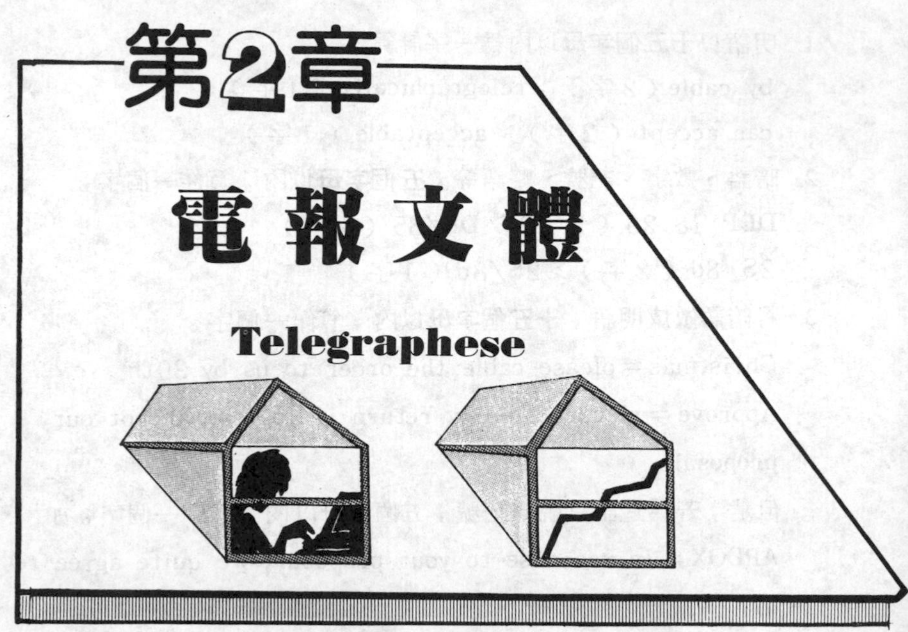

為了節約費用，電報必須簡潔地敍述主旨，於是產生了類似新聞標題的特殊**電文體**（**Telegraphese**）。

例如，普通信文中We will accept your order if you allow us to ship during September的句子，若簡化為accept your order if shipment September allowed亦完全不失原意，若只強調亟欲喚起對方關切的要點，而寫為ORDER ACCEPTABLE IF SEPTEMBER SHIPMENT，則不但簡潔，意思也傳達到了。如此這般，藉著改變語順、詞類，只強調中心點的功夫，使它變成電文體。甚至可能省略 be 動詞、冠詞、介系詞、助動詞、連接詞，僅僅適切地組合名詞、形容詞、疑問詞、動詞（原形與過去式，進行式）而為一強力復簡明的電文體了。

但是，若單單熟悉電文體，却不足以達到期許的效果。首先要(1)具備充分的貿易實務與Business English的知識，(2)熟知交易的本體，(3)英語實力（作文、文法、閱讀之綜合能力），(4)熟語電文相關知識、技巧，綜合發揮以上能力，才能撰寫出有效的電文。並且應了解，如何強調交易現況與將來的展望，才能得到對方的認同，也要能判斷如何誘導對方，才能令他們了解我方的誠意。請看以下的基本句型。

1. 普通信文：In compliance to your letter of 10th, we have opened L/C today.

電　　文：YOURS 10TH L/C OPENED TODAY

省略連接詞、be 動詞。

2. 普通信文：The market here is advancing considerably. Please cable us when you can ship the goods.

電　　文：MARKET ADVANCING CABLE WHEN SHIPPABLE

省略 be 動詞，使用時間副詞，ship 換成形容詞。

3. 普通信文：We will accept your proposal if you delete article No. 9.

電　　文：ACCEPTING PROPOSAL IF NO.9 DELETED

將助動詞去掉，動詞改用進行式，delete使用被動式（過去分詞）。

4. 普通信文：We obtained the export license, but your L/C does not arrive. Please inform us why you do not open it.

電　　文：LICENSE OBTAINED INFORM WHY L/C LATE

obtain 變成被動態，利用疑問詞。省略主詞、述詞。

5. 普通信文：The market here is so active that our stocks are almost exhausted. Please send the goods as soon as possible.

電　文：MARKET ACTIVE STOCKS EXHAUSTED SHIP IMMEDIATELY

省略 be 動詞，使用祈使句。

6. 普通信文：We offer you the goods at the same price, though the market here is strong.

電　文：OFFER SAME PRICE DESPITE MARKET STRONG

換成連接詞 despite 。省略名詞、介系詞。

由以上的例子可以了解，由普通信文變成電文的概要。

其次，要懂得不以 STOP 作爲前後兩句話的界限，因爲 STOP 要多算一字，可用名詞、動詞命令型置於兩句話中間，做爲分界。前面例句 2 、 4 、 5 就是其例。請詳細分析以下例句。

1. YOURS FIFTH ACCEPT MAILING SHIPPING INSTRUCTION CONFIRM

已收到貴公司5日的報價。藉附寄之裝運指示，確認訂單。

2. YOURS Y8321 ACCEPTABLE SUBJECT 85.25 S5812 SHIPMENT END JULY

預備承諾貴公司第 Y8321 號報價單，第 5812 號樣品，$85.25，以 7 月底裝船爲條件。

3. EXTEND CREDIT 6018 END SEPTEMBER PERMITTING PARTIAL SHIPMENT ANDY TYPHOON SHIPMENT UNABLE

請求將第 6018 號信用狀，延期至 9 月底。由於安迪颱風的關係，不能裝船，請允許分批裝運。

4. 有關您 15 日的詢價,告知貴公司五千噸的鋼板，每噸二百五十美元,到漢堡 CIF 價 8 月裝船。以 20 日以前回函抵達本地爲限。大同製鋼發信。House 公司收。將上文寫成電文如下：

(1) L/T（書信電報）

LT

HOUSE HAMBURG

YOURS FIFTEENTH OFFER FIVETHOUSAND TONS

DOLLAR TWOHUNDRED FIFTY CIF SHIPMENT

AUGUST REPLY HERE BY TWENTIETH

DAIDO（18 個字）

(2) Ordinary（普通電報）

雙方熟悉之事物，應該省略。

HOUSE HAMBURG

YOURS FIFTEENTH OFFER 5000 TONS TWOHUN-

DRED FIFTY AUGUST

DAIDO（11 個字）

十一個字，相當於 LT 最低收費二十二個字。速度則以此爲快。

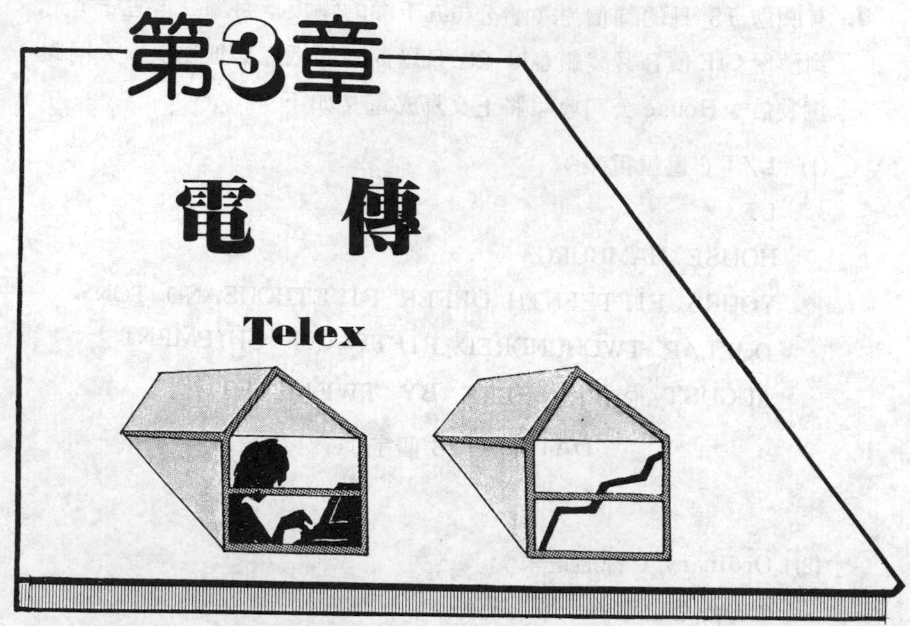

Telex 通稱爲電傳（我國國際電信局稱爲電報交換），係利用附有按鍵的 Teletype （打字電報機）的電信裝置，將電文打製成五單位電碼（5-printer），或六單位電碼（6-printer）的紙帶，透過國際電信局，轉變爲訊號，傳遞給國外或國內裝有相同設備的用戶，再由其設備將收到的訊號譯成原來的電文，五單位電碼的紙條發送器每分鐘可拍發四百零四個字，六單位電碼則每分鐘拍發三百七十五個字。Telex 原爲Teletypewriter Exchange，或Teleprinter Exchange 之簡稱。其通用文體稱爲 Telexese，惟至目前仍未有統一的 Telexese。有關通信費用，請詳見附錄國際電報交換價目表。

Telex 與電話呼叫對方相同，只是一爲口頭，一爲文字交換訊息罷了。而電傳更具有以下的優點：

1. 無人在機旁，照樣可以收報，不受國際時差的限制。

2. 可經由紙帶印製於白紙上，留作記錄，以資憑證。

3. 可以進行筆談會話，如同電話之當場呼叫。

4. 費用按時間計算，比電報、電話費低廉，且明語、暗語均可使用。

5. 可在自己的公司內，直接與對方通訊。

電傳與電報不同之點在於，電傳以時間計費而不是以字數計費，因此電報上，telegraphically（15字）較 by cable （7字）划算，而電傳則相反，by cable 較為便宜。由經濟觀點著眼，就必須從**使用簡短的單字**，及**減少字數**兩部份下功夫。而使用暗語及效益高的單字乃是理所當然的，因此，撰寫Telex者應該具備：

1. 貿易實務及商用英文（Business English）的知識

2. 熟悉交易

3. 英語實力

4. Telexese 的知識

由於分公司、代理公司、合作企業的發達，已經漸漸產生以 Telex為主，以書信為副的趨勢。所以，本著經濟效益來使用 Telex 的概念，不能再等閒視之，整理歸納彼此間的暗語（Code），更是勢在必行。為使字數精簡，常常使用的略字如下：

1. 單位

second = sec	gallon = gal
hour = hr	dozen = dz
minute = min	days = ds
month = mo	kilogramme = kil
ounce = oz	litre = lit
yard = yd	carton = ctn

2. 地名

America = AM	Pennsylvania = Penn
Canada = CA	Hong Kong = HK

Britain = BR
Singapore = Spr
New Zealand = NZ
Tokyo = Tky
Japan = Jap
Philippine = Phln
London = Ldn

3. 普通字

yours = ys
message = msg
Manager = man
immediate = imm
repeat = rt
occupied = occ
advise = adv
agree = ok
please = pls
reference = ref
acknowledge = ack
paragraph = pra
option = opt
including = incl
confirm = cfm
request = rq

將這些縮寫(abbreviations)和暗語及明語混合使用，就產生了 Telexese (電傳文體)。Telexese 還未確立，目前仍屬於各公司內部自行研擬的階段。

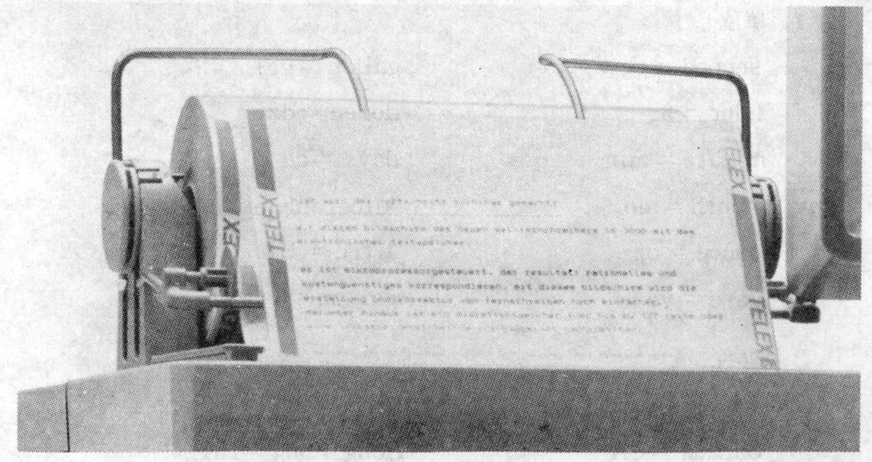

第4章

電傳文體

Telexese

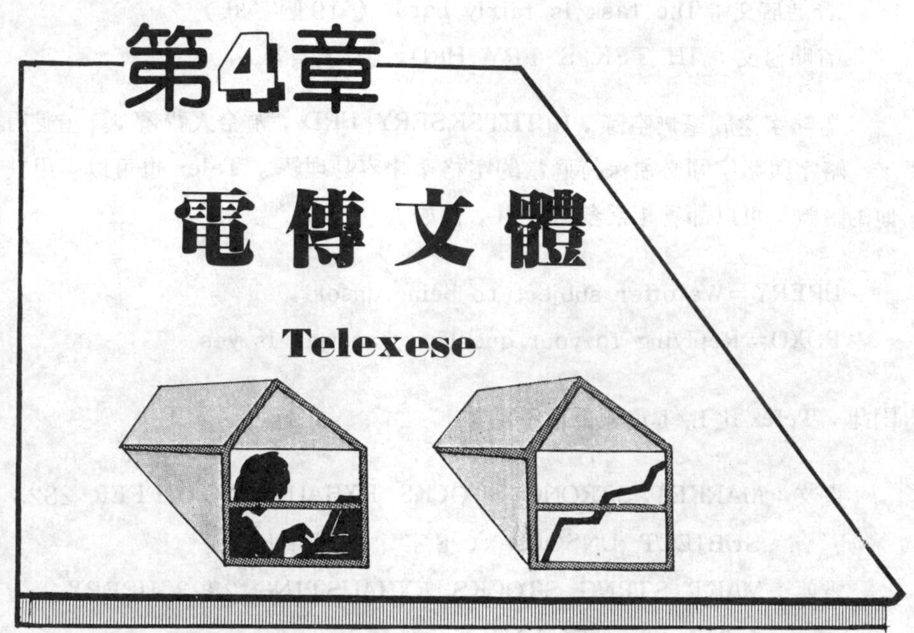

雖然電傳文體至今尚未確立，但一般而言，與電報文體有以下的區別。

電報文體：YOURS FIFTEENTH OFFER 8301 RUBBER SHOES TWOTHOUSAND PAIRS DOLLARS TWOANDHALF CIF NEW-YORK SHIPMENT SEPTEMBER REPLY HERE BY TWENTIETH（18字 116個字母）

電傳文體：YS 15TH OFR 8301 RBER SHOES 2000 PARS CIF $25 NY SHPNT SEPT ANS HERE BY 20TH（17字 60個字母）

談到省略，當然必須要雙方通用者才有利用價值。而且要提醒您注意，即使不完全拼出，也必須有某種可資推敲的憑藉，例如以下的句子：

普通信文：The task is fairly hard.（19個字母）

省略信文：TH TSK S FRY HRD.（12字）

若略字之間毫無空隙，如THTSKSFRY HRD，頗令人費解，不宜使用。略字與略字間必須保持適當的空格，才容易理解。Telex也可以引用其他的暗號，可以節省相當多的費用，例如：

HRERY＝We offer subject to being unsold

POXO＝Replying to your question, answer is yes.

因此，Telex比L/T電報更佔優勢。

電文：MARKET STRONG STOCKS EXHAUSTING OFFER 2823 SUBJECT UNSOLD （8字 50個字母）

電傳：MAKT STRNG STOCKS EXHAUSTING 2823 HRERY （6字 34個字母）

撰寫電文之初，首先要整理出所要傳達的重點，再充分考慮如何簡潔地陳述，有了這種觀念，對Telex業務來說，應該有很大的改善。請參考以下的實例。

[例]：我方6月10日的信函中，告知貴公司，您所提出的減價礙難實現。但是，其後經過費力交涉，得到廠商五十分的降價，這是最大的限度。此地的市場看好，請您考慮我方境況，承諾此事。廠方表示八月以後裝船的話，則不能允諾這項減價，但我方認為若數量龐大，減價仍舊可行。

信　文：In our letter of June 10, we informed you that the discount you requested would be difficult. But we have obtained a 50 ¢ maximum reduction from the manufacturers after the arduous negotiations. The market here is advancing.

Please understand in our situation the above being best. They say they cannot apply the above for the shipment after August, but we feel prices are discountable if the quantity amounts to large.

普通信文相當冗長，若改寫為電文或電傳，透過略字與簡化過程，確實可以減少相當的字數。只是應該彼此充分配合，雙方負責拍發的人員，承做如下的暗語，經常使用，活用，必能創造最適合電傳的文體。

電　文：Ours June tenth discount manufacturers agreed 50¢ despite market which unapplicable after August though similar discount possible if large quantity. （20字 129個字母）

電傳文：Ous June 10 price cut maker agrd 50₵ despit makt unaplicbl shipt after Aug but will agr if larg qty （20字　79個字母）

國際電報交換價目表
INTERNATIONAL TELEX RATES

通報國家 DESTINATION	人工接續 Manual		全自動 Automatic
	首三分鐘 First 3 Minutes NT$	逾此每分鐘 Each Additional Minute NT$	每六秒 Per 6 Seconds NT$
ALASKA 阿拉斯加	336	112	11.2
ALGERIA 阿爾及利亞	456	152	-
ANGOLA 安哥拉	456	152	15.2
AUSTRALIA 澳洲	336	112	11.2
AUSTRIA 奧地利	336	112	11.2
BAHAMAS 巴哈馬	456	152	15.2
BELGIUM 比利時	336	112	11.2
BOLIVIA 玻利維亞	456	152	15.2
BRAZIL 巴西	456	152	15.2
BURMA 緬甸	336	112	11.2
CANADA 加拿大	336	112	11.2
CHILE 智利	456	152	15.2
COLOMBIA 哥倫比亞	456	152	15.2
COSTA RICA 哥斯大黎加	336	112	11.2
DENMARK 丹麥	336	112	11.2
DOMINICA 多明尼加	336	112	-
EGYPT, ARAB REPUBLIC OF 埃及	456	152	15.2
FALKLAND 福克蘭	456	152	-
FINLAND 芬蘭	336	112	11.2
FRANCH 法國	336	112	11.2
GERMANY-WEST 西德	336	112	11.2
GREECE (HELLENIC REP) 希臘	336	112	11.2
GUAM 關島	336	112	11.2
HAWAII 夏威夷	336	112	11.2

通 報 國 家 DESTINATION	人 工 接 續 Manual		全自動 Automatic
	首三分鐘 First 3 Minutes NT$	逾此每分鐘 Each Additional Minutes NT$	每六秒 Per 6 Seconds NT$
HONDURAS 宏都拉斯	396	132	13.2
HONGKONG 香港	264	88	8.8
INDIA 印度	336	112	11.2
IRAN 伊朗	336	112	11.2
IRAQ 伊拉克	336	112	11.2
IRISH REPUBLIC 愛爾蘭共和國	336	112	11.2
ISRAEL 以色列	336	112	11.2
ITALY 義大利	336	112	11.2
JAPAN 日本	336	112	11.2
KOREA 韓國	336	112	11.2
KUWAIT 科威特	336	112	11.2
LEBANON 黎巴嫩	336	112	11.2
LIBYA 利比亞	456	152	15.2
LUXEMBOURG 盧森堡	336	112	11.2
MACAO 澳門	264	88	8.8
MALAYSIA (SARAWAK& SABAH) 馬來西亞	336	112	11.2
MALTA 馬爾他	336	112	11.2
MEXICO 墨西哥	336	112	11.2
MONACO 摩納哥	336	112	11.2
MOROCCO 摩洛哥	456	152	15.2
NATHERLANDS 荷蘭	336	112	11.2
NETHERLANDS ANTILLES 印尼	336	112	11.2
NEW ZEALAND 紐西蘭	336	112	11.2
NORWAY 挪威	336	112	11.2
PANAMA 巴拿馬	336	112	11.2
PERU 祕魯	456	152	15.2

通 報 國 家 DESTINATION	人 工 接 續 Manual		全 自 動 Automatic
	首三分鐘 First 3 Minutes NT$	逾此每分鐘 Each Additional Minute NT$	每 六 秒 Per 6 Seconds NT$
PHILIPPINES 菲律賓	336	112	11.2
PORTUGAL 葡萄牙	336	112	11.2
PUERTO RICO 波多黎各	336	112	11.2
SAUDI ARABIA 沙烏地阿拉伯	336	112	11.2
SINGAPORE 新加坡	336	112	11.2
SOUTH AFRICAN REP. 南非共和國	396	132	13.2
SPAIN 西班牙	336	112	11.2
SRI LANKA(CEYLON) 斯里蘭卡	336	112	11.2
SUDAN 蘇丹	456	152	15.2
SWAZILAND 史瓦濟蘭	456	152	15.2
SWEDEN 瑞典	336	112	11.2
SWITZERLAND 瑞士	336	112	11.2
SYRIA 敍利亞	336	112	11.2
THAILAND 泰國	336	112	11.2
UGANDA 烏干達	456	152	15.2
UNITED KINGDOM 英國	336	112	11.2
UNITED STATES OF AMERICA 美國	336	112	11.2
URUGUAY 烏拉圭	456	152	15.2
VATICAN CITY 梵諦岡	336	112	11.2

INVOICE

NO.________________　　　　　　　　　　　　　　　　　Date:____________________

INVOICE of____

For account and risk of Messrs.____

____

Shipped by____ per_______________________

sailing on or about____________________From____________________to_____________

L/C No.________________________________Contract No.______________________________

Marks & Nos.	Description of Goods	Quantity	Unit Price	Amount
	E. & O. E.			

1

輸出許可證修改申請書
APPLICATION FOR ALTERATION OF EXPORT PERMIT

經濟部國際貿易局
中央銀行外滙局委託之指定簽證銀行 台鑒：
To: Board of Foreign Trade, MOEA.
Appointed Bank on behalf of Foreign Exchange Dept; CBC

日期
Date:________ 修改次數：________
手續費收據號碼：________

下開申請人茲申請修改本行號持有之
We, the undersigned, hereby apply for alteration(s) of the following terms of
輸出許可證第　　　　號之下列條款
Export Permit No.________ held by us.

(第一聯) 由簽證單位存查

欄次 Column	項次 Item	原輸出許可證列載情形 Original conditions in the Export Permit	修改情形 Alterations to be made

注意：未改部份請勿填寫

申請人

(請蓋廠商編號章)
Please Put Your Assignd Number Chop.

申請人簽章 Signature of Applicant

原通關關別：　　　關
原出口報單號碼：

修改編號		檢核	初審

簽證銀行
Authorized Signature

茲證明上述更改
We hereby certify that the above-mentioned
項目本關認為滿意
alteration(s) is (are) found satisfactory to us.

海關簽章
For Commissioner of Customs

第一聯：簽章發給出口廠商

預繳出口外滙證明書
CERTIFICATE FOR ADVANCE SETTLEMENT OF FOREIGN EXCHANGE FOR EXPORT

美　商　大　通　銀　行
THE CHASE MANHATTAN BANK, N.A.
TAIPEI, TAIWAN, R.O.C.

證明書號碼
Certificate No. ________

爲發給證明書事
This is to certify

請蓋分户編號章

發證日期
Date of Issue ________

茲有
that Messrs ________

預繳本行外滙計
have surrendered to us foreign exchange

Amount in figure	

（金額大寫）
for the sum of ________

繳滙方式
in the form of ________ 准抵日後輸出貨品價款 against export shipment at a later date.

說明
Particulars

貨品名稱 Commodity	數量 Quantity	單價 Unit Price	輸出日期 Date of Shipment	輸往地區 Destination

最後有效日期
Expiration Date：

（輸出許可證簽發機關）
Export Permit Issuing Agency：

美　商　大　通　銀　行
THE CHASE MANHATTAN BANK, N.A.
TAIPEI, TAIWAN, R.O.C.

出口記錄
Export record

AUTHORIZED SIGNATURE

日期 Date	簽證號碼 License No.	金額 Amount	餘額 Balance	記帳員 Preparer

(TW) -TRR-0135 4-78 Ptg 3-85 2,000
0010106

上海商業儲蓄銀行

THE SHANGHAI COMMERCIAL & SAVINGS BANK, LTD.

滙出滙款申請書

APPLICATION FOR OUTWARD REMITTANCE

日期
Date

滙出款金額 Amount for Remittance	收款人姓名住址 Name and Address of Beneficiary	
滙率 Rate @		
繳款方式 Settlement □新台幣金額 NT$ …………………… □外滙金額 Foreign Currency Amount ……………………	滙款方式 By means of □票滙 Demand Draft □信滙 Mail Transfer □電滙 Cable Transfer	備註 Remarks:

申請人姓名地址 Applicant's Name & Address

……………………………………

……………………………………

……………………………………

申請人簽章 Applicant's Signature

FO-12 25x4-1 DP.

心得筆記欄

● 在下列各書局可以買到學習出版公司之書籍及錄音帶

● 台北市 ●

重南書局
文翔書局
衆文書局
永大書局
巨擘書局
新智書局
正文書局
弘雅書局
文友書局
博大書局
致遠書局
千華書局
曉園書局
建宏書局
宏業書局
文康書局
光統書局
文源書局
翰輝書局
文化書局
正元書局
天龍書局
金石堂
文化廣場
建德書報社
貞德書報社
百全書報社
聯宏書報社
聯豐書報社
華一書報社
偉正書報社
恒立書報社
中台書報社
建興書局
文笙書局
大中國書局
國聯書局
宏一書局
宏昇書局
百文書局
鴻儒堂書局
廣城書局
學語書局
南陽書局
三友書局
華星書局
新學友書局
來來百貨
永漢書局
力行書局
泰堂書局
金橋圖書股份有限公司
文普書局
力霸百貨
集太祥書局
偉群書局
萬泰書局
明志書局
宏玉書局
興來百貨
文佳書局
自力書局
誼美書局
水準書局
中美書局
頂淵書局
今日書局
長樂書局
德昌書局
敦煌書局
松芳書局
弘文書局
統領書局
啓文書局
永琦書局
鴻源百貨
敬恒書局
新光百貨
益群書局
聯一書局
朝陽堂
六福堂書局
博文堂書局
益民書局
捨而美書局
百葉書局
今博書局
鑫日書局
太華書局
平峰書局
百合書局
朝陽書局
天才學局
久大書
香世界
東利書局
聯合資訊
天下電腦
信宏書局
校園書局
中興大學圖書部
合歡書局
博聞堂書局
政大書局
再興書局
建安書局
文理書局
華一書局
伯樂書局
東光百貨公司
宏明書局
建國書局
中建書局
師大書局
浦公英書局
夢溪書局
時報出版社
宏欣書局
桂冠出版社
九章出版社
開發書局
智邦書局
永豐餘
永星書局
漢昇書局
慈暉書局
達仁書局
新興書局
明志工專
崇文圖書
廣奧書局
進文堂書局
福勝書局
台大書局
書林書局
景儷書局
香草山書局
漢記書局
光啓書局
增文堂書局
富美書局
益中書局
葉山書局
漢文書局
師大書苑
學海書局
克明書局
華城書局
崇暉書局
來來書局
青草地書局
實踐書坊
人人書局
文軒書局
升華書局
大學書局
東成書局
長青書局
玉山書局
亨得利書局
文達書局
光華書局
冠德書局
宗記書局
士林書局
宇文書局
擰檬黃書局
大漢書局
信加書局
勝一書局
兒童百科書局

● 永和 ●

東豐書局
國中書局
宇城書局
潮流書局
文德書局
大方書局
超群書局
文山書局
三通書局

● 中和 ●

景新書局
華陽書局

● 新店 ●

華泰書局
文風書局
勝博書局
文山書局
宏德書局

● 板橋 ●

永一書局
優豪電腦
建盈書局
賢明書局
流行站百貨
恒隆書局
啓文書局
峰國書局
文林書局
文人書局
文城書局
大漢書局
大有爲書局

● 三重 ●

義記書局
日新書局
文海書局
百勝書局
仁人書局

● 新莊 ●

珠海書局
鴻陽書局
文林書局
辰陽書局
崇文圖書

● 泰山鄉 ●

大雅書局

● 淡水 ●

文理書局
匯林書局
淡友書局
國寶書局
匯文書局
中外書局

● 羅東 ●

翰林書局
統一書局
學人書局
三民學局
國泰書局
環華書局
國民書局

● 宜蘭 ●

華山書局
金隆書局
新時代書局
四季風書局
方向書局

● 花蓮 ●

千歲書坊
中原書局
新生書局
精藝書坊

● 台東 ●

徐氏書局
統一書局

● 金門 ●

翰林書局
源成書局
金鴻福書局

● 澎湖 ●

大衆書局
黎明書局

● 桃園 ●

文化書局
中山書局
天寧書局
東方書局

東海書局
大新書局
奇奇書局
全國優良圖
書展藍源德
好學生書局
●中壢●
立德書局
文明書局
文化書局
貞德書局
建宏書局
博士書局
奇奇書局
大學書局
●新竹●
大學書局
昇大書局
六藝出版社
竹一書局
仁文書局
學府書局
文華書局
黎明書局
文國書局
金鼎獎書局
大新書局
文山書局
弘文書局
德興書局
學風書局
泰昌書局
滋朗書局
排行榜書局
光南書局
大華書報社
●苗栗●
益文書局
芙華書局
建國書局
文華書局
●基隆●
文粹書局
育德書局

自立書局
明德書局
中興書局
文隆書局
建國書局
文豐書局
●台中市●
宏明書局
曉園出版社
台中門市
滄海書局
大學圖書
供應社
逢甲書局
聯經出版社
中央書局
大衆書局
新大方書局
中華書局
文軒書局
柏林書局
亞勝補習班
文化書城
三民書局
台一書局
興大書局
興大書齋
興文書局
正文書局
新能書局
新學友學局
全文書局
國鼎書局
國寶書局
華文書局
建國書局
汗牛書屋
享聲唱片行
華中書局
逢甲大學
諾貝爾書局
中部書報社
中一書局
明道書局

振文書局
中台一專
盛文書局
●台中縣●
三民書局
建成書局
欣欣唱片行
大千書局
中一書局
明道書局
●彰化●
復文書局
東門書局
新新書局
台聯書局
時代書局
成功書局
世界書局
來來書局
翰林書局
一新書局
中山書局
文明書局
●雲林●
建中書局
大山書局
文芳書局
國光書局
良昌書局
三民書局
●嘉義市●
文豐書局
慶隆盛書局
義豐書局
志成書局
大漢書局
書苑庭書局
學英公司
天才書局
學英書局
光南書局
嘉聯書報社
●嘉義縣●
建成書局

●台南縣●
全勝書局
博大書局
第一書局
南一書局
柳營書局
●台南市●
欣欣文化社
光南唱片行
嘉南書社
第一書局
東華書局
成功大學
書局部
成大書城
文山書局
孟子書局
大友書局
松文書局
盛文書局
台南書局
日勝書局
旭日書局
南台圖書
公司
金寶書局
船塢書坊
南一書局
大統唱片行
國正書局
源文書局
永茂書報社
天才書局
●高雄縣●
延平書局
欣良書局
大岡山書城
時代書局
鳳山大書城
遠東大書城
天下書局
杏綱書局
統一書局
百科書局

志成書局
光遠書局
●高雄市●
高雄書報社
宏昇書局
理想書局
高文堂書局
松柏書局
三民書局
光南書局
國鼎書局
文英書局
黎明書局
光明書局
前程書局
岃行書局
登文書局
青山外語
補習班
六合書局
美新書局
朝代書局
意文書局
地下街
文化廣場
大立百貨公
司圖書部
大統百貨公
司圖書部
黎明文化
有前書局
建工書局
鐘樓書局
青年書局
瓊林書局
大學城書局
引想力書局
永大書局
杏莊書局
儒林書局
雄大書局
復文書局
致遠書局
明仁書局

宏亞書局
瀚文書局
天祥書局
廣文書局
楊氏書局
慈冊書局
盛文書局
光統
圖書百貨
愛偉書局
●屏東●
復文書局
建利書局
百成書局
新星書局
百科書局
屏東書城
屏東唱片行
英格文教社
賢明書局
大古今書局
屏東農專
圖書部
順時書局
百順書局

現代商業英語與實務

編　　著／卓 美 玲
發 行 所／學習出版有限公司　☎ (02) 2704-5525
郵撥帳號／0512727-2 學習出版社帳戶
登 記 證／局版台業 *2179* 號
印 刷 所／裕強彩色印刷有限公司
台北門市／台北市許昌街 10 號 2 F　☎ (02) 2331-4060・2331-9209
台中門市／台中市綠川東街 32 號 8 F 23 室　☎ (04) 2223-2838
台灣總經銷／紅螞蟻圖書有限公司　☎ (02) 2795-3656
美國總經銷／Evergreen Book Store　☎ (818) 2813622
本公司網址　www.learnbook.com.tw
電子郵件　learnbook@learnbook.com.tw

售價：新台幣一百八十元正

2005 年 4 月 1 日一版七刷

ISBN 957-519-038-6